Motherhood
As
Metamorphosis

Motherhood As Metamorphosis

Change and Continuity in the Life of a New Mother

by

Joyce Block, Ph.D.

A DUTTON BOOK

To my mother Luba, whose love, strength, hopefulness,
and sadnesses fueled my desire to love,
to work, and to understand

A DUTTON BOOK
Published by the Penguin Group
Penguin Books USA Inc., 375 Hudson Street, New York, New York 10014, U.S.A.
Penguin Books Ltd, 27 Wrights Lane, London W8 5TZ, England
Penguin Books Australia Ltd, Ringwood, Victoria, Australia
Penguin Books Canada Ltd, 2801 John Street, Markham, Ontario, Canada L3R 1B4
Penguin Books (N.Z.) Ltd, 182–190 Wairau Road, Auckland 10, New Zealand

Penguin Books Ltd, Registered Offices: Harmondsworth, Middlesex, England

First published by Dutton, an imprint of New American Library, a division of
Penguin Books USA Inc.
Published simultaneously in Canada by McClelland & Stewart Inc.

First Printing, September, 1990
10 9 8 7 6 5 4 3 2 1

REGISTERED TRADEMARK—MARCA REGISTRADA

LIBRARY OF CONGRESS CATALOGING-IN-PUBLICATION DATA

Block, Joyce.
    Motherhood as metamorphosis / by Joyce Block.
        p.   cm.
    Includes bibliographical references (p.).
    ISBN 0-525-24900-1
    1. Motherhood—Psychological aspects.   I. Title.
HQ759.B615   1990
306.874'3—dc20   90-34684
                                                                        CIP

Printed in the United States of America
Set in Palatino
Designed by Nissa Knuth-Cassidy

Contents

Preface

Every woman brings to motherhood her own particular set of hopes, fears, memories, and dreams, and I was no exception. Like many women, before having a baby I expected (though perhaps I might not have admitted it at the time) that in some unidentifiable way motherhood would transform me—tie up any loose ends in my identity, make me a "complete" woman, and rid me of my childish propensities; I dreamed that as a mother I could leave behind me the unfinished business of the past, and never suspected that the past would haunt me as I dared to venture forth into the future. In short, I unconsciously and naïvely subscribed to the notion of "motherhood as metamorphosis."

At the same time that I imbued motherhood with the power to magically change me, I was presumptuous enough to believe that as a mother I would be immune to the conflicts that other new mothers seemed to become embroiled in—conflicts about work, conflicts about separation, conflicts about marriage, conflicts about identity. I was, after all, a social psychologist and a psychotherapist whose area of specialization was the psychology of women, and in the context of my professional life I had heard too much about role strain, "supermom" syndromes, and guilt to imagine that I would be vulnerable to these experiences myself. And so I embarked upon motherhood eagerly, confident that nothing so wonderful as having a baby could disturb my equilibrium, or make me question my sense of myself as a professional and as a woman. The

1

metamorphosis I had anticipated was to be invigorating, never destabilizing.

Motherhood *has* been a metamorphosis, and I believe it is a metamorphosis for many women—but not in the way I thought it would be. I have come to the humbling realization that as much as motherhood is a catalyst of change, it is also the arena in which psychic change proves to be most difficult to achieve. We resist change even as we embrace it.

As mothers, women find themselves reenacting dramas from their distant past. Their own childhood experiences resurface in new forms, and if they are not the adults they thought they were, it is only because they have rediscovered aspects of themselves they have buried but not yet put to rest. In motherhood women are forced to see themselves from a different perspective (everyone else in their lives sees them from a different perspective as well), and if there are surprises in what they see and feel, there is also the uncanny sensation that nothing has "really" changed. There has been an upheaval and a loss of innocence, an actual birth and a metaphoric rebirth, an investment in the future and a reevaluation of the past. And yet, in some intangible but essential way, each woman is the same as she always was, and her experience of mothering reflects that inner consistency.

This book explores women's experiences of change and their experiences of continuity as they become mothers. This dual focus reflects my training as a social psychologist and a psychoanalytically oriented psychotherapist. Social psychology examines how the conditions of life shape the individual's experience of himself and his relation to the world, whereas psychoanalysis explores how the individual shapes his life so as to express his needs and conflicts. The social psychologist in me is sensitive to psychic change in response to varying circumstances, while the therapist is attuned to continuities in personality over time and place. My training in family systems theory has added yet another dimension to my understanding of a woman's experience starting a new family, putting that experience in the context of her and her husband's families of origin.

But I must acknowledge that there were also more personal motives involved in writing this book. Women struggle to integrate motherhood into their previous identities, and again, I am no exception to this general rule. This book is the product of my struggle. By bringing my professional interests and training to bear on my personal experience of motherhood I found a way to create a comfortable balance in my life between change and continuity, thought and feeling—a balance so necessary in the midst of a metamorphosis.

In the process of writing this book I spoke with numerous women about their experiences as new mothers. I wish to thank all of them for their willingness to pause and reflect upon sensitive and sometimes disturbing aspects of their lives. Fifteen women agreed to be interviewed at length solely for the purposes of this study; other women's stories emerged in the context of psychotherapy. Without their detailed reminiscences my theoretical formulations would have had no life.

Although none of the case material I have included is invented (unless explicitly stated so in the text), I have taken the liberty of going beyond the bare facts, extrapolating from the clinical data—analyzing and interpreting feelings and motives for the purposes of illustration. I hope any misunderstandings or misinterpretations I have made will be forgiven; they are inevitable when one person attempts to make sense out of another person's complex experience. In order to protect their confidentiality, all identifying features of the women to whom I refer have been changed.

The women in this study came from diverse backgrounds, but most were middle class, all were older than the average first-time mother, and all but a couple of the women were living with the fathers of their babies. The sample was not intended to be representative of the population of mothers as a whole. Rather than surveying hundreds of women I chose a case-study approach, hoping in this manner to delve deep beneath the surface and arrive at a more meaningful understanding of how motherhood affects different kinds of women, from the inside looking out.

A number of friends and colleagues have supported me in this project, and I wish to mention a few by name. Dr. Florence Denmark, my dissertation adviser, read a rough outline of the book at its earliest stages, and she encouraged me to pursue my ideas. Over the years, Mr. Amos Gunsberg has been instrumental in shaping my understanding of psychological processes in general, and many of my insights about the influence of the past on a mother's present-day experience have their roots in my discussions with him. I am grateful to Sharon Friedman, my literary agent, who was willing to take a risk with a new author; her expertise, her thoughtful comments, and her enthusiasm were invaluable supports from the beginning of the project through to its completion. And special thanks goes to Senior Editor Alexia Dorszynski, whose meticulous but generous reading of the manuscript was always thought-provoking; she was an inspiration in the struggle to achieve clarity. Willa Speiser, the copyeditor, is also to be thanked for conscientiousness.

Kathleen Friedman and I were new mothers together. It was with her that the ideas for this book began to percolate. I will always remember what we shared. My dear friend Ruth Saada consistently voiced confidence in the worthiness of this enterprise as well as in my ability to make my dream become a reality; I cannot thank her enough. And finally, I wish to acknowledge my husband, Henry Weinfield, who lived through the experience with me, and who, through good times and difficult times, has always believed in me, as a woman, as a mother, and as a thinking human being.

1

Motherhood and the
Ghosts of Mothers Past

*Will it ultimately reach the clear surface of my con-
sciousness, this memory, this old, dead moment which
the magnetism of an identical moment has travelled so
far to importune, to disturb, to raise out of the very
depths of my being?*—Marcel Proust, Swann's Way

As is the mother, so is the daughter.—Ezekiel 16:44

One day, while I was walking her to nursery school, my
daughter, who was nearly three years old, asked me in all
earnestness, "Am I going to be Joyce when I grow up . . .
when I'm a big woman?" Amazed and deeply moved by
the naked innocence of her question, I responded, "Of
course not!" and proceeded to explain to her that she and
I are, and would always be, two separate people. "You're
you and I'm me." Whether this explanation made much
sense to my daughter, whose unself-conscious dependency upon me was now more apparent than ever, I can
not know. I suspect, however, that the process of unraveling a mother's and a daughter's intermingling identities is
far more complicated than such a facile explanation might
suggest.

A window into the mind of a little girl in the process of
formulating an identity for herself confirms what psychologists have told us and what many of us know intuitively,
that "in the beginning" it is not altogether clear where
mommy leaves off and where the little girl/baby begins.[1]

5

This is at the "beginning" of course, and under normal conditions, by the time little girls become big women, the question no longer takes that form. Instead, we ask ourselves, as we become mothers, whether we want to mother as our mothers did, and why sometimes we do even when we do not intend to. Who are we anyway? Who do we want to be? And who really were the women we called our mothers? Women often wonder whether motherhood means that they will be gradually transformed into their mothers, and whether that is part of the bargain they struck when they decided to "join the club" and usurp their mothers' role. Attracted by the idea of joining with their mothers in motherhood, they also resist repeating the past "mistakes" their mothers seemed to have made as mothers and as women. The question my little girl raised at the age of three lingers on, camouflaged within the dark recesses of the imagination. It haunts all of us women as we, who will always remain our mother's daughters, become mothers ourselves.

Without being fully aware of it, most women have been preparing to become mothers—if only in the world of their imagination—for years before they actually cross the divide that separates fantasy from reality and have their first baby. Fantasies about becoming mothers incubate inside women from early childhood on. If your own memory for this fails you, or if you can recall only your own distaste for frilly dresses, dolls, and all things "feminine," at age eight, just observe almost any group of three-, four-, or five-year-old girls playing with their dolls, their stuffed animals, or among each other. Mommies, babies, and marriageable maidens (cinderellas, sleeping beauties, snow whites) are invariably the central characters in the dramas these little girls create—and each girl is actor, playwright, and director all in one. These dramas contrast sharply with the superhero adventure stories little boys tend to devise, but if the action on the domestic front appears less grand, the moves are no less deliberate, and the feelings are no less intense. Whether the fantasies boys and girls weave reflect in some mysterious way the differences in their biological equipment or whether they are simply products of a particular socialization experience (women mother, men "work"), or a combination of the two, one cannot help but see that these fantasies are a kind of prelude for what will unfold later in life.[2]

The dramas little girls create mirror and sometimes caricature the real-life mommies and babies they see all around them. The bad witch, the jealous stepmother, the good fairy princess, and the mischievous young girl/baby mythologize the conflicts daughters inevitably experience in relation to their mothers, however much they love and wish to emulate them. In play, the little girl has the freedom to try on all sorts of identities, and she can reverse, and then reverse again, roles that are in reality irreversible. One moment, she can be scolding her naughty baby doll for offenses she herself has recently committed; the next moment, she can be attentively ministering to its every need. In effect, she is rehearsing motherhood by playing mother to herself.

"I told you three times not to pull on the curtains," says a three-year-old girl emphatically to her stuffed bunny rabbit. And then, with an air of indulgent superiority, she adds, "She doesn't know any better, she's only a baby . . . I'm a baby . . . can't walk." Or, "I don't like the clouds . . . they do this, and then they do that, back and forth and back and forth, again and again"—a bizarre, seemingly nonsensical remark that makes perfect sense in the context of her relationship with her mother. Just a couple of hours before, this little girl's mother had expressed irritation with her daughter's constant requests to put on—only to take off and put on again—her various ponytail holders. At the time, the little girl protested against her mother's reproaches for her indecisiveness, and yet soon afterward she would playing "mother" to the whimsical clouds. As to the clumsy, inconsiderate daddy who happens to squeeze onto a corner of the living room couch that doubles as a cradle for the stuffed animal "babies," she implores him not to "sit on the babies . . . you're crushing them!" (She herself has squeezed to one side to give the stuffed animals plenty of space.) And, with a trembling voice, the little girl demands, "Where's her mama?" (referring to the mischievous bunny's mama bunny, as well as to her own mama, who is temporarily out of sight).

In play, sometimes the little girl is the mommy and sometimes she is the baby and her friend (imaginary or real) is the mommy, but most of the time, mommies, babies, and "big girls" have overlapping identities that blend into one another and are constantly shifting. The little girl with the bunny, for example, is mother to her baby rabbit, a baby herself (since the bunny pulls the curtains as she does), and her own mother, scolding and defending the baby with which she is identified. By "reproducing" the mothering she herself has experienced, the girl encompasses her mother within herself as she develops into the woman she will become. Ironically, by incorporating the mother, the girl paves the way for her own separation from this otherwise too-awesome figure.[3]

> *For every woman, there are always three women: 1) girl-baby; 2) mother; 3) mother's mother.—D. W. Winnicott,* Home Is Where We Start From, *1986*[4]

But what do children's fantasies have to do with the *realities* of being a mother fifteen, twenty, or even thirty years later? More than we'd like to admit at times. The little girl/baby and her mommy continue to exist as presences within all women, and they clamor to be heard as the new mother gropes to discover who her baby is and who *she* is now that she is a mother as well as a woman and her mother's daughter. The ghosts of childhood experience disguise themselves in contemporary dress, so that it is sometimes difficult for the new mother to distinguish clearly all the different but familiar voices that echo within her. Often she confuses her voice with the voice of her mother, and the memory she has of herself as a baby blends into her experience of her own baby, whom she feeds, comforts, and leaves hurriedly when she rushes off to work in the morning.

Beyond conscious awareness, the two blur together—the baby then and the baby now—and as if one film were superimposed upon another, the images blur together and it becomes impossible to make out precisely the individual contours. So, for example, when the baby cries with hunger, anger, or delight, its cry may assume a meaning that is not his alone. It may be a sorrowful reminder of the mother's own sense of deprivation, or it may resonate with her own desire to expand, unfettered by the emotional baggage she has acquired in the process of becoming an adult. And then sometimes the baby's cry is just his cry. Although most women consciously identify with their babies, they often do not understand how their identification translates into the particular responses they have.

When a mother's feelings are loving and tender, untainted by anxiety or anger, explanations for her feelings seem extraneous at best. But when negative feelings arise, and they invariably do even among the most devoted of mothers, many women feel guilty and confused. They themselves often sense that there is more going on than meets the eye, and yet they are uncertain as to what it is and feel stuck as they watch themselves and their babies. Consider one mother's overly burdened response to her toddler's angry tears.

Judith, a thirty-three-year-old college-educated woman, acknowledged feeling disturbed and confused about her responses to her two-year-old daughter's fits of temper. Although she knew rationally that she was not to blame for her daughter's crying and that her daughter's rages were normal given her age (these were the infamous "terrible twos," after all), she still felt an urgent, almost desperate *need* to restore harmonious relations between the two of them. This meant smoothing her daughter's ruffled feathers, without compromising her own self-respect in the process.

When reasoning with her daughter proved to be futile—and of course it frequently did under the circumstances, since her words could not be heard, much less comprehended—Judith became outraged and enraged herself. Ironically, her own desperate need to get her daughter to quiet down and listen to reason was as *un*reasonable as her two-year-old daughter's cries of frustration.

Although Judith did not doubt that the experience of dealing with an angry two-year-old was objectively a frustrating one for all involved (the other mothers she knew reassured her that it was), she could not deceive herself into believing that *her* reaction was justified, try as she might. She noticed that her husband, who was not known for his patience, was considerably less disturbed by the tantrums than she, and she asked herself why it was that the very same daughter whom she loved "more than anything in the world" could also make her blood boil more quickly and more furiously than anybody else in her world. How could her warm, loving feelings undergo such a sudden metamorphosis? If there was no *rational* explanation, what was the reason for her response?

Judith's irrational sense of indignation at her daughter's misbehavior is, of course, exactly what her daughter is feeling at that very moment as well. Something in *her* world-experience is not right, and she communicates her outrage loudly and clearly through cries that mount rather than diminish with her mother's solicitous queries. By some peculiar transformation, Judith has come to mirror her daughter's experience. She has joined her daughter in her two-year-old's world, and in this world neither of them has the capacity to understand fully that their momentary disappointments and frustrations are not all-encompassing and will not last forever. Feeling two years old and being two years old are experiences that are probably impossible to re-create at a later time. But feeling like a two-year-old in a thirty-three-year-old body feels ridiculous, in addition to everything else, and under these conditions Judith becomes even more desperate for the "crisis" to be over, and for "normalcy" to be restored.

Although she realizes that she is not helping her daughter learn to deal with frustration by becoming so frustrated herself, Judith nevertheless finds that she is swept along by the momentum of her feelings, which seem to have a mind of their own. Once everything has settled down, and she is thirty-three years old again in mind as well as in body, she experiences a tremendous relief and is unable to comprehend fully how she could have become so embroiled in her daughter's scenes.

Before becoming a mother, Judith never dreamed that she would respond like this to a baby's tantrums—or to anything else for that matter. Moreover, she imagines that nobody, not even her husband, suspects that periodically she feels as if a volcano is erupting within her. She hides it pretty well. Judith claims that although she was known to have temper tantrums as a child herself—"I remember banging my head on the floor when I was very angry, she says"—she is not the "hysterical type" now; or at least she did not, up until recently, conceive of herself as such. In fact, Judith likes to think of herself as the kind of woman who is undaunted by adversity, not prone to panic in times of crisis.

It goes without saying that Judith never reacts this way when someone else's baby is crying. Given that amount of distance, she is able to be sympathetic to both parent and child and philosophical about the inevitability of conflict when raising children. The turmoil remains outside her. When it is her own daughter, however, the cries seem to pierce right through her, and reason succumbs to passion.

In the preceding example, a mother of a two-year-old finds her intense and "infantile" response to her daughter's cries of anger confusing. She senses that what she is feeling has less to do with what her daughter is doing and

more to do with what her daughter's behavior is trigger-
ing inside her, but she is unable to identify precisely what
transports her back to her own childlike state.

By analyzing Judith's inner experience in the context of
her personal history, we can develop a general understanding of how a woman's relationship to her mother
might influence her relationship to her child. The following imaginary dialogue represents a condensation of inter-
pretive work that spanned the course of several months as
Judith explored the possible meanings of her experience
in the context of therapy:

Dr. Block: "Did your own mother respond like that
when you got angry as a child?"

Judith: "No, she responded very differently, at least on
the surface. My mother always seemed to cringe when I
had temper tantrums, and I was told that I had more than
my share. It was as if she experienced my screams as a
slap in the face, but she never raised her voice and never
really lost her temper. Even when my father yelled at her
or berated her unfairly, which he frequently did, she
rarely responded with anger, though it would drive *me*
wild. She'd tell me I was spoiled when I screamed or
cried, and I think she was right, I was kind of a brat. On
the other hand she never really put her foot down or did
anything else to stop it. My mother absorbed everything,
and became quietly miserable."

Dr. Block: "Do you think that when your daughter
screams now you are transported back in time to the
scenes you had with your own mother when you were a
child? Do you temporarily "become" your "beaten-down"
mother and perceive your daughter in the image she
seemed to have of *you* as a spoiled and demanding baby?
Could that be why, despite your better judgment, her
tantrums infuriate you?

Judith: "That could be part of it, but my mother never
yelled back, and I do. She seemed to feel the pain, but she
remained calm, and I certainly do not. There is a part of

me that wishes I were more like my mother, and that when my daughter screams I would just let it roll off my back, but I've always been just the opposite. Even as a child I defended my mother against my father far more vehemently than she defended herself. My father used to say that I was my mother's lawyer."

Dr. Block: "Perhaps then, that is the key. When you hear your daughter screaming unreasonably, as two-year-olds are known to do, you unconsciously revert to the image you have of your mother, an image in which she figured as an object of abuse—you did say that your father berated her, and that you were a spoiled child who threw temper tantrums. Unlike your mother, however, whom you described as a woman who passively absorbed it all, you seem to have vowed to defend yourself (and her) when you feel unappreciated or mistreated. What's more, having identified so strongly with her, you are *prone* to feel unappreciated and mistreated. In mothering your daughter you are still trying to make peace between the little girl you were and the mother you had; you want to be the mother she wasn't, and you want your daughter to be the child you weren't. Then, just when all seems to be going smoothly, pouf, your daughter's screams dispel your hopes that a new era has begun. The cease-fire is broken, and you are ready to attack whoever dares disturb the peace."

By delving even briefly beneath the surface reality of the situation, it becomes apparent that this woman's response is a conglomeration of her experience of herself as a baby, as a mother today, and as the mother her mother was back when. When Judith's daughter yells at her, and her efforts to quell her tears are to no avail, Judith is rendered temporarily impotent. Moreover, she cannot pack up her bags and say "later for you" (just as she was unable to pack up her diapers when she was a dependent baby herself).[5] Psychically, it is a throwback to her past. She feels powerless as a child feels powerless, and the memory of her mother's passivity haunts her; it reminds her that *she* must not absorb whatever "attacks" come her way even if her mother did.

Judith feels what she imagines her mother must have felt throughout her life, but in contrast to her mother, Judith refuses to swallow her anger, acknowledging it instead as her mother never did. But when Judith interprets her daughter's "normal" expressions of frustration and anger in terms of the past, she misinterprets them. If on the surface she responds differently than her mother did, she also reproduces her mother's experience when she responds to her daughter's cries as if they were "slaps in the face" and as if she is a defenseless victim.

The tape is an endless one, and the feelings that are being replayed again and again don't really fit what is happening between this mature woman and her daughter. How could they? They originated at least twenty-five years before this baby was born. As psychoanalyst Joyce McDougall put it, "We do not escape the roles that our unconscious selves intend us to play, frequently using people in our lives today as stand-ins to settle problems of the past."[6]

Because Judith does not *live* in a fantasy world, her response to her willful toddler is what psychologists call "ego-dystonic." In other words, her response feels alien to her and she is painfully aware that there are many pieces missing in the puzzle and that the pieces that are there do not quite fit. She can acknowledge, after the fact, that children aren't "fair" and that they can't always be expected to act reasonably or to consistently reciprocate a mother's love. As she returns to reality after a brief foray into the past, everything falls back into perspective, her child is her child once again . . . until the next incident.

> *Like a Russian doll nesting ever smaller dolls inside of it, I house an infinity of selves.*—Daphne Merkin, Enchantment, *1986*

In theory, by the time we reach adulthood, our identities as separate individuals are more or less stable, and, in fact, psychological development has been traditionally conceived as a movement toward ever increasing independence and differentiation. As babies we may mistake our needs and feelings for those of our mothers, but, if all goes as it should, by the time we are ready to become parents we are relatively clear as to the boundaries that separate ourselves from others and our fantasies from reality. Confusing what we think and feel with what others think and feel is considered an indication of pathology, a failure on our part to progress from a more primitive to a more mature level of functioning—or else a regression in response to stress. This, at least, is the accepted dogma within psychological circles.

Where do the experiences of motherhood fit into this scheme? Many new mothers describe periods when their moods shadow the moods of their babies and when their emotional equilibrium is entangled with their babies' sleep patterns or teething pain. One mother, for example, noted during her interview that she was feeling great this week because her daughter had been in such good spirits. But she cautioned, "You would have gotten very different answers from me last week when she was cranky and clinging all the time." Another woman defended her decision to return to work shortly after the birth of her baby in this manner: "If I'm happy, Maureen is happy . . . I really believe the baby picks up on my feelings."

These new mothers are not simply rationalizing their moods or justifying their behavior, and they are not alone among laymen or among professionals in subscribing to a theory of emotional interdependency between a mother and her baby, though such a formulation is difficult to prove scientifically. Renowned psychiatrist Harry Stack Sullivan, the founder of the interpersonal school of psychoanalysis, has consistently maintained that what he called the "mothering one" unwittingly induces feelings in her infant through a process he calls "empathy" for lack of a more scientific term. In fact, within this school of thought, the transmission of emotion from mother to baby is conceived as the primary factor in the early development of anxiety.[7]

Women who are new mothers not only describe incidents in which their feelings and their baby's feelings seem to mirror each other, but also incidents in which, despite their conscious efforts, they find themselves responding to their babies as their mothers did to them—another form of "empathy" perhaps, but in this case empathy with a figure from the past who lives only in memory. Susan, the mother of a three-year-old boy, prided herself in being responsive to her son's needs, consistently resisting the temptation to impose her will on him even when this inconvenienced her. And yet she reported with a certain amount of horror instances in which she heard herself telling him, in a tone painfully reminiscent of her mother, that there would be simply no discussion about whether or not he would wear a hat or have a last-minute change of menu: "I couldn't believe I was saying just what my mother used to say to me." Apparently, Susan was closely attuned not only to her son but also to her *mother*, and she unintentionally adopted her mother's perspective (even her mother's tone of voice) on how to handle children who resist wearing their hats in winter or who demand hamburger when chicken is already on the table.

When new mothers see themselves in their babies and their mothers in themselves, the peculiar blend of old and new, familiar and unfamiliar, can be unsettling just as any déjà vu experience is unsettling. When they see themselves behaving as if they were the baby rather than the mother, the telescoping of past and present experience can be extremely disconcerting—an unexpected flashback to a distant and buried past. As one woman recalled, "There were a couple of evenings when I just lay on the kitchen floor and cried and kicked my heels"—something she denied ever doing as an adult before becoming a mother. Another woman admitted that once, out of pure frustration with her toddler's refusal to sit still in her stroller, she huffed off indignantly to her apartment down the hall and plunked herself down on her couch muttering under her breath, having left her toddler, stroller and all, in front of the hall elevator to fend for herself!

Surely, when all of these experiences occur—and they are not uncommon—there is a confusion of identities, a loss of distance, or what some psychologists might call a blurring of boundaries. After all, who is the mother, and who is the baby, and who are the ghosts of mothers past? Where does one leave off and the other begin? Would it be fair simply to characterize these women as pathological? Infantile? Regressed? Or is there something about motherhood itself that engenders these kind of responses, ones that are not simply generic responses to stress?

As a mother, a woman returns to an earlier form of relationship that she has probably not experienced since she was a dependent, unsocialized bundle of impulses herself. Since the infant is infinitely dependent as well as limited in his ability to communicate his needs, it is not only considered "normal" for the needs and feelings of mothers and their babies to intermingle and overlap, but "unnatural" when they don't. Although we may no longer speak glibly of "maternal instincts," the infant-mother relationship continues to occupy a special and unique place in our imaginations. This is true for the man or woman on the street as well as for the professional.

Psychoanalyst Margaret Mahler, whose theory of early child development has probably been the most influential, referred to a critically important stage of "symbiosis" between mother and infant, during which time they share a "common boundary" through which they communicate with each other nonverbally. Again, in the context of the mother-infant relationship the ordinary rules that separate normal from pathological are suspended. And Mahler's perspective is certainly not unique. The "good-enough" mother described by renowned pediatrician and psychiatrist D. W. Winnicott is one whose preoccupation with her infant requires her to temporarily withdraw her interest from the world outside the magic circle that envelops them. He speaks respectfully of a stage of "maternal pre-occupation."

It becomes clear, then, that in order to understand women's experiences as new mothers we must temporarily suspend our belief in the received categories of what is normal and what is not and reconcile ourselves to the fact that psychological development does not progress in the neat, linear pattern the diagrams in psychology textbooks might lead us to believe. In fact, many professionals are beginning to suspect that our theories of development need to be reconsidered in light of women's experiences and what has recently been learned from controlled observation of infant behavior.[8] Some of the accepted lore—that the capacity for relatedness predates and hence is more primitive than the capacity for autonomy—may reflect our biases more than "objective" reality, our particular value system more than human "nature." And partial truths based upon observations of men and men's conflicts in a particular cultural milieu may have been mistaken for the whole truth about what it means to become a fully developed human being. For example, Daniel Stern, a psychoanalytically trained psychiatrist in the forefront of research on infant behavior, and Carol Gilligan, a researcher in the social sciences who has investigated sex differences in moral development, have both recently questioned the assumptions of traditional formulations of psychological development, which have focused almost exclusively on the infant's progression from a stage of dependency to stages of increasing differentiation and independence.[9] They have suggested that the capacity for empathy and the ability to understand and relate to another's experience are as important a measure of psychological maturity as the capacity for autonomy and independent thinking. The ability to connect and the ability to be separate are two lines of development that are not mutually exclusive but rather develop in conjunction with one another, and neither is more advanced or more primitive than the other, despite our cultural overvaluation of the rugged individualist, the Robinson Crusoe, and the lone cowboy. If this is the case, and the capacity for relatedness is as late and as complex a development as the capacity for autonomy, then the difficulties many women have in disentangling their identities from their children's are no more "pathological" than the difficulties many men have in sustaining intimacy with other people, even their own babies. They are two sides of the same coin; they are both aspects of the struggle to be singular among many.

Even as we develop separate and more or less distinct identities and learn to understand and communicate thoughts and feelings with ever greater nuance and complexity, earlier modes of understanding and relating to the outside world remain as potentialities within all of us and color our experiences whether we are aware of it or not, and whether we are mothers or fathers or accountants or schoolteachers.

One of the central tenets of Freud's psychology is that as a species we are not nearly as rational or self-conscious as we like to think we are. When we are late for an appointment, when we confuse the name of an important client, when we forget to sign a check, or when we "accidentally" break a family heirloom, we are indirectly expressing our unconscious needs and conflicts. In other words, one need not be "neurotic" to engage in what Freud referred to as the "psychopathology of everyday life." Our dreams, illogical and confused as they often are, provide us with yet another glimpse into the living but "forgotten" past, where reason, as we know it, does not govern our thinking, and black can substitute for white, and "you" and "I" are interchangeable entities.

Since relics from the past are only buried and never lost entirely, we are all vulnerable to the "return of the repressed," as Freud so aptly put it.[10] Since, in becoming mothers, women return via their babies to the stage where it all began, they may be temporarily *more* vulnerable or to put it more positively, more receptive, to the unconscious and unarticulated. Doors shut tightly years before are reopened, and old and new experiences rush into conscious awareness. In her discussion of the normal stages of parenting, psychoanalyst Therese Benedek argues that, as mothers, women tend to relive the conflicts they experienced growing up—conflicts around dependency, conflicts around autonomy and control, and conflicts around sexuality.[11] Though it can be argued that we are all continually reworking early unresolved conflicts rooted in our childhood experiences, it seems that motherhood is an arena that is particularly conducive to the emergence of the "secret-theater self," identified as such by psychoanalyst Joyce McDougall.[12] McDougall uses the metaphor of the theater to speak about an aspect of the self that is generally well disguised: the self that recites scripts written at another time and for other characters, and the self that reintroduces past relationships only to restage scenes from earlier dramas. What follows is one simple example.

Ann, a woman in her late thirties, the mother of a two-and-a-half-year-old boy, likened her own mother to a "well-oiled machine." The youngest of five children herself, Ann experienced her mother as efficient but emotionally unavailable to her during her childhood and adolescence. She recalls shadowing her mother as she conscientiously went about her domestic chores, hungrily soaking up whatever drops of attention she could. It is not difficult to understand why, during our interview, Ann stressed again and again the importance of being what she referred to as a "full-time" mother to her son. In fact, this was a theme that recurred throughout, and nearly everything she had to say about her experience as a mother and her relationships to other mothers was colored by her concern *not* to reproduce her own childhood experience.

Upon giving birth, Ann gave up her full-time job as an editor of a magazine, with no plans to return to work of any kind. What was most noteworthy about Ann was the vehemence with which she spoke about never leaving her son with a baby-sitter for even a few hours and her condemnation of parents who failed, in one way or another, to respond to their baby's needs for tender and continuous contact. In her advice to prospective parents, Ann urged mothers to follow their *instincts* (an interesting choice of word, given her description of her own *mechanical* mother), and to ignore the impersonal, and from her perspective misguided, ideas of the "experts."

Ann's eagerness to be a devoted mother may appear exemplary to some, and she may very well have succeeded in her efforts to give her son the emotional nourishment she never felt she got from her own mother. But her single-mindedness and zealotry appear to have as much to do with her own needs as with her child's. Her mission evolved out of her own experience of emotional deprivation, and her current project is to fill in the spaces she felt her own mother had left painfully empty a long time before.

Mothers as a group are as different in personality as any other group of individuals, but the experience of caring for a baby stirs up early memories and sensations for all and reminds each woman that she was once as helpless and dependent as her baby is now. While dependency and helplessness are universal conditions of infancy, each woman has at her disposal memories of a particular experience of being dependent, and it is these that she will bring to her experience of mothering.

Susan, a woman who had her first baby when she was over forty years old, sensed that her own mother must have had a particularly hard time caring for her during her infancy, when she was most dependent. Reflecting on this impression of her mother, she recalls an incident that occurred immediately after she had given birth to her son, Brendan. While visiting her in the hospital, Susan's mother commented contemptuously on some of the other new-

borns in the hospital nursery, who were sucking on pacifi-
ers. "I raised my children to be independent," she asserted
proudly. Susan was shocked and repelled by the tone of
contempt she heard in her mother's voice directed at the
unsuspecting infants. The incident was disturbing, con-
firming a feeling Susan had always had about her mother,
but had never previously been able to link up to any
specific experience. Susan comes to motherhood relatively
late, and she brings to it her preconceptions, her fears,
and her wishes, which are bound to reflect (perhaps in
negative) her own mother's fear and disdain for the two-
day-old babies in the nursery who were contentedly exercising their sucking reflex.

As mothers some women hope to express the love and
devotion they were never able to express, for any number
of reasons, in relation to their own parents. "My mother
made sure the house was clean, that we were dressed
nicely, and that we had good food, but she wasn't very
warm," says one. Accustomed to stifling their emotions
and adopting an air of self-sufficiency, these women crave
the physical and emotional intimacy that is an accepted
part of the mother-infant relationship. They welcome the
interdependency. As mothers they feel that they have
been given the license to love and be loved unconstrained
by their own mother's inhibitions and prohibitions. For
other women, motherhood reassures them that they are
not only worthwhile human beings—generous, unselfish,
feminine—but also that their individual lives fit into a
larger scheme and that life has meaning beyond the here
and now. "I feel part of a community of women . . . more
normal, more female," says one.

Still other women, grateful for what their parents have
given them, strive to repay the debt they feel they owe
their parents by passing on what they received in the way
of emotional nourishment from the previous generation to
the next generation. As mothers, they feel that they finally have a chance to balance the books. Parents often
have difficulty receiving what their adult children have to

offer them, emotionally as well as materially, and a grandchild can serve as a vehicle through which love and gratitude are expressed indirectly from daughter to parent.
"My mother was just about a perfect mother, and she has
always been my best friend. . . . She would have been
devastated if I'd never had a child. . . . Now I want to be
always there for my daughter Sarah." And finally, some
women valiantly attempt to give to their babies what they
feel they never got in the way of attention, care, intellectual stimulation, or material comfort, hoping of course,
that by proxy they can simultaneously begin to fill in the
holes in their psyches.

Whatever symbolic construction we superimpose on our
relationship with a developing baby, we are bound to get
ourselves in a muddle if the hidden agenda (and most, if
not all, of us are guilty of having some such agenda at one
point or another) serves not only a creative and reparative
function but also to deceive us into believing that the
clock can be turned back, past relationships can be magically transformed, and old wounds can be healed via the
baby. If our mothers never appreciated our achievements
when we were growing up, there is no guarantee that
they will revise their opinion of us when our babies talk
before all the other kids on the block! And, even if they
did, it would not change what was and what lingers on
invisibly inside. Moreover, if we are uncertain of our own
value, our babies can only conclude that they, too, are not
valued for who they really are if we use them to prove to
us otherwise.

> *Daughter am I in my mother's house; but mistress in*
> *my own.*— *Rudyard Kipling*, "Our Lady of the
> Snows"

It is not always clear how a woman's experience in
mothering is connected to her experience of being mothered, and when voices from the past echo through the
chambers of the nursery or the corridors of the office or

wherever a new mother happens to be, they are not always recognized as such. For one thing, there are influences on a woman's experience of motherhood (her partner's attitude, her work situation, and the economic realities of her daily life, to name just a few) that, being more obvious, tend to capture the spotlight and leave the ghosts of the past obscured in the shadows.

While it is easy to see how a husband's or a mother-in-law's or even a friend's response can either bolster or deflate a mother's confidence in her ability to care for a baby, it is often difficult to trace the connecting thread between a woman's past experience of being mothered and her way of mothering now. The path joining past to present is circuitous, and on the surface, differences between the generations are frequently more prominent than similarities: many women work outside the home when their mothers didn't and vice versa; most women expect that their husbands will take an active role in child care when their mothers had no such expectation. These differences are undeniable and reflect important changes in the larger culture that have trickled down into the consciousness of the individual woman, but they tell us little about a woman's internal experience—how happy she is with whatever work she is doing or not doing, and how comfortable she is with her husband's involvement or lack of involvement. Such experiences, invisible to the naked eye, often link one generation to another.

Women do not follow blindly in their mother's footsteps, but all learn from experience, and their own mothers' joys, as well as their regrets, their successes as well as their failures, inform the choices and define the conflicts of the succeeding generation. Psychoanalytic theory is quite helpful in explaining how opposite kinds of behavior are often, in some fundamental way, closely related to each other, since one type of behavior is a reaction against the other. So, for example, an insecure person may be meek and self-denigrating or he may compensate for his poor estimation of himself by being arrogant and devaluing toward others. The surface differences are deceptive and from a psychodynamic point of view, not all that meaningful. Freud provides us with a particularly relevant illustration of this general psychological principle in a section of *Moses and Monotheism* entitled "the return of the repressed." He describes a case in which a daughter conscientiously resists identifying with her mother, and another case in which a son bends over backwards in order that he might live his life as differently from his father as possible. The father was unscrupulous; the son, a paragon of virtue. And yet, despite their efforts to be their parents' opposites, traces of their early identifications with these same parents emerge years later. What was repressed during childhood resurfaces in adulthood as the children become parents themselves and the underlying similarities between parents and children are exposed. Following is an example of how a mother's influence may manifest itself through its opposite.

Kate, sixth in a family of ten children, reported that her mother became overwhelmed with the responsibilities of caring for her children and developed a serious drinking problem. (Kate's case will be discussed at length in the following chapter.) In direct contrast to her mother, who had reluctantly abandoned her graduate studies in biology to care for her children, Kate began a new job during her pregnancy, and returned to a full-time work schedule almost immediately after the birth of her baby. Although there is no doubt that Kate is a responsible and loving mother, and that her baby's well-being is her first priority— "Maureen comes first," she says—her own mother's experience as an unhappy full-time mother was a pivotal one for her. "If I'm happy, Maureen will pick it up," she says knowingly, having been an unhappy witness to her own mother's frustration and sadness. Kate is hyper-vigilant about not falling into the trap her mother did and would rather err in the opposite direction than be drowned as she saw her mother drowned, first in her family and then in alcohol. "I wish I didn't have to travel with my job," she says, but she has never considered leaving her job or jeopardizing her position by refusing to travel even though it means being away from the baby more than she likes.

Although most women feel that the bond they have with their mothers strengthens as they become mothers themselves ("I'm much more tolerant of my mother . . . I understand now what she had to deal with" is a frequent refrain), many women consciously approach mothering intent on being quite different from their mothers at least in certain specific ways. If their descriptions of themselves and their mothers are relatively reliable (and that is admittedly a big "if"), women do, in fact, become very different kinds of mothers than the mothers they experienced growing up. In most cases, however, it is not without some struggle, and most often there is a blending of the positive and negative influences.

Susan, the forty-four-year-old mother of three-year-old Brendan, was brought to tears when during our interview she described the internal tug of war she experienced one night when her son was just five weeks old. It was three o'clock in the morning, and Brendan had been crying intermittently throughout the night—to be nursed, to be cuddled, to be walked. This was not new; in fact, most nights had been spent rocking Brendan, walking Brendan, or otherwise soothing him to sleep. Exhausted from this schedule, which was no schedule at all since Brendan's awakenings were at irregular times, Susan decided early in the evening to begin to try and change the pattern before it developed into a habit. Perhaps, she thought, if she did not respond immediately to his first cry (once he had been fed and put back in his crib), he might be able to soothe himself back to sleep. Didn't some of the "experts" stress the importance of helping the baby develop the ability for self-soothing? Realizing that her son might be a bit young for that, and that her own need for sleep entered into her decision to try something new, Susan admittedly felt uneasy. What was really in "the best interest of the baby"?

Susan could almost hear her mother's voice coolly advising her to let him cry himself to sleep, but this familiar voice only confused matters further. Susan had a vivid recollection of the cries emanating from her younger brother's room when he had been just a baby and she was already old enough to be concerned for him. Her mother had pointedly ignored his screams,(it was supposed to build character), and Susan hadn't known what to think about it all at the time.

Lying in bed, wide awake, her baby crying in the next room (now for five minutes), Susan suddenly knew what *she* wanted to do. Bounding out of bed, she hurried into her son's room and picked him up. His cries stopped almost instantly in response to her touch. Rocking him in her arms, walking back and forth throughout the darkened apartment, she became overwhelmed with contradictory feelings. Tenderness overflowed and blended with sorrowful longing to produce a sweet sadness that was pleasure and pain all in one.

Retrospectively, Susan understands that in soothing her son, she was also soothing herself as a baby, and because her own mother had been incapable of giving so freely of herself, Susan was moving beyond her mother. Having released herself from her mother's painfully tight clasp on her emotions through this act of tenderness, she was able to experience an intense sweetness, which her emotionally constricted mother had deprived herself and her children of. Susan's sadness was for herself as a baby, a baby who had never got what she was now able to give to her son. It was also a sadness for her mother, who had been and was still stuck. By allowing herself to give more than she had received, Susan was leaving her mother behind, and this was sad as well as tremendously exhilarating. Susan felt as if a burden had been lifted from her shoulders, a burden she had carried with her everywhere without knowing how much it had weighed her down and darkened her vision.

*   *   *

Judith experienced her mother very differently from Susan, but her inner dialogues and conflicts also reflect her struggle to understand her mother, transcend her mother's limitations, and give to her mother, now deceased, what she was unable to do when she was alive. Two separate but related incidents illustrate her metamorphosis as a mother and her mother's daughter.

The first incident occurred a few weeks after the birth of her baby. She had been home alone with the baby the entire day, which in itself was still a novel experience for her on two counts: she was not used to being home at three-thirty in the afternoon for any reason other than being bedridden, and during the first week or so after the baby was born, there was a near-continuous stream of visitors. So this was a unique opportunity for reflection. The afternoon sun was flooding the apartment as her infant lay in its crib asleep, a tranquil expression on its face. She "puttered around the house" (a phrase she recalled her mother having used to describe her own domestic activity) and marveled at how pleasing it was to see the daytime sun illuminate the room after so many years of working under artificial lights. She recalls having felt blissful, reveling in the opportunity to simply *be*, and wondering why on earth it had seemed so terribly urgent to her to have a "career," and to carve a place for herself in the world of work. Had she actually been so misguided as to believe that that was the only one worth inhabiting, she wondered to herself. At that particular moment, such a worldview seemed so patently narrow, cold-blooded, and alien. How and why did she come by it?

At some point in these musings, images of her mother, with a characteristically wistful and lost expression on her face, surfaced, incongruous with her own newly discovered experience of inner contentment. How might she understand that expression on her mother's face when it contradicted her own experience as a mother? She didn't feel wistful or lost. Quite the contrary, she felt blissful and grounded. Judith began to question whether she had been wrong in assuming that her mother's look reflected a yearning to do more with herself than just "putter around the house." "After all," she thought, "what could be more satisfying to me than this puttering, when I know that my baby is resting happily in the other room?" Perhaps her mother's sadness had a different origin altogether, or was a complicated mixture of things, having relatively little to do with being at home, taking care of the house and family. Things seemed to be falling into place—at least for the moment. Wasn't her own drive to be "more" than a housewife related to all these memories of her mother, which had haunted her throughout her adolescence? More reflective than when her day began, she still felt unusually contented when her infant awoke from its nap, and her thoughts turned to more practical matters.

Three weeks later, incident number two: bleary-eyed from lack of sleep, and frustrated literally to tears at having been unable to quiet her irritable baby, who was crying for no discernable reason, Judith suddenly flashed back to the first time she saw her own mother cry. She remembered how upsetting it was for her at age five ("It must have been earlier than that") to see her mother cry, particularly since it seemed somehow to be her own fault. And then, under the mounting pressure of her baby's inconsolable screams, she felt, for the first time, that she could truly understand why neither she nor her mother had been able to hold back the tears. "She tried so hard, and I am trying so hard, and yet try as we might we fail in our quest to eliminate pain, frustration, and unhappiness." The promise of Nirvana has been broken.

Still tearful herself, Judith felt shaken and confused, but convinced nevertheless that the intensity of her response to her baby's cries had less to do with her baby and more to do with her mother. Once the crying had ceased and her baby was peacefully nursing, she realized that one source of confusion during the incident, which was surely not the first of its kind, was that she identified simultaneously with the baby in her arms, with the image of her

mother crying and frustrated, and with the image of herself as a young child, terrified at having seen her mother
so unhappy and feeling impotent to make it all better. She
recalled that, in the heat of the moment, she silently
vowed not to be like her mother—unhappy and frustrated—
but also not to allow her innocent baby to suffer the
sadness that she herself had felt as a little girl seeing her
mother so unhappy. "Why can't you be calmer and more
loving to her when she is irritable?" she asked herself
guiltily, identifying with the baby and the child within
her. But this again was only part of a more intricately
detailed picture. She also identified with her mother, a
woman who never quite emerged from her shell, a hungry child herself, who had never received the appreciation
and respect she deserved.

It is not coincidental that on this afternoon it occurred
to Judith that she should give her office a call to remind
them that she was still interested in returning to work,
and that she did *not* plan to resign when her leave of
absence was up in a couple of months. "My mother always warned me never to put all of my eggs in one
basket. Unfortunately for her, she did, and unfortunately
for me, I was the basket in which she placed her dreams.
We both suffered on that account." Judith knew that she
didn't want to be away from her daughter all day, every
day, but after that episode she began to think of ways to
return to work part-time.

For Judith, being happy and having a happy daughter
is an expression of her love for her mother. She is creating
the kind of life her mother longed for but never had, and
this is her gift to her. When something goes awry, however, when her daughter is miserable and she feels impotent to alleviate her misery, she feels that she is slipping
into her past rather than reshaping it and making it all
better. At that point, her loyalty to her unhappy mother
demands that she part ways, rather than follow directly
behind in her footsteps.

2

Becoming the Mother You Had (Or Never Had)

Our mothers model for us what we do and do not want to be, and generally we incorporate both the positive and the negative as we develop our individual styles of mothering. In this chapter we will explore in more detail the paths a number of women traversed, starting from their early experiences *being mothered* by their particular mothers to their experiences *mothering*. For the purposes of illustration, the women discussed in this chapter will be roughly divided into two groups based on their contrasting experiences as daughters: women who perceived their mothers as having been too distant and not tender enough, and women who perceived their mothers as having been too enmeshed and not separate enough. Their experiences along the dimension of disengagement and enmeshment are what they hold in common, but as we shall see, each new mother transforms the raw material of what she got as a daughter to create her own distinct and multifaceted relationship with her baby.

Women who remember their mothers as having been cool and distant are frequently determined to give their child the warmth and understanding they feel they didn't receive when they were young. The baby must not feel neglected, invisible, or inconsequential. They often find that having a baby gives them the freedom to love and be loved unconditionally for the first time in their lives. Sometimes, however, there is the worry that they, like their own mothers before them, do not and perhaps even cannot give enough of themselves. (A baby cries for more when they have already dipped into their reserves and given all that they can.) Still hungry for affection themselves they are haunted by the phantom of the "bottomless pit" that can never be filled, within themselves and within their babies. Torn by their desire to give but also wary lest they not be sufficiently given to, these women can become extremely self-critical when they find that, as mothers, they, too, are not always loving or attuned or available.

Gina, thirty-one, is the mother of a three-year-old girl. Gina completed a master's degree in business prior to having her daughter. She described her own mother as a severe and emotionally distant woman—"She never stopped to find out what it was like to be me; it was more like 'clean your room.'" And Gina remembers feeling invisible and emotionally undernourished. During most of Gina's childhood her mother worked full-time in a factory, and her remaining waking hours were spent cooking, cleaning, and generally maintaining the home. Although she made sure that Gina's clothes were always ironed neatly for school, and that there were always home-cooked meals at regularly designated hours, Gina's mother rarely paused long enough to discover who her daughter was on the inside, nor did she find time to indulge in the more tender aspects of mothering. At least this is how Gina remembers her. Over the years, Gina learned to assert her existence by challenging her mother at every juncture, and though this only served to justify her mother's harsh manner and confirm her suspicions that firmness rather than tenderness was what her daughter needed, her behavior assured Gina of a clear and intense mother-daughter connection.

Gina's experience as a child insinuated itself into her experience as a mother in the following manner. Gina returned to part-time work when her daughter, Laura, was one and a half. Although she was pleased with the compromise she had struck between work and motherhood and felt comfortable that Laura had made an easy adjustment to her mother's absence from home, Gina nevertheless questioned whether she was satisfying (or even capable of satisfying) her daughter's emotional needs.

Her insecurities appeared to be unrealistic, stemming more from her past experience than from what transpired in the present between her and her daughter. Unlike the mother she remembers having had when she was growing up, Gina is unequivocally very interested in getting to know her daughter. She is well attuned to subtle shifts in Laura's moods and interprets them empathically. However, Gina notices every minor lapse in her own attentiveness, and since the standard by which she measures herself is weighted heavily against her, she tends to be her own worst critic. She is as unsympathetic to her own shortcomings, sometimes losing sight of the forest for the trees, as her mother was when she was growing up. (If only she had been perfect, then maybe her mother would have taken notice of her; if only she were perfect now, then maybe her daughter would never whimper.)

As a mother herself, it is evident that Gina luxuriates in the love and adoration her daughter feels for her, something she never felt she got enough of in her relationship with her mother. But being the center of her daughter's universe makes her feel uneasy, as well. Her daughter is not *her* whole world—her husband, her work, even her domestic chores demand her time and attention. Gina knows intellectually that this is as it should be, but. . . . When her relationship to Laura bears even the slightest hint of a resemblance to her mother's relationship to her, Gina cannot stifle her doubts about whether she is giving her daughter enough of what she didn't get from her mother.

As a new mother, Gina is forced to come to terms with her disappointment as a daughter, because it has colored her perceptions of herself and her emotional resources. Although feelings of disappointment with her own mother nag at her and challenge her to do things differently with

Laura, they simultaneously lead her to doubt her ability to do precisely that. Sometimes Gina wonders whether she was wrong, after all, to have felt ignored as a child. Perhaps, she argues with herself, she took it too personally when her mother was preoccupied with practical matters. Was she unrealistic, as all children tend to be at times, in expecting more from her mother? But then again, she argues back, if she wasn't wrong, and her hardworking, well-meaning mother did neglect her emotionally despite her virtuous and self-sacrificing manner, how can she be sure that her daughter does not also feel neglected when she does not give her the undivided attention she clamors for? And how can she be sure that her daughter isn't right? Until Gina can recognize her mother's shortcomings without condemning her for them, she will remain a harsh critic when it comes to her own imperfections as a mother, and her perceptions of the present—her own behavior and her daughter's—will be clouded by its ambiguous relationship to her past.

Diane, too, expressed fears that despite her conscious intentions she may be unable to put her own selfish desires aside and give her son the attention he needs. Diane describes her mother as a depressed and withdrawn woman who, shortly before giving birth to Diane, lost most of her family in Europe during World War Two. Whenever Diane finds herself among family but momentarily miles away, lost in her own thoughts, she is jolted out of her reveries by the memories she has of her mother staring off into space, physically present but emotionally inaccessible to her. Prior to becoming a mother, this was not a problem for Diane, because there was simply more time and space to drift off into her own private musings, and nobody seemed to suffer on that account. But now she is aware that when she temporarily checks out, so to speak, she is ignoring her son, who is energetically trying to capture her attention, and this disturbs her. It is all too familiar. Her need to retreat periodically from the fray of domestic life into her own thoughts is a part of Diane's character that is not easily modified. Perhaps that is one reason why she waited until she was forty to have a baby. As a mother whose own mother was emotionally remote, Diane is amazed and relieved to see that she has been able to bend to her son's needs as much as she has, but she remains somewhat wary of her ability to transcend the mother within her.

Often the secret, unarticulated worries new mothers bring with them to motherhood are unreasonable, reflecting the difficulty they have disentangling their identities from their mothers' identities more than anything else. Other times, however, their worries have some basis in reality, for after all, each is her mother's daughters and has incorporated aspects of her personality. The family resemblance cannot be denied. One dilemma these women (who recall their mothers as having been overly distant or cold) experience may be expressed in the form of the following question: "If I don't *always* feel loving and I don't *always* want to bend over backward for my baby does that mean that I'm being cold and inflexible like my mother?" Since most of the time it is not a question of *always* or *never* but rather of "What is too much?" and "What is not enough?" there is no simple solution to these troubling questions, no yes or no answer by which to allay these women's anxieties once and for all.

In contrast to this first group of women, who felt neglected as children, there are those who remember their mothers as *overly* dependent upon their children for intimacy and emotional contact, and sometimes this over-involvement in their children's lives went hand in hand with a dependency upon their husbands for economic security and social standing. As mothers, these women are often sensitive to potential threats to their sense of separateness and are determined to preserve their independence by maintaining interests outside of their baby and family. In contrast to Gina or Diane, these women are more worried about being overly consumed by their involvement in other people's lives (their baby's, their husband's) than about being too selfish, too unyielding, or too self-absorbed.

Elizabeth is a woman who vocalized specific concerns on becoming a mother, when she allowed herself, as she never had before, to become completely dependent upon her husband financially. Since her particular situation illustrates well how past experiences color, sometimes to the point of distortion, present experiences, it is worthy of further attention.

Although Elizabeth and her husband were in complete agreement that she should stop working and complete her graduate studies after the birth of their first baby (they did not need the extra money she had been earning by working part-time), she found herself anxious at the idea of relinquishing her financial independence, even temporarily, despite the fact that in terms of dollars and cents her earnings had actually amounted to relatively little. What was causing the difficulty was the symbolism she attached to earning her keep.

Elizabeth's mother had devoted her life to cultivating her intellectual interests and talents and to raising her children. To the dismay of her husband, marketing herself was distinctly not one of her talents. And according to family lore, Elizabeth's father sacrificed his own aspirations to live the life of an artist—"sold his soul," went into business, and assumed the responsibility of being sole breadwinner. A good provider, her father also brought home with him from the office a fair amount of bitterness and the atmosphere became thick with mutual resentment. Ultimately the arrangement became intolerable for both husband and wife, and the marriage dissolved after more than thirty years.

Middle-aged at the time of the divorce, Elizabeth's mother was even less able to support herself than she had been twenty-five years earlier. She floundered for a while—the family (including Elizabeth) went into therapy, the country house was sold—and Elizabeth's mother now lives reasonably well on the interest. A happier ending than most, perhaps, but her mother's experience left Elizabeth cautious about embarking on a similar journey, all expenses paid.

Elizabeth had always been very attached to her mother, and though there was a period during adolescence when Elizabeth's sexual precocity threatened to rupture their very special relationship, drawing her into an alliance with her father, Elizabeth continues to be quite openly identified with her mother. Nevertheless, when motherhood suddenly thrust Elizabeth into a situation in which she found herself entirely dependent upon her husband financially, conflicts she had always had about her mother and her mother's ill-fated relationship with her father were stirred up.

Unlike Elizabeth's father, Elizabeth's husband enjoys his work enormously and does *not* seem to resent his role as exclusive wage-earner. Unlike her mother, Elizabeth has supported herself, is not naïve about matters of money, and is pursuing a degree that should give her the skills to earn a good living in the not-so-distant future. However, these realities do not entirely relieve Elizabeth of the internal pressure she experiences. Her position as a new mother, dependent upon her husband for her social standing and economic security, is reminiscent of her own mother's position vis-à-vis her father, despite the very real differences in their situations and their personalities. Consequently, she feels that she is paddling in dangerously familiar waters and must be on the alert for shifting currents.

Elizabeth tries to distance herself psychologically from her mother, or at least from certain dependent aspects of her mother's life. She affirms her independence by patently refusing to dress the part of a "middle-class" woman, supported comfortably by her husband. "I get pleasure in being in contrast to our apartment" (luxurious by any standards); "I'm dissociated from it." She even cultivates "an extra *lack* of fashion." The conflict Elizabeth experiences as a new mother is not only about money and social standing, and it is not only between her and her husband, but it is about dependency and autonomy, her own and her mother's.

When, upon looking back, a woman is convinced that her own mother's identity was buried in the process of mothering, she may worry that she, too, will wake up and discover that she has submerged herself and stifled her creativity in motherhood and may need regular reassurance that *her* head is still above water. Afraid of becoming a consumed and consuming mother, such a woman may actually lean over backward in the opposite direction and distance herself unnecessarily from her baby or from other mothers, vigilantly guarding time and space for *her*self. Rather than infantilizing her toddler, as she perhaps was infantilized by her mother, she applauds his growing independence and is less sympathetic than she might be to his need to regress periodically. The fear of giving too much and plunging in too deep is often an unreasonable one, reflecting a woman's ambivalent identification with her overinvolved mother more than her actual relationship to her baby and other aspects of her life. But, realistic or not, her fears of turning into her mother can propel her forward in one direction and then backward again in the other.

In psychological terms, new mothers can become embroiled in the classic approach-avoidance conflict. As they distance themselves from their mothers in order to avoid making the same mistakes they feel their mothers made, they find themselves being pulled back; they are their mothers' daughters, and how can they betray (and it can feel like a betrayal) that early bond? But, as they are drawn in closer, and the identification with their mothers becomes too dominant a strain in their lives, they resist being engulfed once again, and so the pendulum swings.

Thirty-five-year-old Laura, a government worker and mother of a boy who is two and a half, is a good example of a woman who remembers her own mother as having been overly involved in her children's lives, to the detriment of all. Laura describes her mother as the kind of adult who is really a kid among the kids. Unable to distance herself from her children, she found it impossible to be a parent and to take an authoritative stand, with the result being continual chaos and intermittent explosive outbursts. From Laura's point of view, her mother's overinvolvement in the emotional ups and downs of her children went hand in hand with her ineffectuality.

Laura lost respect for her mother because her mother, so closely identified with each of her children, was unable to impose order upon a household that was brimming with adolescent conflict. Consequently, she is intent on doing things differently now that she is a mother herself. She does not want to lose respect for herself, nor does she want her son to think of her as ineffectual. Therefore, Laura makes every effort to avoid the emotional messiness characteristic of her experience growing up; if anything, she is overly conscientious about setting clear limits and establishing inviolable boundaries between herself as parent and her son as child.

On the level of daily life this manifests itself in a tendency for Laura to be less patient than her husband, less likely to tolerate lengthy negotiations with their son when he does not want to brush his teeth or go to bed: all in all, a less "democratic" approach to parenting. This difference between herself and her husband would be less troubling were it not for the fact that Laura is not altogether comfortable with her no-nonsense approach to mothering. She is critical of herself when she is impatient with her son, admires her husband's sensitivity to their son's need to have a say in how things get done, and at times feels genuinely confused about whether she is being too strict or her husband is being too indulgent. Fearing that her two-year-old might inveigle her into a battle of the wills in which she might waver and lose too much ground, as her mother frequently did before her, Laura resists the battle with a vehemence that only lets her know that in some circuitous fashion she is reenacting her mother's experience.

Ironically, her tendency to make snap judgments rather than negotiate or flounder around for solutions reminds Laura of her mother, who was not only childlike but also arbitrarily dictatorial in relation to her children. This was how her mother tried (unsuccessfully) to regain her footing and prop up her faltering position of authority. Paradoxically, in Laura's effort to distance herself from her mother's way of mothering, she finds herself relying on the very same maneuvers on which her mother relied, after having allowed herself to slip into an emotional swampland.

Women who perceive their mothers as having been overly involved in their children experience to some degree or other a common dilemma that may be expressed in the form of the following question: "If I let down my guard, surrender some control over my life and my feelings, and allow myself to enter fully into motherhood, does this mean that I will sink into oblivion, and lose my sense of myself as well as my child's respect as my sad and frustrated mother did before me?" The conflict around control and autonomy expressed by this question is one that may seem to have been resolved years earlier, often during adolescence, when in response to a mother's engulfing involvement a daughter religiously establishes a separate identity for herself. At that point she may have drawn clear and secure boundaries around herself and allowed nobody to tamper with them. Upon having a baby, these boundaries are no longer respected and they are no longer realistic. They keep too much good feeling out and prevent important information from coming in. New lines must be drawn, and in the process feelings break through with an intensity that pries open the doors these women shut so firmly years earlier. The old conflicts about being separate and being intimate, giving and holding back, rooted in the early mother-daughter relationship, demand new resolutions.

*　　*　　*

In this section we will examine more closely the divergent paths taken by a number of women. Beginning with each woman's experience of being mothered in a particular fashion, we can identify traces of her past experience as a daughter that surface (sometimes in disguise) in her experience as a mother. By this process, we can begin to understand, from a psychological point of view, the origins of the particular set of conflicts each woman grapples with as she incorporates motherhood into her identity as a woman.

When Charlotte, thirty-five and the mother of a three-year-old boy, was asked how she would have liked her mother to have been different, she responded by relating the following joke, one told to her by her mother:

> An Irish woman, Mrs. O'Shea, is talking to a priest when a woman passes by with her eight children. The priest says, "God bless Mrs. O'Grady, there she goes with her eight children," and Mrs. O'Shea says, "I wish God had blessed me with eight children." And the father says, "Why, Mrs. O'Shea, didn't God bless you with children?" And she says, "Yes, by God, thirteen of them."

Charlotte is one of eight children herself and has carried with her into her adulthood the feeling that she missed something important being one of many, herded around with the "flock" by her loving but overburdened and ultimately distant mother. Charlotte described her mother as a "loving, lovely, but pained" woman, overwhelmed by the responsibilities of caring for her eight children. "Stretched thin," she was unable to give any of her children much in the way of individualized attention, and Charlotte's memories of time spent with her mother during her childhood generally include the family as a group.

Having perceived her mother as the Burdened One, Charlotte became very protective of her, and the special relationship she carved for herself was as her mother's buffer and alter ego. "I knew that she was in pain, and that her life was difficult and that I wanted more from her and that she couldn't give it. . . . She named me after her . . . she identified with me and used me as a buffer for the pain and stress in her life. . . . I wanted to protect her against feeling guilty or feeling inadequate or sad." However, as is always the case when a child tries to cure a parent's spiritual suffering, Charlotte was unable to resolve her mother's problems for her, particularly since she seemed to bring some of them on herself. "I remember her telling me that since she took care of children a lot when she was growing up, the one thing she didn't want to do was to have a lot of kids herself." Charlotte is convinced that "popping out more babies" was a way in which her mother simultaneously dealt with the stresses in her life and created more stress for herself. Her mother confided in her once that she wished she had finished high school and continued on to nursing school. But she hadn't, and as it turned out, her children "were all she had." Paradoxically, they were her solace as well as her burden, what gave her life meaning and what kept her from fulfilling her dreams.

Charlotte's mother's contradictory feelings about being a mother (her children were everything to her and she sacrificed everything for them) were naturally transmitted to Charlotte, who had since childhood assumed responsibility for her mother's happiness and unhappiness. Being her mother's confidante conferred on Charlotte special powers to soothe, to comfort, to make amends, but it also rendered her particularly vulnerable to feelings of anger when her efforts were unsuccessful and feelings of guilt when she wished to disengage from the struggle to make her mother happy.

During her late adolescence and early adulthood, Charlotte made a conscious effort to separate herself from the family group, and discover who she was and what she wanted for herself—or at least that is how it appeared to

Charlotte in retrospect. She decided to leave her hometown, pursue a graduate degree, settle in New York City, and marry outside her family's religion, and in this manner she differentiated herself from her parents as well as from her siblings.

When Charlotte became a mother at the age of thirty-one, after having established a professional identity for herself within an "egalitarian marriage," the old conflicts having to do with being a separate person and a loyal daughter at the same time were stirred up once again. These were conflicts she admittedly had not completely resolved during her childhood and adolescence—and conflicts her mother had not resolved satisfactorily for herself a generation earlier.

When Charlotte became a mother she resolved to give her baby all the individualized attention she had longed for but rarely experienced directly in her relationship with her mother. In her role as her mother's confidante she approached this kind of intimacy, but the attention was on her mother and her mother's needs, rather than on herself and her own needs. In contrast to her mother, she wanted to be available to her son when he needed her, and in contrast to her own experience of being lost in a crowd of children, all clamoring for a scarce supply of attention, she wanted her son to have the chance to develop his unique talents, at his own pace, with her support and encouragement. This was all very well and good in theory, but it posed a problem for Charlotte, because in her commitment to giving her son what she herself had not had as a child, she lost touch with what she needed for herself as an individual apart from her son. She mothered her son as she had attempted to mother her mother and as she had wished (and still wishes) to be mothered herself.

Charlotte did not return to half-time work as she had planned, and it was only with considerable ambivalence that she began to work one morning a week when her baby turned eight months old. Charlotte found herself feeling anxious and guilty when she spent time away from home, whether it was for work or for pleasure, because this meant that she was taking time away from her son. However, she also felt depleted by her responsibilities caring for Ted and periodically exploded at her husband and at her son when she was feeling ungiven to herself.

Ironically, Charlotte's angry outbursts reminded her of her mother, whose tired and beaten-down expression would suddenly become transformed as her eyes flashed with anger and bitter frustration. Her mother had frequently resorted to yelling, presumably because unless she exploded she simply was not heard at all. But the similarity between Charlotte and her mother only intensified Charlotte's feelings of shame and guilt when she could no longer contain her anger or smother her resentment. This did not coincide with her image of the mother she wanted to be.

There is little doubt that Charlotte was a devoted and creative mother, rocking her colicky baby for hours at a time during the first three months of his life and playing with her toddler on the floor for days on end. Now that her son is nearly three years old, few can rival her ability to enter into his world and engage in imaginary play. Since becoming a mother, however, Charlotte has sensed that she has slipped back into another mind-set, one in which the needs of others—the group of her siblings, her mother, and now her son—almost invariably take precedence over her own needs. This internal reshuffling of priorities met with some resistance, since she had worked so hard to create a sense of herself as a worthwhile individual during her young adulthood.

Finding a balance between giving and taking, between being connected and being separate, is a fundamental task of mothering for all women. But for Charlotte, balancing her own needs as an individual with the needs of her son and family was a particularly difficult problem because her own mother had never quite resolved the problem in her own life, and everybody in the family was affected as a result. They heard her regrets and witnessed her weariness day in and day out. Charlotte described her mother as a woman who was able to give but unable to take, at least not before things reached near-crisis proportions. Charlotte believed that this was the source of her mother's pain and bitterness and the antecedent for her own chronic feelings of not being taken care of.

Just as her mother felt frustrated at being unheard and uncared for, so, too, Charlotte feels at times deprived and bitter, questioning whether her husband is doing enough for her or for the family. She traces some of her bitterness back to her mother, but it is difficult for her to disentangle the past from the present. Drawing a parallel between herself and her mother, she recalled that her mother "had to yell really loud to be heard and I mean more than physical hearing, I mean emotionally for anyone to hear, and I think for me I have to get to as bitter a point as I do in order to recognize that I have emotional needs that aren't being met."

Charlotte is aware that a tendency to eat compulsively and to go on spending "binges" (something that was never a problem before she became a mother) is one way in which she expresses her feelings of deprivation, but she finds it difficult to satisfy her needs more directly. She notes, moreover, that during her childhood she was nearly anorectic and that her refusal to eat was her way of distancing herself from her engulfing but emotionally unnourishing family. Eating compulsively takes on an additional meaning in this context; by bingeing, she continues her mother's tradition of not asking directly for what she needs, and she rejoins the fold by mirroring her mother's frustration rather than challenging it at the source. When this happens Charlotte is re-creating the emotional environment in which she grew up.

As a mother, Charlotte is, like most women, remaking and repeating her past relationship with her own mother. She has transcended many of her mother's limitations and has actively striven to give her child more of what she didn't have enough of when she was growing up herself. In her efforts to remake the past she has become a mother who is exquisitely attuned to her son's individual needs and has structured her life so that he does not experience himself as she did—one of a flock, faceless, and hungry for attention. Ironically, as her mother's daughter she received good training in sensitivity to the needs of others.

However, the differences between Charlotte and her mother should not obscure the underlying similarities. In her devotion to her son, her own definitions of who she is and where she wants to go have become blurry, and, just as her mother felt overwhelmed and bitter, Charlotte, too, is haunted at times by feelings of deprivation that she expresses indirectly by overeating or overspending. While her mother had eight children and she has, at this point, only one, the demands Charlotte has placed upon herself, to give and not to take, re-create the emotional climate of her childhood. Perhaps, as much as she has moved away from her mother's style of mothering, she feels the need to reasssure the weary mother within her that she remains a loyal daughter who breathes the same atmosphere and who has not strayed far from the nest.

Kate is also from a large family—in fact, she was the sixth in a family of ten children—but though she, too, experienced her mother as "spread thin" and insufficiently involved with her when she was growing up, Kate's experience of her mother was, in other ways, quite different from Charlotte's. Consequently, Kate came to motherhood with very different expectations for herself and her baby.

Kate's mother was doing graduate work in biology and teaching the G.I.'s returning home from World War II when she fell in love with Kate's father and got married. At that time it was rather unusual for a woman to be studying for a doctoral degree in biology, but as Kate understands it, her mother was an exceptional woman

. and very committed to her work. After the birth of each of her first two children she returned to her studies and her teaching, leaving her children in the care of her mother. But once the third child was born and the family had relocated to the Midwest on account of Kate's father's work, this arrangement was no longer possible. Kate is convinced that her mother experienced the transformation of her life as a major loss, but the consequences would not become apparent until years later.

According to Kate's description, in the beginning, her mother applied herself industriously to the task of motherhood. She was always busy, never idle. She made sure all of her children were dressed well ("She made all of our clothes for us") and had all the cultural and educational advantages she herself valued so much ("We were given piano lessons, dance lessons, and she took us to museums. She even took four of us on a trip to Washington D.C."). But Kate sensed that her mother yearned for something more. "She would have loved to have gone off on her own," says Kate; she took flying lessons at one point, but of course she couldn't literally fly off, much though she might have wished to. After all, she had ten children, and her husband had no domestic inclinations.

Kate's father offered her mother little in the way of emotional support—his motto was "children should be seen but not heard"—and Kate believes that her mother lost her "sense of herself" in her solitary quest to provide a culturally rich environment for her ten children. The emotional cost of "constantly giving and never getting anything for herself" was high, and when Kate was twelve, her mother began drinking heavily, or at least that was when it became obvious to Kate. Her mother's alcoholism, which ultimately led to her hospitalization once her children were old enough to insist that she take care of herself, created an atmosphere of instability within the family and fractured the very foundation of harmony and culture she had endeavored to lay. She took flight metaphorically, and, since her husband was only peripherally

involved in family life, her children had to fend for
themselves.

"Chaos and contradiction" is the way Kate characterized life in her family, but the contradictions make psychological sense. A conscientious but deeply frustrated
woman who single-handedly raised her ten children with
minimal emotional support from her authoritarian-minded
husband, Kate's mother was also one who could forget to
pick up her daughter from a Brownie meeting, and who
was "oblivious" to the fracas going on right before her
eyes. "It would be hell in our house, just hell; my mother
would be drunk and my father would scream and yell,
and it was agonizing for every one of us. . . . We used to
call her Eve White and Eve Black. She would be this
loving, lovely woman that everybody in the world would
just love, and as soon as she had a sip, or even smelled
alcohol she became Eve Black . . . a ranting and raving
lunatic."

Whatever ambivalence Kate had and still has about her
mother—and her descriptions of her are overflowing with
contradictory memories and feelings—Kate does not seem
to blame her mother for her alcoholism, her emotional
volatility, and her unreliability. She came away from her
experience as a daughter wishing only that her mother
could have been a happier woman. "We got as much out
of our mother in terms of passing on the good, the information, the education, the intelligence, everything that
anybody else would ever get, and I think that both my
parents did as good a job as any parent's could ever do in
bringing up their children. . . . Every family has problems
. . . I just wish the two of them would have been happier,
with themselves, internally." This will be significant in
shaping Kate's expectations for motherhood.

Kate has a master's degree in business ("All of us had
careers; my sister's a doctor"), and before she became
pregnant she ran her own company. When she found that
she was pregnant with her daughter, Maureen, she decided to shut down the company as soon as possible (it

was in the process of folding anyway) and secure another position before her condition became too obvious to prospective employers. Kate quickly found another job in her field, hiding all the while, until it was no longer possible, the fact that she was expecting a baby.

Up until Maureen's birth, Kate continued to work full-time and then some, often getting to the office at 7:30 A.M., and when her husband was at night school, not returning home until 9:00 P.M., and she was unwavering in her desire to return to full-time work after the baby was born. Kate did in fact return to work after ten weeks (Maureen was born by cesarean, and this accounted for the "delay"), and though her hours are somewhat attenuated (she generally gets to the office by 9:00 and returns home by 6:30), she has only missed work a couple of times during the fifteen months of her daughter's life.

In comparison with Charlotte, Kate appears relatively free of conflicts regarding her work outside the home; She says, "I always wanted a career and always thought I'd be very successful in what I did." And yet, despite her long hours away from Maureen, Kate does not hesitate when it comes to identifying her priorities: her daughter takes precedence over her work. This is not a contradiction for Kate, since she is convinced that her daughter's happiness hinges on her own feeling of well-being, which in turn is inextricably linked to her work and her sense of self-respect. "My mother had very little confidence in herself. . . . If you don't respect yourself, you can't possibly get respect from others, and I think that because she didn't respect herself at all, she got very little respect from all of us."

Kate is fiercely committed to not repeating her mother's life pattern. Kate knows first-hand how destructive it can be for a woman to submerge herself entirely in motherhood, and how, ultimately, everyone in the family pays dearly for her "selfless" devotion. "Eve White" and "Eve Black" are two sides of the same coin. And yet, despite their differences, she remains her mother's daughter. Ac-

knowledging the stresses of coordinating her schedule
with her husband's and the baby-sitter's, Kate is, after
fifteen months of motherhood, pleasantly surprised at
how little difficulty she has had juggling career and motherhood. She appears to be genuinely unfazed by the frenzy
of her daily life. Kate finds that her experience being
mothered by an unpredictable, unavailable mother was,
oddly enough, good preparation for motherhood. "All my
life I've lived in a very chaotic situation; I grew up in
chaos, and that's probably what I'm most comfortable
with. . . . I had to deal with it. . . . I can be flexible . . . if
something's hard one day, I know that the next day it will
be all right."

Kate is explicit about not wanting to be the kind of
mother her mother was; nevertheless, it is evident that
not all of her mother's influence was negative. Although
she describes her mother as frequently having been oblivious to her children and acknowledges that at a certain
point her mother so abdicated her responsibilities that her
children had to learn to mother themselves, Kate has
come to value the qualities of independence and flexibiity
she was forced to develop at an early age. As a mother
herself, she is proud of her ability to maintain a relatively
laid-back attitude and has little admiration for the overly
solicitous mothers she encounters who worry about
every whimper and every scrape. Being a survivor herself,
Kate finds herself less prone to panic. Other mothers may
"get crazy" when their infants put anything and everything into their mouths, but Kate can say, "I see what we
survived, and I'm sure I put a lot worse in my mouth."
For Kate to "get crazy" would be tantamount to condemning her mother of child abuse, and she is not prepared to
do so.

Although Kate greatly resented the fact that her mother
was so undependable and does not want her daughter to
worry about whether *she* will be there to pick her up from
a Brownie meeting, she also marvels at how well she and
her siblings turned out despite it all—"We grew up being

fine upstanding citizens instead of junkies and crazy people." Perhaps her conviction, based upon her own experience as a child, that children are quite hardy little creatures, explains why Kate appears relatively free of conflict at having left her daughter for long hours from a very early age (with a carefully chosen baby-sitter). Then again, given her mother's experience as a mother, and her own experience as her mother's daughter, she was psychologically unprepared to do otherwise; not working would have been out of the question for her.

There are certain parallels between Kate's and Charlotte's experiences as daughters. Both women described their mothers as having been overwhelmed by their responsibilities caring for their numerous children, who seemed to "pop out" despite their conscious wishes. Both women characterize their mothers as having been "stretched thin," as women who gave until they were depleted, as women with limited ability to ask directly for what they needed to sustain themselves. But there were significant differences as well, and Kate's solutions to her mother's conflicts were not Charlotte's. Charlotte's mother continued on a steady course; she felt bitter perhaps, but there were no major crises in her life. Nor was there a clear path she could have taken to fulfill herself more than she did as a mother, certainly not one leading her outside the context of her home; she came from a poor and uneducated family, where her experience as a mother was just what would have been expected. Her dreams of a different life were just that—dreams.

Kate's mother, on the other hand, was educated, financially well set-up, and had established a professional identity for herself before she became a mother. Having worked prior to having her children, the requirements of motherhood came as more of a shock. Her losses were real, not simply fantasies. Oscillating between extreme devotion to her children and obvious neglect, Kate's mother plummeted to far greater depths of despair and expressed her unhappiness in more radical terms. On becoming a mother,

Kate decided to take the path her mother had begun to take and then diverged from. By choosing to work full-time she is saying, in effect, "Since I would have been a happier child if my mother had been a happier person, my daughter will also be happier if I allow myself the freedom to have a life apart from being her mother."

Women who experienced their mothers as overly protective or overly involved in their lives when they were children bring to motherhood a different set of preconceptions about what it means to be a mother and how it feels to be a dependent child. But knowing that a woman experienced her mother as overly involved in her life is just the first step to unraveling the connecting threads that join her experience of mothering to her experience of being mothered. As we have observed, Charlotte and Kate responded very differently to the experience of growing up essentially alone, unattended to at the deepest level, one among many. They defined the "problem" their mothers had somewhat differently, and used different strategies in their efforts to construct a happier life for themselves and their children.

So, too, there are bound to be similarities as well as differences between women who describe their mothers as having been overly enmeshed in their lives. What many of these women seem to hold in common, however, is a sense that their mothers harbored a certain amount of resentment toward them precisely because they occupied such a prominent place in their universe. The logic behind their mother's experience is somewhat paradoxical, but seems to go something like this: having "unselfishly" devoted their lives to their daughters, these mothers feel that it is only fair to expect that their daughters will make it up to them in one way or another. This is what they were led to believe when they decided to make motherhood their raison d'être. But when their daughters do not succeed in making them happy—and, alas, their flesh-and-blood daughters are never quite what their mothers dreamed them to be—their sacrifices are stripped of their presumed meaning, providing grounds for bitterness and disappointment. Dependent on their daughters for a sense of their own vitality, mothers such as these experience their daughters' individuality and separateness not only as threats to the mother-daughter relationship but also as threats to their self-esteem.

Cheryl was purportedly too "unconventional" as a child ("My mother told me I was more than she could handle"); Laura was too "independent"; and Rebecca incurred her mother's wrath when she refused to be "dressed like a doll" as a child and insisted on washing her hair more than her mother deemed necessary or appropriate as an adolescent. The specific content of their mothers' complaints seems to have been unimportant; the blanks could be filled in any number of ways. What was important was that their supposed "imperfections" were experienced by their mothers as personal assaults, betrayals of an unwritten contract seamlessly bonding mother to daughter.

Rebecca offered some insight into a process that, in her case, seemed to span three generations of women. Rebecca's mother always spoke of her own mother, who had died when she was a young woman, in the most glorified terms—she was the perfect mother, who deserved to have a perfect daughter, who in turn deserved to have a perfect daughter herself, and so on, and so on. Rebecca believes that because her mother idealized her grandmother she placed unrealistic demands upon herself to be perfect, never questioning the feasibility of actually achieving this goal, and Rebecca became the measure of her success or failure. Rebecca's "imperfections" challenged her mother's shaky belief in her own worthiness, and this she could not endure. Rebecca felt the repercussions of having inadvertently shattered her mother's dreams throughout her childhood. "I obviously was not the perfect child . . . and my rebelling against having bows in my hair got her *very* frustrated."

Women who felt that they were the center of their

mothers' lives experienced their mothers' love and concern as something they could depend upon in times of need, but also as something that suffocated them both, crowding out their individuality. This is because the love was not unconditional or really unselfish, but instead given with the implicit understanding that some intangible something was expected in return. Daughters were expected to fill in the gaps in their mothers' psyches and become what their mothers needed them to become—whether their mirror image or their polar opposite.[1]

Laura's description of her mother is paradigmatic: "She is a person who assumes emotional responsibility for everything and every person around her. She could feel responsible if her kids were complaining about the snow. . . . She wants to be in the center and fix everything and yet not have to feel like she has to fix everything. . . . She would absorb whatever you were feeling. If you had a bad day, she would take that, feel responsible for that, but feel the pressure of feeling responsible for that and dump it back on you."

Not every woman responds the same way to growing up in that kind of emotional stew. Cheryl, a woman whose experience will be described in more detail later, characterized herself as extremely attached to her mother, who to this day continues to remind her to wear her galoshes when it's snowing. But other women characterized their relationships with their mothers as quite the opposite—remote or combative. This is only further evidence for Freud's assertion that opposites often reflect underlying similarities.

Laura recalls that from early on she continually challenged her mother's authority, and that rather than feeling close to her intrusive mother, she was in a constant tug of war with her. After all, she reasoned, how could her mother command her respect and assume a position of authority when she felt just what her children felt and was all too willing to take responsibility for everything, including the bad weather? "There was nobody there to guide and to direct. . . . She felt like a kid herself. . . . I would have liked her to be less reactive and absorbing, an adult, instead of one of us." The ongoing battle between Laura and her mother functioned as a defense—it allowed Laura to maintain a safe distance and still feel connected to her mother at the same time.

Rebecca, the only child of a forty-one-year-old elementary schoolteacher, also claimed that although her mother was "extremely overinvolved" with her, she was never very close to her mother. Reacting against her mother's efforts to control all aspects of her life (including how frequently she washed her hair), she devised her own set of rules and conventions (which she adhered to religiously), and was thus able to preserve a sense of control over herself. Ironically, by fighting fire with fire, Rebecca incorporated into her own personality the very qualities of her mother from which she sought to free herself. With a mother hovering ever so close, Rebecca distanced herself, in what she characterized as a "reaction formation" (a psychological process whereby a feeling is transformed into its opposite).

Given Rebecca's experience with her mother, it is not surprising that her concerns about protecting her space and time enter into her relationship with her baby. As a mother, Rebecca does not hesitate, as some other women do, to impose a certain amount of structure on her baby's life, and she acknowledges that the structure is for her own sanity as much as for his. She feels that "you have to make time for yourself and realize that you continue to have needs." Her approach to sleep problems is just one example of this general style. "Parents have to get that under control. It is like their first step to asserting themselves as parents. . . . If they can't get a good night's sleep themselves, they are not going to be able to function."

Rebecca returned to work three days a week when her son was two months old, and she was back to a full-time work schedule by the time he was five months old. Although shortly thereafter she quit her job to take another position in which her hours were somewhat shorter than full-time and where there was greater flexibility in scheduling, it was not without some ambivalence. Rebecca is decidedly not one who allows herself to be easily influenced or diverted from her chosen path, but as a mother she bent the rules: she compromised, and got off the "fast track" she had put herself on some time ago. These changes did not come easily to her and are testimony to her love for her son and her ability to transcend the past. Given her history and her personality it is evident that Rebecca's greatest difficulty as a new mother was the internal struggle she waged with herself to become less "goal-directed," more flexible, and more tenderhearted.

Having learned to defend her territory at her mother's knee, Rebecca can be as tough with her son as her mother was with her, but she is not altogether pleased to see her mother's qualities reflected back at her when she pauses to take a good look at herself as a mother. "I think sometimes this thing about rules and structure is a little excessive, and that I'm reacting against my mother and at the same time I'm adopting some of my mother's behavior." Rebecca wonders how she will respond when her son becomes more willful, more rebellious, and demands even greater compromises of her. Will she be able to see her son for who he is, or will she respond to him as she would to the image of her mother threatening to take over her life?

Women often experience a mother's overinvolvement and overprotectiveness as a form of control, and it is for this reason perhaps that the daughters of overinvolved mothers are acutely sensitive to situations in which they feel that they are losing control or that someone else is edging toward the "driver's seat." Their mothers too frequently crowded them out of their own lives and tried to make their decisions for them. When, as new mothers, conflicts around being controlled and controlling emerge in relation to a baby or in relation to a spouse (whose varying perspective on the child must also be reckoned with), it strikes a familiar but dissonant chord. The child still living inside the mother resists being pressured by the new baby, while the mother of the new baby identifies with him and empathizes with his fierce desire to assert his will. The ensuing conflicts revive earlier editions of similar conflicts about yielding control that these women enacted years before in relation to their mothers; for instance, the when, where, and how of sleeping, eating, and toileting are obvious points of contention. A baby's preferences are often distinctly not its mother's.

Before becoming mothers, the three women in our group of women who had characterized their mothers as overly involved had all established themselves in careers and were all progressing up the proverbial ladder of success. Highly committed to their work, all three had planned to return to full-time employment within the first six months of having had their babies, and all of them did. Not working was unimaginable; juggling everything was a far more appealing prospect. As daughters, each had fought, sometimes bitterly, to carve out a space for herself alone, a space in which she could blunder or excel—at her own pace, on her own momentum. As new mothers, each struggled to defend this space and still leave room for the more tender, more fluid, and less predictable experiences of motherhood. We will examine the case of Cheryl in greater depth.

Thirty-nine-year-old Cheryl is the mother of a nearly three-year-old boy. She described her mother as having been overinvolved and distant at the same time, over-involved in the sense that "everything I did was her sole interest," distant because she was not fundamentally happy as a mother and appeared to take little pleasure in her children—despite their being everything to her. Cheryl's mother never worked outside the home, and Cheryl wonders whether her mother might not have been happier if she had had interests outside of her children. "She's one of these people who understands why women work, and I suspect it is because she herself would have liked to."

Growing up with a mother who was "a worrier," a mother who absorbed herself in every wrinkle of her life, a mother who noticed every blemish, Cheryl developed into a child who, from her own description, had a classic case of separation anxiety. She screamed when she had to go off to kindergarten, and her mother jokes that when the time came for her to go to college she was not much different. As a child, Cheryl was "completely attached" to her mother, and yet, as is often the case with children who have separation anxiety, she described herself as "rebellious" and "very independent." (We might speculate that her anxiety served as a check on her growing sense of separateness and autonomy, and that her rebelliousness was in turn a reaction against her overly dependent relationship with her mother.)

Even now, these opposite strands in her personality are inextricably linked with one another, and Cheryl is uncertain as to how much her childhood experience of intense dependency was a reflection of her mother's dependency upon her, rather than of her dependency on her mother. She recalls that as a child she was frequently concerned about her mother's well-being, as well as about her own, and she remembers feeling somewhat comforted by the thought that, were her mother's mother to die, she, Cheryl, would be there to take care of her mother. As an adult, Cheryl dismisses her concern for her mother as a childish projection, an egocentric fantasy, but it may well be that her fearfulness as a child was for her mother's emotional survival *as well as* for her own. A mother's overinvolvement in her child's life places an enormous burden on the child to feel responsible for her emotional equilibrium, since every move the child makes seems to have a direct effect on its mother's mood. Under these conditions, it would be difficult for Cheryl to disentangle her worries from her mother's, or to be certain who was feeling so needy and so insecure as she prepared to go off to school. Despite, or perhaps because of her early difficulties separating from her mother, both physically and emotionally, Cheryl came to cherish her freedom to shape her life according to *her* wishes. "I'm not the kind of person who goes with the flow," she says. This commitment to maintaining her autonomy has served her well in her professional development: she took initiative in her work as a university professor, applying for government grants, organizing and adminstering specialized programs, assuming leadership roles.

Before having a baby, Cheryl worked long hours at the university, and yet she enjoyed being able to indulge herself when she was so inclined—she might take a day off from work to nurse a cold in bed, propping herself up with pillows and mindless magazines. But whether she was driving herself or pampering herself, it pleased her that it was pretty much up to her to choose what she did at any given moment. Psychologically this suited her; it allayed her fears of being intruded upon and manipulated. In effect, she was mother to herself.

Marriage did not pose a threat to Cheryl's preferred mode of operation, and she managed to preserve her hard-won sense of autonomy in her relationship with her husband. She maintained an active social life apart from him and would often visit with women friends on the weekends or evenings after work. She stated unequivocally that in those days the evening was hers to do with what she wished, and her husband raised no objections. With such a premium placed on freedom, it is not surprising that she postponed becoming a mother until she was well into her thirties.

Cheryl's mother had never worked outside the home; Cheryl's mother breathed her children's air and not her own; Cheryl's mother wanted something different; and Cheryl was committed to doing it all very differently when she became a mother herself. She knew that she would return to a full-time academic work schedule before her son was six months old, and did, although her anxiety was only compounded by the pressure she experienced from neighborhood women who had not returned to work, let alone to full-time work, after they had had their babies. Cheryl never contemplated doing anything but what she did, and despite her mother's anxious concerns, and subtle intimations that all was not as is should be, she knew intuitively that on some deeper level her mother supported her continued pursuit of her career—how could she not, when she clearly would have liked to have had one herself?

But if Cheryl's experience as her mother's daughter fueled her desire to continue working outside the home, it also cast a shadow on her experience mothering. Admittedly carrying on the legacy of the "worrier" mother, Cheryl had a special noise-sensitive machine installed in her son's nursery just in case she did not hear him immediately when he awoke during the night, and while she was breast-feeding she tormented herself when, on account of work, she had to miss a feeding. She pumped her milk and was unreasonably fearful that her milk would dry up.

Cheryl had reacted against her own mother's worrying intrusiveness by becoming a dedicated professional and finding a husband who gave her the freedom to come and go pretty much as she pleased, so when she became a mother she found the loss of personal freedom most difficult to endure. It re-created an earlier time in her life when encroachments on her personal space were constant, and there were no clear boundaries separating her life from her mother's. "I have no free time to do the things I like to do . . . I'm on call all the time." In fact, from Cheryl's perspective, ninety percent of the arguments she and her husband have had since the birth of their son express in some manner their mutual feeling of deprivation in this regard. "It all boils down to each one of us trying to carve out a twenty-minute niche for our own."

Because of her own experience as a child, Cheryl is hypersensitive to any signs that her son Jesse may be having problems separating from her. Consciously making every effort not to replicate the relationship she had with her mother, she tries to ignore her mother's admonitions that she should stay home every Saturday night as she herself did faithfully when Cheryl was a small child, even though this is exceedingly difficult for her to do when Jesse's screams resound through the halls as she and her husband edge themselves out the door after long, drawn-out, but not always reassuring good-byes.

Cheryl cannot help but be of several minds. On the one hand, she argues with the mother inside herself that she, unlike her mother, is giving Jesse a positive message: she is letting him know that she has confidence in his ability to withstand a certain amount of frustration, and confidence that he will be okay even if his desires are occasionally thwarted and his parents have needs and interests apart from him. Cheryl consciously tries not to give Jesse the double messages she feels she must have received from her mother when she was young; she leaves the house cheerfully, without the commiseratory, "Oh, I know you're really sad mommy's leaving." When Cheryl's mother used to say that to her, it always seemed to function as a self-fulfilling prophecy, almost an injunction from her mother to her to *be* sad, to disintegrate. Then her mother would be obliged to stay behind in order to put Cheryl back together again.

On the other hand, the anxious child within Cheryl echoes her mother's pleas, and implores her to stay home— *always*. Jesse's crying at two years of age reminds her of her own anxious tears at five and even older, and with mixed feelings she recalls her mother's implicit message that she, Cheryl, was all that her mother lived for. Her mother's unstinting devotion continues to tug at her. She wonders whether she is spending enough time with Jesse, and whether she *should* be feeling as her mother felt— that her child is her life. Where should the line be drawn?

As a new mother, Cheryl is struggling to accommodate opposite aspects of her personality so that she can remain loyal to herself, loyal to her mother (who, despite her failings, has always been there for her), and attuned to her son, whose individual needs are sometimes difficult to disentangle from everyone else's, past and present. She both wants and does not want to be the overinvolved kind of mother her mother was. Consequently, she is and she isn't.

Cheryl adores her son, can become consumed with worry when he expresses the slightest distress, and feels so guilty at the idea of leaving him overnight that she has not attended the conferences she customarily attended before he was born. Yet she openly admits that she cherishes whatever free time she has away from her son, more perhaps than some other mothers who worry less about their child's every move when they are with them. For Cheryl, her private time away from the family is essential to her sense of self; it is revitalizing. It is only then that she feels free to listen undistracted to her own voice, and it is only then that she can stifle the nagging sensation that she should be attending to someone else's.

Cheryl worries about Jesse's clingy behavior and wonders if he clings more than other children his age. Hypersensitive in this regard, perhaps she just notices it more in him. She questions, somewhat facetiously, whether there isn't a genetic basis for separation anxiety—she read some such article recently in *The New York Times*. But that is not the issue here. The particular focus of her concern as a mother expresses her own psychological makeup and the contradictions and questions she has brought with her from her experience as the daughter of her mother. She is not convinced that she can be involved with Jesse without being consumed, and she does not always trust herself to know the point at which separateness turns into neglect. She asks herself whether it is sufficient to love and be loved without being glued together by guilt and mutual dependency, and whether Jesse will love her enough if she doesn't make him her whole life. "My mother kept me tied to her, and in certain ways it worked for her. . . . We [speaking for herself and her husband] don't want to do such a good job parenting that Jesse *never* feels guilty and never calls." Although this is said in jest, it seems to reflect a real fear. Freud is convincing when he argues that jokes are just one more window into the unconscious workings of the mind. Surely this one is.

The ghosts of mothers past have all kinds of faces, and lest we forget, in our efforts to understand and tame the ghosts we fear and dread, many of the faces are reassuring, supporting, and nourishing. "I still think of my mother when I'm sick," Laura admits, and Elizabeth knows that her mother is the only person in the world with whom she can talk endlessly about minor, but to her mind highly significant details of her daughter's development. Nancy, who returned to her full-time job on Wall Street when her daughter was two months old, manages to temper her guilt and anxiety over leaving her daughter each morning and remains relatively unflustered when she loses her baby-sitter on a day's notice; she carries within her an image of her own mother, which sustains her. Her mother was devoted to her children, but motherhood was not her entire life; she was *never* overprotective or clingy, but Nancy always considered her to be her "best friend." Her mother's success at creating a balance in her life inspires Nancy to do the same.

Not a woman I spoke with failed to point out her mother's strengths as well as weaknesses, and even the most critical among them mentioned such qualities as intelligence, energy, a commitment to her family, or the ability to endure. Even Ann, whose angry feelings toward her mother were ignited by her own experience mothering —"It was like putting a match into an oil pit"—expressed gratitude toward her mother for teaching her a love of nature and a respect for all forms of life.

But whether a woman feels that her mother was "pretty perfect," or in some way or other unable to respond to her needs as a developing child, most women become more sensitive to the kinds of pressures their mothers must have experienced when they were raising their children. This awareness of what it must have been like for them softens some of the rough edges that continued to grate in their adult relationships.

Surprised perhaps when they observe themselves behaving like their mothers and in a manner that is less than ideal, women find that they are less likely to blame their mothers simply because they failed to be what they would have liked them to have been. This is not an uncommon phenomenon. Psychologists have found that people tend to blame other people's failures on personal inadequacies, but when it comes to explaining their own failures they are more sensitive to the influences of external factors that prevent them from performing as they might want to.[2] So, while a woman who is not yet a mother herself may attribute her own mother's inattentiveness to her mother's inadequacies as a person—for example, her cold indifference to her children's needs, or her dependent personality— she may feel it incumbent upon herself to revise her explanation when she observes that *she* is not always perfectly attuned to her child or sufficiently objective. Unless she wants to characterize herself also as cold and indifferent, clingy and dependent, she will have to reconsider why her mother was the way she was. Experiencing the demands of motherhood firsthand diffuses blame and inspires humility and hence empathy.

Although becoming a mother stirs up buried memories of being mothered and provides an impetus for revising and/or reenacting the original family drama, it also allows the original cast of characters to lay to rest old battles and relate to each other on a different basis. The scene of the drama has shifted to another arena, and the unresolved conflicts between a mother and a daughter no longer need to be ironed out between *them*. There is a new mother and a new baby, and whatever threads were left hanging from the previous relationship will be picked up and transferred onto the new generation. It follows that while many women feel closer to their mothers after becoming mothers themselves, they also feel less dependent, and hence less easily disappointed or hurt.

Since having a baby, Gina, for example, is better able to accept the fact that she never was and never will be the center of her mother's universe, and moreover, that her mother is still more likely to criticize her than to praise her. She no longer flies off the handle when her mother comments unfavorably about the condition of her hair, or the manner of her dress. Perhaps this is because Gina feels secure that in her relationship with her own daughter she is loved, and she finds this extremely gratifying; she likes to be needed, and now she is. The object has shifted, and her mother has diminished in importance.[3] "I can see I was one of many parts of her life, and now she's one of the many things in my life. . . . She's only one person, not everybody."

By becoming the mother you had (or never had), you encompass the past within yourself and feel empowered. As Nancy Chodorow has pointed out, the "reproduction of motherhood" serves a dual function: it preserves a woman's relationship to her mother and her past but simultaneously allows her to carve an identity of her own, and in this way it sets her free.[4]

3

Life with Baby: A Radical Transformation of Time and Space

To see a World in a Grain of Sand
And a Heaven in a Wild Flower
Hold Infinity in the palm of your hand
And Eternity in an hour
—William Blake, "Auguries of Innocence"

A Day in a Life: Before and After

The texture and rhythm of life change dramatically for new parents during the first year of their first baby's life, and generally it is the new mother's daily activities that are most affected by the birth of a baby. This is true whether or not a woman continues to work outside the home, since almost invariably it is the mother who assumes primary responsiblity for the daily care of the new baby.

The way we move through time and space defines who we are and what we value, but it is not until our habitual patterns are disrupted that we are even aware of how deeply ingrained our habits are and how difficult it is to adjust to a new scheme of things. On becoming a mother, a woman suddenly enters a world in which the customary rules governing time and space no longer apply.

At birth, a baby knows only the present, and only gradually does it develop a crude understanding of the past and the ability to anticipate the future. Even at the age of three, a child's conception of time consists of relatively diffuse categories; last week and yesterday blend together, and next week may as well be next year and vice versa. If on Thursday, Friday is tomorrow, why isn't Friday tomorrow the next day? Utterly grounded in the present, and with limited capacity to move through space on his own, a baby, and even a young child, is a captive to his momentary feelings. Tomorrow's pleasures give him little consolation today. He lives by what he can see, hear, touch, or smell at a given point in time, and yet his understanding of what he sees, hears, touches, or smells is so different from our own that he might as well inhabit another planet. What the baby imagines is real is real to him, and from his perspective his parents are omnipotent and omniscient; "the world" is mediated through their activity.

We all begin this way—that is, we all begin as babies, unsocialized and innocent of how things happen (what makes mommy appear or disappear, and how long it will be until summer). Over time, however, we undergo a gradual but profound metamorphosis; for most of us, the baby's relationship to time and space is alien to our own. As new parents, we need to acclimate ourselves to the new culture our baby brings with him to the family. Love and feelings of attachment inspire us to enter into his world and rediscover what we have long since forgotten. At the same time, however, we know that we must continue to live as adults, in an adult world, partaking of adult pleasures, and this means that at some point we need to gradually impose aspects of our adult culture and our adult language on our newest family member. But how soon and how much? What can he teach us about time and space, and hence about life, that we have lost in our eagerness to "grow up," in our sometimes frantic quest for money, recognition, power and respect?[1] And what does he have to learn in order to live peacefully among others? Without being conscious of it, each mother grapples with these fundamental human questions.

Before one becomes a mother, it is difficult to imagine how a woman with a baby spends her time at home. For the mother, the ordinary, predictable kinds of clutter that fill up large portions of a typical work day in the outside world do not infiltrate the inner sanctum of the home. Train schedules, small talk with fellow workers, window shopping, and eating at restaurants are simply not a part of her everyday reality. Although it is often a relief to be rid of such clutter, it can also be hard adjusting to not having all that familiar stuff around; it has kept us company for a long time.

Of course, there are specific activities, such as feeding, diapering, cleaning up, and playing, that mothers do with which we can easily identify, but somehow the parts don't add up to the whole; it seems, before the fact, that it would be impossible for an entire day, which consists of at least sixteen waking hours, to be filled up with just feeding, diapering, playing, and cleaning up, sometimes without even venturing more than three blocks from home. Yet the day *is* filled up, and though there may be fewer identifiable "events" (and none that are suitable to mention at a cocktail hour), the feelings, both positive and negative, are often quite intense, and take up a lot of psychological time and space. There is constant opportunity for diplomacy, leadership, and creativity, though not of the sort that will command public attention or respect.

A thirty-seven-year-old doctoral student and mother of an eighteen-month-old girl, Elizabeth bemoans the limited opportunity she has for intellectual stimulation and "adult" forms of communication. "Sometimes I feel there are no subjects left in my head, that I haven't had any interesting, new experiences. What would I talk about if I went to a dinner party?" Rachel, who works in a retail business she owns with her husband, notes that although she is completely engrossed in being a mother when she is at home with her eight-month-old son (she has returned to work three days a week), she sometimes feels as if she is "brain dead." And Susan, a consultant for a state government, who did not have her first child until she was forty years old, put it this way: "Being a mother is the most difficult job I've ever had, bar none, but also the most gratifying. There's a kind of intimacy, a way of knowing someone that you don't even have with your husband."

When one lives with a baby, time is punctuated by bursts of activity that are followed by unpredictably long stretches of quiet. The boundaries between day and night, mealtime and worktime, playtime and bathtime are constantly shifting, and basic bodily functions—eating, sleeping, defecating—that ordinarily occupy a peripheral role in the lives of healthy adults occupy center stage. This means there is less time and less space for other thoughts and activities, and privacy and "time for oneself" are no longer basic rights but luxuries, indulgences.

Let us compare how a "typical" day unfolded for Judith before she had her baby with her "typical" day as a mother, at home with her baby six months afterward. The difference between the two days is not purely a matter of what she does or where she spends her time; after all, this varies from woman to woman and from day to day with or without a baby. What distinguishes time spent at home with a baby or young child from time spent working "in the world" is the pacing, the punctuation marks, the use of language (verbal and nonverbal), and the emotional atmosphere. What are the events of the day? Who initiates them? Where are the boundaries separating one event from another? One person from another? In short, how is the day structured or not structured, in time and in space? These elements combine to create distinct atmospheres, so that time spent at home *feels* fundamentally different from time spent outside the home at work.

We can identify certain fundamental *dimensions* of living that seem to be affected by the birth of a baby: predictability and control over daily activities, freedom of movement and autonomy, experiences of intimacy and separateness, and the extent to which verbal/rational and nonverbal/

emotional channels of communication are relied upon. Within the descriptions that follow, passages relevant to each of these dimensions are italicized.

Prior to having the baby, Judith had been working in a large city hospital as a mental health professional. Her work in the hospital involved counseling psychiatric patients as well as *regular* staff conferences, seminars, and extensive paperwork *documenting what she did and when she did it*. Living some distance from her job, she needed to be on her way to work by seven-thirty every morning. *She liked to be on time*, and if she left the house later than planned she would feel anxious when a train was unexpectedly delayed and obligated to squeeze herself onto an already overcrowded car. Leaving so early gave her *little time with her husband* in the morning (she always left the house well before he had to), and sometimes they disagreed about her obsessive need to be *punctual*, but she preferred to leave early and *be sure*, rather than hope that everything outside of her control ran smoothly. And of course it was ultimately her decision.

Being up at six-thirty every weekday morning allowed her time for a quick shower and a bite of breakfast with her husband, who roused himself expressly for this purpose. Of course breakfast was rushed, but it was a time for them to finalize their plans for the evening, and, more important, a time for a small measure of intimacy—a look and a touch—before *going off in separate directions*. If there had been some harsh words the night before, it was also a time for reconciliation, albeit an abbreviated one.

Judith prided herself on her ability to get everything done in the morning (even making the bed and brewing fresh coffee), and on good days she left home feeling that *everything was well under control*. Despite her complaints about the long subway ride, *she found the travel time between home and work emotionally nourishing.* Sometimes she took the opportunity to mentally *review* what had happened at work the previous day or to *anticipate* the activities of the day before her. More frequently, however, she would let her thoughts wander here and there. Once the crowds had thinned out a bit and she was able to find a seat, she would take out her book, picking up where she had left off the previous evening. On the train she relished in the opportunity to *immerse herself completely in another world* and be *oblivious to the world around her.* Since the time she had begun making her long commute, *she had finished more novels than in all the previous years since high school.*

Often *Judith met other people* from the hospital where she worked, and she developed a few subway acquaintances—people with whom she spoke only during their commute to and from work. These were pleasant enough exchanges, though sometimes she would have preferred a solitary journey. Of course, there were days when the train did not come on time, or when everyone had to disembark in the middle of nowhere on account of a track fire. On those occasions she would nervously check her watch, wondering, along with everyone else on the platform, whether she would make it in to work on time, and cursing silently to herself about the inefficiency of the subway system and the wasted tax money. Generally, however, things went more or less *according to schedule,* and when the trains were delayed *she knew she could always run the distance from the station to the hospital* and avoid arriving at work too late.

On a typical day, Judith *knew before starting out how she would spend the next eight hours.* Meetings with patients and staff were *scheduled at specific times,* and though emergencies did come up and meetings were unexpectedly canceled, there was usually some give in one direction or another. Someone might have to wait, she might have to have lunch at 1:30 or 2:00 rather than the usual 1:00, but *there were relatively clear guidelines* as to what she should do in any particular circumstance, and she had some choice about when she chose to do what, as long as it all got done in good time.

Her *contact with her fellow workers* was in most cases relatively superficial, and it was a *consistent* and *predictable* part of her day at work as much as anything else. Personal small talk and catching up on the latest hospital politics provided *a temporary reprieve* from the more intense work of the day. She could talk for fifteen minutes or five depending on her level of interest and what she needed to get done that day. Her office had a door, and she used it to regulate the amount of contact she had with fellow workers during the day. *Her privacy was respected* when her door was completely shut, and *everybody knew the difference* between a door slightly ajar and one which was wide open. *Nobody seemed to take offense* if she wished to keep her door closed more than some of the others, though she suspected that some of her coworkers felt that she was a bit overly conscientious, maybe even stuffy. But it didn't really matter. *The rules of behavior were informal but rarely violated*, and she felt that, within limits, *she had control over her contact with others. Depending upon her mood and her work load, she could choose to have lunch at her desk by herself or join a group and go to the diner or Chinese restaurant across the street.* The fact that more often than not she spent her lunch hour at her desk poring over a report or chart was *simply an expression of her personality*.

On a typical workday, as five o'clock approached, Judith knew she could and probably would start packing up to go home, but she also knew that this was largely up to her. If she wanted to finish that chart note she was working on or that article she was engrossed in, there was nobody there to tell her she couldn't or shouldn't. Her husband generally expected her home around six-thirty, but *she could always give him a call* and say she would be half an hour late; he wouldn't mind as long as they had no specific plans for the evening. Then again, *she could always bring some work home and finish it up after dinner, at her leisure.*

On a typical day, Judith left the hospital promptly at five o'clock. *She had come to a logical point* in her charting, she could break off and easily pick up the thread the next day. So, reversing her tracks, she *put aside her work*, and, with a sense of relief at being able to *leave it behind till the next morning, she emerged from the vault* in which she had spent the last eight hours and headed for the subway. The trip home had a rhythm all its own. Waiting on the platform for her train, chatting with a subway acquaintance, and, during the last stretch of her journey, resuming her book where she had left off that morning, *she gradually made the transition from public to private life.*

Judith arrived home at six-thirty, and her husband was not yet in, so before beginning dinner *she glanced at the morning paper*, which she had not yet had a chance to read. Dinner by seven-thirty, an argument with Steve about something that had transpired at work, a couple of phone calls, *listening to a new record*, an apology for the harsh words over dinner was the way the evening unfolded. Mentally exhausted, but *wanting some physical intimacy*, Judith and her husband *retreated to bed at ten-thirty and were asleep for the night not long afterward.*

After having the baby, Judith took a child-care leave, with the option of returning to her full-time job after ten months. A couple of months after her daughter was born she resumed working just a few hours a week, teaching at a university and doing private consultation. By choice, over the next several months she was home full-time caring for her baby three out of the five weekdays. The days she did work outside her home she was gone for no more than five hours at a stretch. Her daily life had changed radically, though of course she was fundamentally the same woman she had been just a short time ago. Here is a description of a typical day at home.

Judith was *awakened by her daughter's cries* at six o'clock that morning. She brought her into bed, as had become her custom, and nursed her back to sleep without disturbing her husband, who did not need to awaken for work until seven-thirty. Dozing off alongside her happily sleeping baby, Judith roused herself just in time to shut off the alarm. She was pleased that she managed to wake her husband without disturbing her daughter's sleep. While he was showering, she ever so slowly disentangled her arm from beneath her daughter's back and edged herself off the bed, scarcely breathing lest the movement disrupt the tranquility of the scene.

If the truth be told, her concern over preserving her daughter's sleep was not exclusively motivated by a concern for her daughter. After all, Mara would have plenty of time to nap later on in the morning or afternoon, or whenever; *there were no definite plans for the day, anyway*. But now, Judith *hoped* (note the element of uncertainty and unpredictability) that she would sleep just one half hour more so that she could make her husband some breakfast without juggling her daughter on her hip while she was doing it, and *perhaps* even get to sit and talk with him for a few minutes alone before he had to leave for the day. They had always had that early morning time together before the baby came, and it was nice to have it now sometimes, if at all possible. But on this morning, just as Judith had poured the first drops of water into the coffee filter, she heard her daughter's cries. It crossed her mind that her husband's unconsciously heavy tread was responsible for awakening the baby, and she felt somewhat exasperated at his relative disregard for their daughter's sleep, but then his thoughts were obviously elsewhere, and who could blame him? How could he know how important those few minutes without the baby were to her? *Finishing the breakfast preparations with the baby in one arm* was not so difficult after all (she did not want to be put in the baby seat, that was for sure), and the *three of them* sat at the table while Steve gulped down his coffee, grounds and all, and Mara took a second breakfast *at Judith's breast*. The minutes together, all three, were brimming with warm feelings, adult talk, more baby talk, and finally with good-byes. *No need to make plans for the evening, they knew; "We'll be here."*

After Steve left, *a calm* settled upon the house. Judith could picture Steve rushing down the street to the subway, grabbing a newspaper at the local newsstand, running down the subway steps as he heard the train pulling into the station, but *the scene was far removed from her own immediate experience.* Here at home with her baby, *there was no reason in the world for her to rush at all.* She cleared the breakfast dishes, but they could easily have waited. There were things to do—marketing, laundry, *maybe* a visit with a nearby friend—but the day lay stretched out before them, and as long as Mara was playing happily on the floor with her airplane rattle *nothing had to be "done" just then.*

Being a creature of habit, and a woman who habitually keeps busy, Judith started to wash the dishes, an activity that allowed her to collect her thoughts and roughly sketch out in her mind the day's plans. She was accustomed, after all, to having some such time and space to herself in the morning when she used to commute to work. But, this morning, no sooner did she turn on the water than she heard *a whimper and then a wail* in the living room where she had left Mara peacefully playing a few moments before. She ran in, leaving the water still running, and discovered that Mara had managed to inch her way into a corner behind the door but was unable to back herself out. Almost reflexively, *her eyes filled with tears* as she rescued her daughter from the dilemma she had gotten herself into. It was wonderful! Mara had actually managed to move herself across the room in the space of a minute. What persistence! What will! And yet, how expressive of her helplessness and dependency. *Flooded with her feelings,* Judith glanced at the clock. It was only fifteen minutes since Steve had left for work; she couldn't telephone him yet to let him know of their daughter's latest achievement. Instead, she repeated her exclamations of excitement to Mara, who seemed to share some, though certainly not all, of her feelings with her. She *danced around the house with Mara in her arms, inventing an idiotic verse in the process, because there was no other way to express the mysterious blend of delight and sadness the event had elicited.*

When Judith decided it was time to shower—the morning excitement had tapered off, the dishes were done, naptime was approaching, and a trip to the supermarket was on the agenda—*she positioned the baby seat in the doorway of the bathroom* so that she would be able to hear Mara through the noise. Mara didn't particularly like the baby seat and liked the playpen even less, but now that she could navigate across the room, Judith didn't feel comfortable leaving her free to roam out of earshot. Showers were another reason why she was so intent on not awakening Mara before breakfast. *It was so much easier to shower when Mara was asleep*, and with Steve still at home she could even close the door and allow herself the luxury of five exhilarating minutes. *Now she felt rushed to get out, to get dry, and to free her daughter, who, with outstretched arms, was clamoring to be released from the despised baby seat.*

Eleven o'clock. Should she try to get the grocery shopping done before putting Mara down for a nap? She would have loved to go outside for a little walk and get some fresh air; she had never liked staying in all morning. But leaving now meant that Mara would probably not go down for a nap until twelve-thirty, and possibly then would not wake up until two o'clock or even later. What with nursing and changing her diaper it would probably be too late to pay a visit to Alexandra, another new mother and new friend who lived in the neighborhood. Her son was probably napping already, and Alexandra might not want to wait until late afternoon to get together. *What if* Mara fell asleep in the Snugli on the way home from the supermarket? Would she wake up when they got home and not nap at all? *Would she then be too cranky to take out?* The last time she had missed her nap she ended up falling asleep in Judith's lap at five o'clock, just when they had to pack up and head home. After that incident, Judith had vowed to try to get Mara to take her nap at the regular time. *Maybe* the stroller would be a better idea *because if* she fell asleep in the stroller *she might* continue to nap once they returned home. Of course then she would be all bundled up and would wake up in a sweat. . . . And on and on.

Pausing in these ruminations to look out the window, Judith saw that there was still some snow on the street, an additional factor to be given serious consideration. *Snow made navigating with a stroller*, particularly one laden with groceries, *a virtual impossibility. The snow clinched it.* The freedom of movement the Snugli permitted her more than compensated for any of its disadvantages. Mara was still relatively light, five or six pounds lighter than her friend's baby of similar age, and Judith had developed no back problems yet. Moreover, both Judith and Mara loved bouncing securely along the streets together, *body to body.* So, the Snugli it would be, *and if Mara fell asleep* on the way home, as she was known to do, *and if that interfered* with her napping, so be it.

Judith decided to telephone her friend before leaving the house to see whether she wanted to make *tentative plans* for later in the afternoon. *Tentative plans were made, depending on how the next couple of hours progressed in both households.* Forty-five minutes and one diaper change later, mother and daughter were bundled up and ready to go. Back at the house by noon, it was not until nearly one o'clock that the groceries had been put away and lunch was made, what with peeling off all the layers of clothing and discovering that not only did *the diaper need changing but that a soiled stretchie and undershirt needed to be rinsed out as well.*

Mara was just beginning to eat solid food, and *though most of the mashed bananas and cereal ended up on her bib, it was still a novelty and a delight to see her sitting up and eating in her high chair almost like a real person. Judith looked forward to mealtimes. Feeling a bit foolish, but wanting to do it all the same, Judith took out the camera to try and capture some of Mara's quizzical expressions, which were impossible to translate into common English. She thought again of calling Steve at work to tell him about Mara's morning adventure and to share with him her enthusiasm for Mara's newly acquired tastes in food, but she figured it could wait and was convinced that something would definitely be lost in the telling.* Steve was probably in a meeting anyway.

By two o'clock *Mara had nursed herself to sleep, and with painstaking care Judith lifted her from her lap into her crib, cursing to herself when the railing did not lower immediately and hoping once again that her daughter would continue to sleep now that she had untangled herself from her embrace.* If she slept, then Judith would be able to clean up the bananas that had landed on the floor before they hardened. *Maybe* then she could make herself a sandwich and a cup of coffee. She might even be able to take a look at the newspaper. Judith had tried reading the newspaper while nursing Mara, but turning the pages without disturbing her was virtually impossible, so *she only managed to read the first few paragraphs of a number of different articles. This had only whetted her appetite for more information, which, given the circumstances, she was unable to obtain.* But maybe now. . . . Starting the book she had borrowed from a friend seemed *too open-ended a project;* it was better to set more realistic goals—a couple of articles, maybe one phone call.

Mara slept for more than an hour that afternoon, and this was *unstructured, free time* for Judith, something she always looked forward to but often had difficulty shaping to suit her needs. And then, since becoming a mother, *her most pressing needs seemed to revolve around the baby.* Everything else seemed to pale in significance. Judith was not used to having unstructured free time for herself at home (she certainly never had this when she was working full-time or when she was in graduate school), and now that she had some she couldn't decide whether she should flounder around, uncharacteristically, or impose a structure that would have to be *modified again and again to accommodate her baby's changing schedule.*

Judith found it *difficult to relax or immerse herself fully in an activity* while her daughter was napping, because she *never knew exactly when Mara would actually awaken.* (On the subways, in the days when she commuted to work, she always knew when her stop was coming up, and so became easily absorbed.) *Sometimes the nap hour lasted only forty-five minutes; at other times it was extended to two hours or more. It varied from day to day, and there was no way of predicting. Obviously Judith's preference on a given day for more or less free time was not taken into consideration.* Never having had a high tolerance for loose ends, Judith felt uncomfortable knowing that at any moment she might have to put aside what she was doing and abruptly switch gears in order to focus her attention on the baby. Her desire to see a task through to its completion served her well at work, but now it only was a source of frustration.

Suppressing the impulse to fill up her time immediately with a specific "task," Judith read a little, sat and daydreamed a little, and gave some thought to what she was going to make for dinner that night. She decided to try something different and dice up some chicken and vegetables for a new Chinese-style recipe. By three o'clock she was *tiptoeing* into the nursery hoping Mara would wake up (she felt personally replenished and missed her company). Perhaps they could even manage to pay Alexandra a visit, assuming she was still in the mood for a visit so late in the day. Mara woke *and nursed*, and after Judith had telephoned Alexandra once again to reevaluate afternoon plans, they dressed, and *carefully, so as to avoid slipping in the icy snow*, walked the five blocks to Alexandra's house to pay her and her baby a brief visit.

Judith had seen Alexandra only two days before, but they were both eager for company that afternoon. *It was the first adult contact each had had all day.* They shared with each other the details of their days, which included what each baby did, how each baby slept, and what they ate, as well as their own thoughts and feelings about work, husbands, and motherhood. *It was all very personal.* Though they had met only five months before in their obstetrician's office, they felt as if they had known each other for years. Upon leaving, Judith made *tentative plans to meet Alexandra the following day; they'd talk in the morning.*

Home again by five-thirty, *eagerly awaiting the arrival* of *"daddy,"* Judith was pleased that she had already done most of the dinner preparation while Mara was asleep, since by this time of the day Mara demanded a lot of attention. Usually when Steve arrived home *(after much anticipation)*, dinner would follow shortly afterward. And since tonight Mara was cranky, it seemed best to start bedtime preparations as early as possible. *Maybe she'd be asleep by eight and there would be some time to talk.* An irritable exchange over dinner (Steve failed to comment on the new recipe and was insufficiently excited over Mara's creeping across the room earlier that day) added to Judith's *feeling of urgency* about getting Mara off to bed. *She wanted to have time alone with her husband.*

By nine o'clock (because of her late nap) *Mara was asleep in Judith's arms, and once again Judith lifted her daughter, ever so gently, into her crib, holding her breath so as not to awaken her, tiptoeing out of the room, acutely aware of every creak in the floorboards.* There was still some time to talk, though a good hour was spent venting and then soothing the hurt feelings left over from dinner. Exhausted by ten-thirty, Judith retreated to bed, wishing she had the energy to open that book her friend had lent her over a week ago, but knowing that she didn't. A kiss (all was resolved, but Steve was going to stay up a while), and before dropping off to sleep *the wish that this would be a night in which Mara would sleep right through till morning (they were more frequent now than two months ago).*

The Dimensions of Change

Predictability and Control

I don't think I've ever felt so strongly, the love, the frustration. . . . There is an overwhelming intensity,

and on good days having her is a combination of falling
in love and Christmas. . . . But, if you had gotten me
last month every response would have been different.
Every answer is very much colored by her behavior. . . .
Last month I didn't know whether I could cope anymore.
—Deborah, thirty-five, mother of an eighteen-month-
old girl

Ordinarily, adults in our culture are accustomed to being able to predict with a good degree of accuracy the events of a day, a week, and certainly the next hour. This is as true for women as it is for men. Predictability allows for the planning and structuring of time and fosters within us a sense of control over our lives, as well as our moods. Having breakfast at seven-thirty in order to catch a train at eight and arrive at work by nine with ample time to prepare for a ten o'clock meeting is just the most mundane example of a daily routine an individual may devise so as to minimize anxiety and maximize a sense of control over a largely uncontrollable universe. Although nobody can control the train service, and most of us who work in organizations have little control over the timing of a morning meeting, we can pretty well determine when and how quickly we eat breakfast and which train we will be ready to meet.

Even young children become wedded to certain routines and rituals—a particular story before bed, brushing teeth after and not before the bedtime story, a certain arrangement of stuffed animals on the blanket. If a parent accidentally alters the wording in a favorite and familiar story, or thoughtlessly rearranges the stuffed animals to make room for the little girl whose bed they inhabit, that little girl will not only notice the disruption of the familiar, but will protest and reinstate the old order until *she* is ready to create a new one.

The content of our routines and rituals varies, and some of us are more attached to them than others, but all of us engage in some form of routinized and ritualistic behavior because it seems to reassure us that our universe is ordered, not random, and that we are in some way masters of our destiny. Even our social conventions—our greetings and rules of etiquette—relieve us of the burden of constantly having to renegotiate our relationships with others. The perfunctory "Hello, how are you?" with which we greet an acquaintance sometimes feels like a hollow and meaningless form, but we are taken aback when our acquaintance does not respond with "fine," as expected. The ritual is there to contain—or mask—otherwise messy feelings so that all can proceed with the work of the day.[2]

But being able to predict and control moment-to-moment reality is generally *not* the experience of new mothers, and consequently feelings, which were hitherto bound, spill over. Caring for a baby or young child requires a high tolerance for uncertainty and imprecision, a healthy respect for the irrational within us all, and the ability to loosen control temporarily without losing control entirely. While books on child development are invaluable guides that can help mothers predict what their babies will be doing over the months and years ahead, they are useless when it comes to predicting what a baby will be feeling, doing, or needing from one hour to the next, let alone from one day to the next week. Will she nap today? At eleven or twelve? Will she play nicely with her toddler friend or will there be constant struggles over every toy? Will I have to cancel my plans at the last moment when it starts to pour? Will he like the beach, or will I have to take him back inside after half an hour? Will he have a tantrum in the middle of the street if I insist we leave the park before dark? And what shall I do then?

Of course, babies vary in their activity levels as well as in their ability to tolerate eating in restaurants, new sleeping quarters, and new people. And this too cannot be reliably anticipated beforehand. (Many people who, prior to becoming parents, were convinced that a baby's personality is predominantly a product his environment, and more specifically his upbringing, find themselves suddenly reconsidering genetic theories of personality when their babies manifest undesirable and seemingly otherwise inexplicable characteristics.)

Some babies, at least during the first few months, can be taken nearly everywhere—to study groups, to the office, to the museum. They sleep or quietly take in all that is going on around them and allow their mothers to maintain a sense of orderliness. Most women have heard of such prodigies, and some even expect that as soon as they recover physically from the birth their lives will return to "normal." (Isn't that what modern motherhood is about? Weren't so many of the restrictions our mothers experienced unnecessary, merely a function of a particular cultural milieu?) Usually, however, this does not happen, and after an initial grace period parents of even the most placid baby must make major adjustments as he learns to crawl and discovers several months later that he has the power to say no.

Diane, a first-time mother, age forty who planned to return to her job as a hospital administrator after a two-month child-care leave, had heard from a friend that the first few months of motherhood can be a good opportunity for afternoon moviegoing. Her friend's baby had apparently slept contentedly in his mother's arms through many movies. Looking forward to this herself, Diane was sorely disappointed when her baby was unable to tolerate more than five minutes in a darkened theater, and she was at a loss over who or what to blame. Who can predict? And who can anticipate that there is so much that cannot be predicted or controlled, particularly when prior to motherhood, life seemed to be falling into place?

What complicates matters and makes the adjustment even more difficult is that women often question whether they are somehow to blame if their babies do not conform to their image of the "ideal, well-adjusted baby" and worry, moreover, that other people will also judge them on this basis. A mother need not be "neurotic" or particularly insecure to question herself in this manner. There has been a tradition within psychology, but also within the culture as a whole, to focus exclusively on the shortcomings of the *mother* when children appear to be having problems. Therefore, if some women berate themselves when their babies are not "perfect specimens," it is part of a cultural gestalt, not simply a reflection of their individual pathology. Is my baby so active because I overstimulate him? Or am I constantly playing with him because he is so active? Does he cry when I leave him because I've been too overprotective? Or am I so protective of him because he has difficulty separating? All of these ruminations add up to the same basic question, the question that people have asked themselves since Job, whenever they or someone they know encountered a misfortune: Can bad things happen to "good" people? Am I master of my fate, and therefore to blame for all that befalls me or by extension my child?

Psychologists have found that people want to preserve a belief in a "just world" because otherwise life feels too random, too unpredictable. But if the world is just, "good" mothers should be rewarded by having "easy" babies, and "difficult" babies are only evidence that a mother has not been good enough. This kind of reasoning is not only fallacious but also far from consoling.[3] Understanding the interaction between a mother and her baby is always helpful, but assigning blame rarely is, whether it is the mother or the baby who is designated the guilty party. Mothers do well to cultivate a high tolerance for ambiguity, because there are no black-and-white solutions to the conflicts that invariably arise when the desires of the baby are not the mother's desires, and his needs are not her needs.[4] It is wrenching to be frustrated by someone you love, and so much simpler when the "good guys" and the "bad guys" are in separate camps altogether and victory is unambiguous. For most mothers, however, such polarities are patently false, there are too many gray areas, and thus life with a baby is emotionally very complicated.

Living in a world where meanings are ambiguous and behavior is often irrational and unpredictable is difficult to reconcile with the informal and formal training most women as well as most men receive in school and in the marketplace. Predictability and control are, after all, what a scientific and technological world aspires to. Taming the irrational forces of nature, vanquishing disease, and systematically gathering information so that we can predict more accurately everything from the weather to the population in the year 2000 are some obvious examples of the way the impulse to take control of life manifests itself in our culture.

Prior to becoming mothers, women do not need to question their participation in this cultural tradition any more than men; they share a common heritage. But as women and men embark on parenthood together, their perspectives begin to diverge, reflecting changes in the quality of their daily lives. Suddenly "gender" becomes a discriminating factor. A woman who has spent an entire day at home with her baby or young child and has more or less adjusted herself to his rhythm will have difficulty readjusting her focus once again so that she can empathize and respond to her husband's fundamentally different experience at the office; and of course the reverse is also true—try as he might, her husband will not fully appreciate what her day at home has been like from the inside looking out. His sense of certainty is incongruous with her experiences of life's ambiguities. Thus we can anticipate that these transformations in the organization of time and space have profound implications for the marital relationship. But more of this later.

For some women, the loss of predictability and control over the details of daily life is more than compensated for by the feeling that as mothers they are ultimately in charge—the home is their domain, and there is no boss or bureaucracy to which they have to account. As one woman put it, "The spontaneity is gone . . . but the choices are up to you." She and others like her feel more, not less, in control of their lives now that they are mothers, and decisions having to do with the children or the home are incontrovertibly their decisions. They are relieved that they no longer need to be directly concerned with money, status, and other forms of worldly power, and are happy to have found their own sphere of influence. As in the more traditional arrangement between husbands and wives, they feel that they can exercise their will and express their individuality most fully as mothers.

Particularly when a woman has experienced pressure from peers or from family to work or socialize more than she actually wished to, motherhood comes as a liberating experience. If she has derived little satisfaction from her work, she may discover that motherhood gives her a license to bow out gracefully; her desires to remain at home or work part-time or return to school at some point in the future are legitimized.

This is not, however, a universal experience by any means. Many women relish their work and the financial and psychological freedom it gives them to pursue whatever leisure-time activities they wish to, within their means. Shortly after becoming mothers, they become acutely aware of how much they took for granted the freedom they had to come and go at will, and how all the assumptions have to change now that there is a baby. This is the experience whether or not they continue to work outside the home:

"I no longer own my day."
"My time is not my own."
"I can't necessarily do what I want to do; I have to convince my two-year-old that it's what he wants to do too."
"Other people are controlling my life . . . my child, my husband, my baby-sitter, my mother."

This kind of remark is repeated again and again.

"Just as I think I'm running on schedule, Jesse has an accident in his diaper, or there's a big cleanup, or my baby-sitter's late."

"If there's a meeting I suddenly have to attend at seven-thirty in the morning, and I can't get Tom out of his crib to bring him to his baby-sitter, everything falls apart from the start of the day . . . it puts enormous pressure on us . . . so more and more I'm rearranging my schedule so I don't have to deal with it."

"My schedule revolves around the baby-sitter . . . Why do I have to be the one who cuts corners and races around like a crazy person?"

Paradoxically, new mothers feel simultaneously more *and* less in control of their lives, more *and* less free to express their individuality, more *and* less spontaneous in shaping their day. Psychoanalyst and pediatrician D. W. Winnicott captured both sides of this paradox of motherhood in his 1964 book addressed to new mothers, *The Child, The Family, and the Outside World*. While he asserted, as some women continue to assert today, that "nowhere else but in her own home is a woman in such command," he never indulged in a romanticized view of mothers and babies and their relationship and was acutely aware of the restrictions imposed on a new mother's freedom.[5] "A baby comes along, wanting his own way as babies do. By wanting his own way the baby is upsetting the apple-cart. . . . The apple-cart is the young mother's newly found independence of spirit and newly won respect for what she does of her own accord. . . . Therefore, each new child is a threat to your own set-up, your carefully constructed and well-maintained order of things."[6]

New mothers today are, on the average, older and more established in their "independence of spirit" than the new mothers Winnicott was addressing in 1964. Whether this difference makes the adjustment more or less difficult for women now is arguable.[7] Most women voice some lingering nostalgia for the days when, even as married women, they could come and go as they pleased. Yet many are also convinced that it would have been even harder to have given up that kind of freedom at an earlier stage in their adult development. The older a woman is, the more she has evolved set ways of doing things; but having had ample time to sow her wild oats and live "of her own accord," she may feel more ready to bend to the desires and needs of her baby. There is no closure to the problem, and as difficult as it is to hold two contradictory feelings at the same time, that is the psychological reality for most mothers who wish to give of themselves unstintingly and also wish to enrich themselves and fulfill their dreams of adulthood.

A baby's needs and desires are often difficult to predict, let alone control, but upon becoming mothers women find that their own responses—to the baby as well as to the changes in their lives—are also not always what they expect or would like them to be. As mothers they discover new aspects of themselves and their personalities and rediscover old ones. They are often unprepared for their own oscillations and ambivalences.

Most women are surprised at the intensity of their feelings, the positive as well as the negative. In the privacy of their own homes, within the intimate circle enveloping them and their babies, they find that "the heart has its reasons, which reason does not know," to quote Blaise Pascal, the seventeenth-century French philosopher, and that feelings prevail over reason and logic. "Instinct" theories are resurrected to explain otherwise irrational responses. Even the scientifically inclined admit that their objectivity is greatly compromised when fleeting but powerful emotions sweep over them. "To someone who is up twenty-four hours a day, a day seems forever," remarks Diane, whose baby had colic and who also happens to be a social scientist and hospital administrator. "When the baby smiled at the nanny, I had to kill that feeling of jealousy . . . because I know that it is the best thing. . . . I'm not an intense person and I didn't expect those intense feelings of love and jealousy," admits Nancy, a mother of a four-month-old who has returned to her full-time job as a financial consultant. "When I feel he's rejecting me it's like a rocket going off inside," observes Susan, a doctoral student in psychology who is also the mother of a three-and-a-half-year-old boy. "Jesse and I enact the oedipal crisis every day. He's smitten and I adore him," laughs Cheryl, a college professor who is the mother of a two-and-a-half-year-old boy. All of these women work outside their homes; all of them need to maintain an air of professionalism at work; and this means that the tumult beneath the surface needs to be carefully kept in check, put on hold.

Being forced to contain and compartmentalize their feelings in order to conform to the decorum of the work environment has its advantages and disadvantages. On the one hand, it provides women with the opportunity to put their experience as mothers in the larger perspective of their lives and to put the nursery and the playground in the larger perspective of the world outside. After having distanced themselves thus, they may be able to return to their babies feeling less burdened and more objective. On the other hand, however, some new mothers who work outside the home feel that they need to dissimulate on the job, and pretend to be someone they no longer are and perhaps never will be again. When this happens, life in the public sector is not a welcome refuge from motherhood, but an additional source of strain and alienation.

Not having anticipated how they would feel as mothers, some women who originally planned to return to full-time jobs end up revising their work plans, often after much vacillation and inner turmoil, when they find that they enjoy being home with the baby—"doing nothing" —more than they had imagined possible. "I don't mind walking to Lamston's and doing something I would ordinarily view as mindless," observed Rebecca, a woman who modifed her work schedule so that she could have Fridays home with her baby. Others admit that contrary to what they expected, they feel anxious and guilty when they have to go on overnight business trips, and though their feelings may not correspond to what they *think* they should be feeling, or what they thought they would be feeling, they persist nonetheless. Although Rebecca admitted that she enjoyed the unstructured time at home with her baby, running errands, doing what she defined as "nothing," she also admitted to feeling embarrassed at having modified her work schedule to accommodate her baby. Having always identified herself as a feminist, she held fast to her belief that mothers can have careers too and that women should adhere to the existing norms of the workplace if they want equal opportunities. But when theory had to be translated into practice, and it was her and her baby, rather than a woman and a baby in the abstract, she slowed down, changed jobs, and made sure that she left work promptly at five—though there was always a twinge of guilt and a hint of regret when she did.

Shifting Boundaries

> *They came to her, naturally since she was a woman, all day long with this and that; one wanting this, another that . . . She often felt she was nothing but a sponge sopped full of human emotions.*—Virginia Woolf, To the Lighthouse

Through the character of Mrs. Ramsay, a woman who epitomizes the "feminine" element, Virginia Woolf expresses the experience of many women who are mothers. Time for oneself is a scarce commodity for mothers, and questions about leisure time invariably bring a chuckle, a look of puzzlement, or an ironic remark.

Within the frame of an already fluid existence in which hours bled into one another and bodies overlap, the new mother learns that there are often no definite boundaries to the day. Her caretaking activities extend into the evening and often into the night. The usual five o'clock or seven o'clock or even ten o'clock work curfew has no meaning for a baby, whose needs cannot be turned off or postponed to a more convenient time. Because a baby or young child does not understand time and space as adults do, a mother can't reassure herself or her baby that she will make up the time she takes for herself the following day. Although women have the power to choose how they will structure their time as mothers (often much more than they do on a job, where a higher authority decides for them when and what things need to be done), they feel more obligated than ever to govern themselves according to the needs and desires of another person—namely their baby.

Many women who have previously worked twelve- or even fourteen-hour days admit that caring for a baby can be even more emotionally exhausting than working at a job, even if it is equally if not more gratifying. This may be because women feel more able to regulate their "work" when it is paid work, done outside the home. They can *choose* to stay late on a given day or *choose* to call it a night if they are no longer in the mood to work late or if a friend proposes dinner out at the last minute. When it is not a labor of love, nobody (including the woman) expects that her devotion should be unlimited.

Similarly, there are few jobs in which a woman can expect to be called out of bed regularly in the middle of the night; with our new technology, it is possible to screen phone calls if we choose not to be interrupted when we are eating, making love, reading, or simply enjoying some privacy. When we turn on the answering machine or shut the door, it is with the understanding that there are few things so urgent that they can't wait. Even with an unsympathetic boss, we can usually make the assumption that, as an adult, he understands that tomorrow is another day and that good-bye does not mean forever; we generally need not worry whether he will feel abandoned or neglected if we leave for the day, or deny him one of his requests. With a baby, we can't assume as much. How can we be sure that this helpless little creature in our care does not really *need* us to rock him, cuddle him, play with him even if he is fed, dry, and it is two o'clock in the morning? Surely he cannot discriminate very well between a pressing need and a preference. He asks for it; clearly, he wants it. It is up to us to judge, but how can we be sure that our desires—to go back to bed, to talk to another adult undisturbed by constant interruptions—are "fair and reasonable" in his terms? Even a three-year-old communicates his desires with an urgency that is difficult to dismiss or postpone.

Even when the nature of work outside the home is not always predictable or controllable and the level of involvement varies from day to day or week to week (for instance, Laura, a political lobbyist, noted that what she had to do on any given day at work depended in large part on what was on the front page of *The New York Times* metropolitan section), there is always the option of changing jobs, or if need be, calling in sick. We can set limits more easily at work because most of us come to the humbling realization that even if we miss a day things do *not* fall apart, the center *can* hold. (We may hold a unique position but we are not indispensable, and the job is not the only job in the world.) Having such options—to quit, to call in sick— even if they are never actually used, allows us to *feel* in control even if we do not exercise our power and choose to live under pressure and in chaos.

With motherhood the situation is very different. The "work" is inextricably linked with our deepest feelings of attachment, and these feelings complicate matters when boundaries and limits need to be set. In most work situations a framework already exists that structures and regulates activities as well as interpersonal relationships. There are formal and informal rules of conduct, and it is not difficult to distinguish between desirable and undesirable behavior.

The new mother, on the other hand, is allowed (or forced) to construct her own framework; it is largely up to her to create her own system of relationships, and this includes how she organizes time and space. It is up to her to decide when "no" means "no" and when it is negotiable. There is no authority hovering in the wings to do it for her; there is nobody there to affirm that what she feels at any given moment is reasonable or to help her resist acting on her feelings when they go against her better judgment. The opportunity to make this kind of decision—and there are continually new variations to be considered, so there is rarely a sense of closure—can be a source of gratification as well as anxiety.

The psychoanalyst Erich Fromm points out that people do not always feel comfortable having the freedom to direct their own lives, let alone the lives of others.[8] With the freedom to choose comes the risk of failure and the accompanying feelings of shame and guilt. Precisely because there are no blueprints for how to be a "good enough mother," there is ample room for individualized and creative solutions, but also for self-doubt and self-recrimination.

As we shall see in a subsequent chapter, the lack of free time, time to do whatever one wants to do without worrying about whether this is okay with anyone else, is at the heart of many marital conflicts. These often surface after a couple of months, when it becomes clear to everyone that the "normal" routines of family life have been disrupted, but no new mode of operation has been worked out to everyone's satisfaction. For example, the new father may come home after a "hard day on the job" and assume that he has finished his work for the day and is entitled to structure the evening as he likes. Or perhaps he expects to take a break, relax, read the paper, have dinner, and resume his work once the dishes have been cleared from the table and he has read a story to the baby. The new mother, whether she has worked outside the home during the day or not, *knows*, without anyone having to remind her, that the way in which her evening unfolds is largely not up to her, and though she may be very reluctant to give up any of the time she has to be with her baby in the evening, she may also find it disturbing that her husband assumes, unless otherwise informed, that his work day is over when the evening has just begun.

Because her baby-sitter was unexpectedly delayed, Julie, who works eight hours a day, six days a week, as a chef in the restaurant she and her husband own jointly, brought her ten-month-old son with her to our interview, which took place in her restaurant. Although her husband was also "free" and at home at the time, Julie's "time to herself," not his, was sacrificed, and it was with some struggle that she managed to amuse their fidgety baby while simultaneously reflecting upon her experience as a new mother. Bringing the baby along was not what she had planned to do; it was inconvenient, but something came up and something else had to give and the time she usually reserved for herself before beginning her day at work was the obvious choice for her and her husband. The rules governing this choice and others like it were never made explicit, but they nevertheless dictated how they responded in concert to the unexpected.

The internal pressure women experience to carry on even when physically exhausted and emotionally spent is fueled by intense love and the potential for intense guilt. The baby's cry, or a husband's tired and reproachful glance, often echo a woman's own qualms about taking time for herself or setting limits on the demands others make on her time and space. When good and reliable child care is both costly and hard to find, and husbands need to be asked to help (since they rarely volunteer their services themselves), practical, psychological, and interpersonal constraints conspire with one another, and the new mother rarely feels free to take a day or an evening or even a couple of hours off. If not objectively, at least psychologically, her freedom to say "no more" has been attenuated. "When I'm away I miss her, when I'm with her all the time I wish she would go to sleep," says one mother about her baby daughter. This epitomizes the internal contradictions many women wrestle with all the time.

Moving Forward in Time and Space: Pacing and the Relationship Between Process and "Progress"

I'm not on the fast track anymore.—Rebecca, thirty-seven, mother of a one-year-old boy, expecting a second child.

Especially for the new mother who does not resume her previous work schedule once the baby is born, the quality of time as well as the quantity undergoes a radical transformation. What marks the passage of time when the hours on the clock have lost their former significance, when 9:00 A.M. could just as well be 10:00 A.M. or 8:00 A.M., when there is no meeting to make, no precise schedule to follow, and no clear break for a coffee or a lunch? There are new markers, but if a woman tries to relate to time as she did in the office or in school she may not recognize them. It's a new system altogether.

In the marketplace, we are working against deadlines, and if we are conscientious we know there is no time to waste. Other people are depending upon us to get our work out expeditiously. A report must be completed—otherwise it cannot be handed in. A sale must be made—otherwise nothing has been gained from two hours of talk. Papers must be graded and handed back before the next exam. The end, rather than the means to the end, the goal, rather than the process that leads up to reaching it, are the focus of our attention and the measures of our successes or failures. From the standpoint of the market-place time is money, and anything that constitutes an unnecessary delay is wasteful, an indulgence, an impedi-ment to progress. Of course, speed is not everything, and a quickly typed letter with numerous typographical errors is not applauded. But all other things being equal, the faster, the better.

In caring for a baby or small child, all our definitions of what is progress and what is a wasteful indulgence must be reconsidered every step along the way to becoming a person. Is there value in taking fifteen minutes rather than five to get out the door? What about thirty minutes? Or even forty-five? A mother may just want to get the clothes on and leave so that the whole day isn't "wasted" doing the grocery shopping, but what about her baby? Are we wasting her time when we rush her and forget that *how* she gets on her clothing is as important as how quickly? When does she have to learn that time is limited and that there is a future as well as a present? What is too fast too soon, and what is too slow and too scattered?

Building slowly, layer upon layer, waiting, seeing once and then seeing again but with slight variations, feeling intense surges of emotion, and then calm—this is the activity of mothering, though we are not used to defining activity in this way; these are the events of the day, though there are few discrete incidents to report. A mis-chievous smile, a luncheon of peas, the discovery of toes, a loud and tearful interlude, and a sudden calm are the highlights of the day. It is a different way of being.

Some new mothers find it extremely difficult to adjust to a slower pace because what an individual "accomplishes" defines how valuable he or she is in the world outside the home. A doctor can point to the number of patients seen in a given day, just as a professor can point to the number of articles published in scholarly journals, or a salesclerk can add up the number of dresses sold. Mothering can't be quantified. What transpires between a mother and baby is in the moment, lost in the retelling, the unwritten history.

For women who do not return to work outside the home it is a question of leaving behind a "culture" they are familiar with and acclimating themselves to one that has very different customs and a very different system of measurement. For women who continue to work, there is a continual parleying back and forth between one system and another, at the risk of confusing the two and inappropriately applying one set of rules and standards to another set of circumstances.

When women are unable or unwilling to modify the way in which they ordinarily do things, even when it is incompatible with a baby's rhythm, they find themselves in a perpetual tug of war with babies and toddlers who cannot help but slow them down or pull them off track. Difficulties adjusting are not limited to women who continue to work outside the home, though the pressures these women experience are most obvious, since they need to get out of the house early in the morning and they know that if they allow a two-year-old to put on her boots "all by herself" they will miss their train and arrive late for work. There are some women who resist changing their style of living because they are afraid that they will lose everything (their work, their friends, even their identities) if they relax their grip and allow themselves to breathe in a new atmosphere. Most of the time, however, the adjustment is difficult simply because women are well schooled in the "masculine" virtues of the marketplace, and like men, they resist giving up what they know best.

Ann, who has chosen to stay home with her child full-time, continually wrestles with herself in an effort to contain her impatience with her two-and-a-half-year-old son, who naturally makes her wait while he insists on putting his sneakers on himself. Though disenchanted with the publishing world, which she characterized as a

world run on "hype and greed," Ann continues to be
acutely aware of the ticking of the clock—even though
most of the time it is irrelevant to her job of caring for her
son. "Being on time has always been very important . . .
and somehow I can't find the patience to wait calmly."
This becomes a problem when, even in the playground,
Ann finds herself very conscious of the passage of time.
Sitting with the other mothers and chatting feels like a
waste to her, and "killing time" has always been intolerable. Despite her desire to devote herself full-time to mothering, Ann's inner clock continues to tick according to
business time, and try as she might she cannot muffle the
sound.

Many women become impatient with their toddlers for
the numerous delays—in the bath, in the street on a cold
day, or just getting out the door—and then feel guilty
afterward. Toddlers justifiably resist being rushed. They
cannot begin to comprehend what all the hurry is about
and will often put up quite a fuss if they feel that their
sense of time is being violated. Celia describes the conflict
she experiences each morning as she walks her two-and-a-
half-year-old daughter, Vicky, to her nursery school. She
knows that the walk to school is an important time for her
and her daughter, and that a happy separation will set the
tone for her day as well as for her daughter's. But Vicky
often dawdles, and since she resists getting out of bed
earlier in the morning, there are limits to how much
dawdling can be permitted. Celia has a job to get to; as a
single mother who is her child's sole support, Celia frequently ends up urging Vicky to either walk faster or
allow herself to be pushed in her stroller—which is tantamount to imprisonment. Vicky feels, but does not truly
understand, the time pressure (what does she know of
work and nine o'clock?), and tempers flare. The tension
seems inevitable under these circumstances; it can feel
unmanageable when guilty feelings add fuel to the fire.

Celia admits that sometimes she "gives in" to her daughter's demands, some of which are unreasonable, partially out of guilt, partially to avoid a scene, and partially to give her the opportunity to exercise her will, which is thwarted so much of the time. Is she being flexible, or allowing herself to be manipulated? These are the questions Celia asks herself, and she isn't always certain how to answer them. The struggle around pacing becomes a conflict about giving versus giving in.

While some women resist modifying their tempo to accommodate the slower rhythm of a baby or young child, other women err in the opposite direction. They abandon themselves so completely to the enterprise of mothering, denying themselves their own perspective on time and space and life in general, that they end up feeling stifled and frustrated. They become so flexible, so willing to allow their babies to dictate their every move, that they lose their center of gravity. "It was like dying and being born again . . . it was a total upheaval." (This is how Roseanne, a thirty-four-year-old business executive, described the first two and a half years of motherhood. Previously intent on climbing the corporate ladder, she chose not to return to work after the birth of her daughter.

Intimacy and Isolation: Expanding and Contracting Space

> *The influence of two bodies on each other is inversely proportional not only to the square of the distance, but possibly even the cube of the distance between them.*
> —*Edward T. Hall*, The Hidden Dimension

In his landmark study *The Hidden Dimension*, Edward Hall brought to popular attention the ways in which people use space to satisfy fundamental psychological needs for separation and intimacy.[9] Psychologists interested in nonverbal behavior have observed, moreover, that we define our relations with others by the physical distance we maintain and by the extent to which we allow ourselves to touch and be touched. High-status people—

supervisors—are more likely to touch and less likely to be touched than low status people—employees; and, significantly, sex differences parallel differences in status, with men being more likely to touch and women being more likely to be touched.[10] While cultures differ as to how much physical contact is considered appropriate under various circumstances, every culture has its own set of unwritten rules reflecting what its members experience as comfortably close and what they experience as invasive.

Hall does not specifically discuss the spacing between a mother and a baby (which like everything else varies across cultures), but according to his classification scheme, the time mothers spend with their babies includes more than the usual amount of close intimate distance. The physical intimacy not only *reflects* the nature of the relationship, but also *determines* it and must contribute to some of its intensity.

With the birth of her baby, the new mother must adjust to changes in her relationship to space—the space that separates her body from other bodies and the space that encompasses the world all around. What was always close by—the feel and smell of those she loves—is even closer, and what was always distant—the friend who moved across the country—can scarcely be seen over the horizon. "Near" and "far" are terms that must be redefined. Some spaces shrink and others seem to expand. At home with a baby, a mother literally narrows her perspective, if only temporarily, and adjusts her inner lens so that her baby remains in sufficiently sharp focus. In relation to the baby, life is stripped to its bare essentials—joy and sadness, pleasure and pain, love and anger. Everything outside is embellishment.

There is no other relationship in which the unspoken rules governing "personal space" are so flagrantly disregarded, much of the time willingly and joyfully, but some of the time out of respect for the needs of the dependent infant, not the needs or desires of the mother. Being the emotional center of a child's universe is gratifying and flattering, but it is also exhausting and even tedious at times, and many women find that they yearn, as they never did before, for a few minutes to be *entirely* alone, even if it is in the shower or simply alone among strangers in a supermarket or on a bus—just to have that invisible bubble around them that says unambiguously to all around "Do not disturb."

Securing this space is not so simple. You cannot explain to an infant or even a toddler that you need a few moments to yourself, even if it is in the next room, or behind a book, or simply listening quietly to a record. Talking uninterruptedly on the telephone, going for a brisk walk, or browsing in a bookstore are out of the question. "I need to have something for me separate from her. . . . He [referring now to her husband] walks to work alone, he can read a book on the train . . . have lunch every day with a friend. . . ." During the first several months just having an uninterrupted meal with a lap free feels like a luxury; every bite is relished, every sip of unjostled wine savored.

What used to feel very intimate—sitting across the table from your husband, talking intently, and gazing passionately into one another's eyes—is often not physically close enough for a mother and a baby. Smiling and gurgling at each other across a table frequently feels too removed. Skin-to-skin contact is the medium of exchange best understood. Smelling, touching, nuzzling with a baby on and off, perhaps all day and into the night, is a kind of close physical contact adults are not accustomed to having outside of lovemaking. Immersed in a world of bodily sensation, pleasurable and unpleasurable, women may feel saturated by the end of the day, uninterested in sexual contact or any other forms of physical intimacy, to the dismay and indignation of their husbands, who do not share their experience.

While mother and child are in closer proximity than

occurs in any other relationship, life beyond the nursery can feel very far away. The distance between a woman and her best friend who lives across town and who works from nine to five every day is objectively the same, but subjectively very different. With a baby at home, venturing out for an evening dinner with or without the baby feels too far. One is at the mercy of the elements, and on a stormy day "far" might mean outside the immediate neighborhood. Even in good weather a cranky baby or even a normally high-spirited one means that the quiet café down the street that plays classical music while people sip cappuccino in the late morning is as remote as its Paris equivalent, as inaccessible as a friend's country house (which used to be referred to as "only" a four-hour drive door to door).

Changes in the organization of time translate into changes in the organization of space. Since moving from one place to another is always very slow and involves considerable forethought ("Do I have enough diapers? Wipes? Food? Drinks? How long will he last in the stroller? When will he need to nap?), many women find that they spend much of their time with the baby in familiar, easily accessible places. Deborah, a professional woman who worked for many years with a disabled population, drew a parallel between the experience of being a mother and the experience of being physically disabled. Both the mother and the physically disabled person inhabit a world in which their mobility and personal freedom are relatively restricted. "To always to have to walk out the door with a stroller, with a baby, with a diaper bag, with a bottle. Looking around the neighborhood saying 'Oh, that store is too crowded; I can't get in,' or 'Uh oh, there are stairs,' and then the anxiety comes over me."

The zoom lens has temporarily been shelved. The baby is in close-up, and the details in the room are vivid, while the landscape is a blur, if it is not cut out of the picture entirely.

Sleep

*When I invite friends for dinner on the weekends I
am happy that they can spend some time with my
daughter and thrilled at how quickly she is getting to
know all of them. But when eight o'clock rolls around
and we're ready to sit down to eat I want her to be
asleep; otherwise I can't fully relax. Nobody else seems
to feel any urgency about getting her to bed before
dinner, but I am quite a stickler in regard to the curfew
I have set in my head. Once we have completed all the
stories and other nighttime rituals, and I have said
what I hope will be my final good-night, I am always
conscious, at least during those first crucial minutes, of
the noise level in the living room. I'm wondering whether
a loud burst of laughter will awaken her, or induce her
to get out of bed once again in order to find out what is
going on out there without her. My husband gets
irritated, but I continually remind him to keep his voice
down. He's oblivious to all that goes on within me at
these times. Frankly, I'm not going to stop reminding
him. That time and space with my friends is just too
important to me.—Judith, thirty-three, mother of a
two-and-a-half-year-old girl.*

When time and space are at a premium, how and where
a baby sleeps, during the day as well as during the night,
assumes enormous significance for the whole family. Sleep,
the baby's and the mother's—and the two are inextricably
linked—is the one respite from the near-constant physical
contact a new mother has with her baby when she is at
home. It is a rare father who shares equally in basic
caretaking (feeding, bathing, changing, holding), and so
whatever other additional responsibilities fathers may shoulder, they generally have more space for themselves. Therefore, even the most doting mothers discuss at length minor
variations in how their baby is sleeping or not sleeping.
Since a baby's sleep pattern has a profound impact on the
amount of time and space a mother has for herself, interactions around sleep serve as analogues of a woman's

struggle to balance her needs apart from the baby with her needs as a mother and the needs of her baby.

Rachel is a twenty-eight-year-old woman who works three days a week in a business she owns jointly with her husband. She is the mother of nine-month-old Zachary. Rachel appears to be markedly free of conflicts or anxieties and quite pleased with the balance she has struck between her time with and her time away from her son. She identifies her son's erratic sleep pattern (he has never slept through the night) as the single most difficult aspect of mothering. Finding herself exhausted and irritable at having to get up at least a couple of times each night to nurse her son, who also resists napping during the day, she and her husband decided to follow the advice of her pediatrician and try the latest method of helping children overcome sleep problems. Two weeks passed, and though Zachary was sleeping for longer periods throughout the night, he also cried whenever he was in the vicinity of the crib. The cure seemed worse than the disease, and Rachel came to the conclusion that it was *her* need and not her son's that he sleep through the night and that her "sanity wasn't that important if he were going to be nuts." Judging from her demeanor, Rachel's sanity is still intact, and she has not sacrificed herself unduly. She has, however, reconciled herself to being perennially exhausted. But Rachel is no martyr and no "supermom." She seems to have made a point of replenishing herself through other channels and at other times. A loving and a particularly relaxed mother, Rachel had no qualms about identifying her favorite time of the week as the morning when she goes to work and leaves her son with her husband for the full day. That morning is her time to be really alone, she explains, and it is then that she feels most rested.

Roseanne, the thirty-four-year-old mother of two-and-a-half-year-old Emma, had considerably more difficulty reestablishing her equilibrium after the birth of her daughter, and one of the problems was that she never succeeded in securing time and space just for herself. Roseanne was an assistant vice-president in a bank before she became a mother, and although she planned to return to her position after a six-month leave of absence, she never did; it was only when her daughter reached the age of two that she began to work one day a week outside her home.

An injury at birth that required her daughter to receive intensive physical therapy and daily exercise for a number of months had complicated matters for Roseanne and made it particularly difficult for her to leave her daughter in someone else's care even for a few hours. Even after the injury was healed, feelings of guilt and responsibility prevented her from taking any regular time or space for herself, though she acknowledged the desire to do more than "change dirty diapers" all day long.

Roseanne's ambivalence about taking time and space for herself emerged in relation to her daughter's erratic sleep patterns, and her response to this was emblematic of her responses generally. After months of sleepless nights, Roseanne described herself as "a zombie," unable to function day or night. But it was only when, on account of fatigue, she could no longer follow the exercise regimen prescribed for her daughter, and it became clear to her that her *daughter's* well-being might be jeopardized by her condition, that she considered setting limits on what she could give. Like Rachel, Roseanne tried to follow the advice of one of the "experts" in helping parents with their children's sleep problems, but without the emotional support of her husband, she was unable to tolerate her daughter's cries, and once again resigned herself to life as a "zombie" for the next several months.

In contrast to Rachel, Roseanne had no comparable "morning to herself," no time away from home, during which to refuel, and the physical and psychological ramifications were apparent. Although her daughter is nearly three years old, Roseanne still seems very weary, and her memories of the first year and a half of motherhood are still vivid and full of anxiety and pain. At the time of the interview, Roseanne was anticipating a winter vacation and looking forward to enrolling her daughter in the children's day camp, where she would eat in the children's dining room: "It's not a vacation for me if I don't," she said. But whether she will make room in her vacation for this kind of time and space for herself apart from her daughter remains an open question. Her husband will surely have a significant part to play in the choices she makes. Roseanne's situation is unique to her, but the conflict she experienced is a fundamental one for new mothers, and sleep is only one vehicle through which it is expressed.

Vacations: Real and Imaginary

> *"Mothers always exaggerate," said Ridley. "A well-bred child is no responsibility. I've traveled all over Europe with mine. You just wrap 'em up warm and put 'em in the rack."*
>
> *Helen laughed at that. Mrs. Dalloway exclaimed, looking at Ridley:*
> *"How like a father! My husband's just the same. And then one talks of the equality of the sexes!"*
> —*Virginia Woolf,* The Voyage Out

Just as the holiday season can be a time of turmoil when people's dreams of what the holiday *should* be like interfere with their ability to enjoy what *is*, vacations and weekends (which are in effect, mini-vacations from work and scheduled responsibility) can also be tense times, with or without a baby. Simply because vacation time is the time we have designated for relaxation and "fun," we tend to feel that it is our right and obligation to indulge ourselves and to be free of our normal responsibilities. On vacation, on weekends, in the evening after the dishes are washed and put away, we not only give ourselves permission to follow our fancies but feel that we *should* be able to do what we want to do. We have paid our dues, so to speak, and we feel entitled to relax and enjoy ourselves. The "tyranny of the shoulds" afflicts us all sometimes, and psychoanalyst Karen Horney warns about the sense of entitlement that accompanies it in her analysis of "neurotic" strivings for perfection. But when we are preoccupied with what *should* be, we resist accommodating ourselves to new and changing circumstances, and this makes it impossible to enjoy leisure time with a baby or young child."[11]

A baby knows nothing of our inner constructions and cannot understand that one of the prerogatives of being an adult is that during certain specially designated times we can allow ourselves once again to be as carefree as children. A baby is as much a baby on vacation, on the weekend, and after-hours as at any other time of the day or year. Consequently, it is under these circumstances— when we feel that we are supposed to have time and space to do what we wish—that the transformations in pacing and mobility are even more glaring.

Many women experience an internal tug of war when they realize that they must substitute new leisure-time activities for the old pleasures that they are accustomed to. But what's more, they frequently find that they clash with their husbands about how to structure and enjoy their free time together as a family. Even when new mothers feel willing to forgo museum trips, Sunday brunches, restaurants, movies, car rides, and European vacations in order to accommodate a baby's needs and preferences, they find that their husbands are often more reluctant than they are to do so and less flexible. Either the men are less aware that changes have to be made now that there is a baby/toddler/young child who has to be considered, or else they are more confident that the baby/toddler/young child can and should learn to accommodate his needs to the needs of his parents. Although many new mothers hate it, and are aware that their marriages suffer on account of it, they find that invariably they, not their husbands, are the ones who are cast in the role of party-pooper or fuddy-duddy. Sensitive to the baby's need for consistency and regularly scheduled meals and naps, they unwillingly confirm the age-old stereotype that women are less adventurous than men. One woman's vacation may be illustrative.

Judith describes herself on a train, speeding through the Italian countryside. Her three-month-old baby is in her arms asleep, and her husband is by her side. Thirty-five years old at the time, she hasn't been to Europe for over ten years. When she was last there, she lived alone in Paris, working as an au pair, taking time off from ordinary life in order to "find herself." Her memories of Paris include cafés, museums, and aimless wandering through city streets at all hours of the day and night. Now, she returns to Europe with her husband and her infant under very different conditions. Yet she still feels adventurous and even carefree as she settles into the compartment in anticipation of the eight-hour train ride ahead of her. She is quite pleased with herself, and pleased that her baby requires nothing in the way of nourishment but breast milk, of which there is ample supply. In a somewhat self-congratulatory manner she wonders to herself why other people frequently become so stodgy and cautious after having children, when here she is, speeding through the Italian countryside and a responsible mother all the same. . . . Gradually the compartment fills to capacity, until the aisles are overflowing with passengers. Good-natured and boisterous, they spill into her already cramped quarters. Cigarette smoke is thick in the air as her baby awakens prematurely from her nap with a scream that is scarcely audible admist the hubbub. Surrounded on all sides by well-meaning but curious strangers, she does her best to quell her baby's hunger without exposing too much bosom to the young man across from her whose knees are nearly touching her own. Feeling squashed, embarrassed, and now furious with herself for not having even considered bringing along formula, she has just reached her breaking point when her husband unwittingly delivers the final blow. He mumbles something about going to the bathroom to stretch his legs, and makes his escape, leaving her and her nursing infant to fend for themselves in the claustrophobic cell in which she is fated to be confined for the next seven and a half hours. Abandoned and immobilized, she is eager to vent her feelings of impotent rage on her husband—he being its only possible target. He returns to the compartment after twenty minutes offering her a drink, an innocent look upon his face. This is the beginning of their vacation.

Through a New Lens

Since mothers generally assume primary responsibility for the emotional and physical well-being of their children whether or not they work outside the home, the birth of a baby requires a reexamination of their relationship to time and space. Freedom and autonomy, control and predictability are no longer taken for granted. Reason defers to the power of emotions, and feelings are no longer accorded the position of stepchildren in the family of ideas. As mothers, women are forced to reconsider definitions of intimacy and to devise means of preserving a modicum of privacy without violating their baby's needs for consistent physical and emotional contact.

Becoming a mother gives a woman the license to live and to "play" without being continually concerned with "productivity" and quantifiable results; to be with her developing child is sufficient unto itself—or so she is told. But motherhood also demands that a woman cultivate a high tolerance for ambiguity. It is difficult to evaluate how one is doing as a mother, particularly since what transpires over the course of a day, a week, a month, or a year reflects not only the quality of mothering but a host of other factors, the baby's developmental stage and his innate constitution to name just two. Feedback from the baby is a highly unreliable source of self-evaluation, since it can raise a woman's self-esteem to unrealistic heights one moment only to catapult her into the depths of self-doubt and frustration the next. And, unlike other jobs, for which there is at least some financial remuneration, public recognition for a job well done is not forthcoming to mothers on any regular basis. The results of good mothering are often intangible.

Under these potentially chaotic circumstances, in which slow and fast, near and far, success and failure, pleasure and displeasure are seen from the perspective of the adult woman *and* from the perspective of the baby, the new mother knows more about life, but is also more uncertain of what she knows and how she can integrate her contradictory experiences. The responses a woman receives, both positive and negative, from her husband, from her family, and from her peers therefore become more significant to her than before. And friendships, old and new, thrive or disintegrate according to their ability to adapt to these relatively unstable conditions.

4

The Initiation into Motherhood: Communion, Alienation, and Competition

The human being, at all times, from the first kick in utero to the last breath, is organized into groupings of geographic and historical coherence: family, class, community, nation. A human being, thus, is at all times an organism, an ego, and a member of society and is involved in all three processes of organization. His body is exposed to pain and tension; his ego to anxiety; and as a member of a society, he is susceptible to the panic emanating from his group.—Erik H. Erikson, Childhood and Society, 1950

The Initiation

After having always been "an outsider," you have finally applied and been accepted for lifetime membership in a universal Society. There was of course the customary seven-month delay between being notified of your acceptance and its effective date, but this gave you time to acclimate yourself and others to your new status. Eager to absorb any information that could be even remotely relevant to what lay ahead, you found yourself suddenly surrounded by Society members of all ages and occupations, whose fervor about the Society was equal to yours, and who willingly recounted their own early experiences and advised you accordingly.

111

Since becoming a full-fledged member, you have noticed that strangers stop you on the street, in the supermarket, on the bus; they smile, strike up conversations, tell you intimate details of their life histories. Neighbors you passed for years in the elevator without ever having exchanged more than a nod of recognition now linger with you in the hall, even ask if you would like to drop in for a cup of tea one afternoon, and offer you unsolicited advice. Moreover, everywhere you go, people tell you stories—funny, sad, and horrifying. Differences in social status, ethnic background, and educational achievement recede in importance; the world seems smaller and there is considerably less privacy; you are more exposed, but more comfortable in your nakedness.

Now that you are a member of the Society, you find yourself spending more of your free time with other members, and when you meet new people you wonder about their relationship to the Society, and, if they are not members themselves, you wonder what they think of you, and whether they intend to join in the future. Sometimes in social situations you unintentionally gravitate to other members, as they do to you, and when you talk with each other, the conversation tends to lead back to things related to the Society. Although you are hungry to exchange new information, or simply review old news again and again, you are also sometimes bored, and look out of the corner of your eye at nonmembers and feel pulled in their direction. You have seen how insular some members have become, and you begin to feel waves of claustrophobia.

To your surprise and regret, since becoming a member of the Society you have had less contact with people who are not members, even those with whom you still feel most intimate. This is a source of both sadness and anger. You find yourself feeling alienated from the Society at times, but it is too late to withdraw your application, and membership is irrevocable.

Conversely, you also find yourself feeling alienated from nonmembers, knowing that they couldn't possibly be interested in the details of Society life. And yet these details occupy much of your thinking now. Shouldn't you be making more room for other concerns? Could you, indeed, if you wanted to? Misunderstandings, jealousies (yours and theirs), and the constraints of time and space widen the gulf that divides you from nonmembers. Is it possible to bridge the gap? How important is it to try? Is the Society sufficient—a world unto itself? And aren't you still the same person you were just a short time before?

You turn to other members of the Society in your search for answers to these and other questions. Aren't they, after all, the most likely candidates to share your perspective and understand your conflicts without judging you too harshly for your weaknesses? It is then that you discover the schisms within the Society itself (it is a group as any other is, and its members are heterogeneous, competitive, and ideologically diverse), and your feelings of communion and transcendence are tempered by feelings of alienation and competitiveness.

This is the initiation into Motherhood.

Communion, Alienation, and Competition

I'm a member of this universal club. . . . I immediately have something in common with everyone [who is a mother]. Even on some peasant farm in Mexico I would feel connected to people because I have a child now. . . . My advice to new mothers is to find a mother's group. It's really important to be able to sit around and talk about diapers without feeling self-conscious.—Rebecca, thirty-seven, mother of a one-year-old boy

When I meet mothers in the playground, there is a sense that everyone's trying to figure out who the other is. . . . As a group, I don't want to have anything to do with the other mothers, though on an individual basis they are okay. I feel very alien, and my impulse to stay away is stronger than my curiosity.—Elizabeth, thirty-seven, mother of an eighteen-month-old girl

I think there is an undercurrent of competition in the relationships between working mothers and nonworking mothers. For example, when Jesse had trouble separating, the other mothers I knew made me feel that he was having the difficulty because I worked. . . . I like them very much—we have good times together—but it's funny, they never said that the reason he spoke before anybody else was because I worked! I think it would be better for me to be with other mothers who work . . . but they are too busy!—Cheryl, thirty-nine, mother of a two-and-a-half-year-old son

Contrary to the popular and perhaps peculiarly American ideal of the "rugged individualist" who is sufficient unto himself and who never for a moment wavers from his chosen destiny, it is generally recognized by sociologists and social psychologists that *nobody* lives in a social vacuum, and that people's behavior, beliefs, and feelings about themselves are influenced, more than most of us would like to believe, by the conditions they find themselves in and the people with whom they associate and identify. Inasmuch as our ideas and values influence our choice of friends, the reverse is also true, and our friends unwittingly shape our ideas and values.[1]

While we often conceive of motherhood as a turning point in the life of an individual woman, laden with personal meanings and associations, it is also an inherently public experience, and as such can be compared with initiation into any social group or role. A woman's identity as a new mother shapes and in turn is shaped by the relations she has with other people, mothers and nonmothers alike.

Motherhood functions as both a "universal club" and a "sorority," thereby engendering in women a paradoxical sense of communion with the world and alienation from it. As a "universal club," motherhood liberally embraces women of all denominations, regardless of their social status. But as a "sorority" it is exclusionary; nonmothers, women and men alike, are by definition "outsiders," members are expected to be loyal adherents, and deviation from the "group culture" is discouraged. As a result of these anithetical tendencies stemming from motherhood, women find that as new mothers they simultaneously expand and contract their circle of friends and acquaintances, oscillating between feelings of communion and isolation, intimacy and alienation, solidarity and competition.

Although some women emphasize one side of the polarity more than the other, the experience of motherhood appears to be inherently fraught with contradictory feelings about the self in relation to the world (the larger culture as well as the culture of mothers) and the self in relation to the past. Consider Ann and Denise, both women in their thirties who left their full-time careers, one in business and one in publishing, to stay home full-time with their babies, each of whom is now two and a half years old. While motherhood enhanced Denise's feelings of belonging and relatedness, it forced Ann to confront her feelings of spiritual isolation and solitude.

"Having Madeline is a real icebreaker," said Denise. "I feel like I'm back in college, and I've met a lot of people. Before I had the baby most of my interests—computers, sports—were more typically male. I found that I didn't have a lot in common with other women. Once I had Madeline, I became very interested in things that interest other women. . . . I feel more feminine." As a mother, Denise allowed herself the freedom to open up, both socially and psychologically, relaxing the tight grip by which she had previously kept her feelings in check. People expected her to be brimming with emotion, as they never did when she was working in business, and she responded in kind. Without having to step outside her immediate neighborhood, she was welcomed into a small community of other mothers, who spontaneously offered support and company.

Ordinarily a reticent woman who kept her personal concerns and opinions to herself, Denise was inspired to reciprocate the advances of the other mothers and to share intimate aspects of her life with relative strangers. Shortly after her baby was born, she joined a mother's group consisting of six neighborhood women who met at alternate houses on a weekly basis. As this only whetted her appetite for regular contact with other mothers, she expanded her social network further to include a second mother's group outside her immediate neighborhood. While prior to having had the baby she never imagined that she would be anything but bored to tears discussing diapers, sleep habits, and the latest Fisher-Price toys, she unabashedly soaked up the information and the support the other women offered her in their weekly gatherings. She no longer felt estranged from these women whose interests now corresponded with her own, nor did she worry about whether they perceived her as an outsider. In an atmosphere of mutual support, Denise felt less embarrassed about expressing her feelings and voicing her opinions, and her characteristic social awkwardness was no longer so prominent a feature of her personality.

Denise thinks of her mother as having suffered from social isolation as a result of living in the suburbs without a driver's license, dependent upon her husband and her children to shuttle her here and there. As she struggles to come to terms with the legacy of her mother's insular existence, she resists her "natural" inclination to keep to herself and to her immediate family, relishing in her newfound connection to a larger community of women. This deep sense of connection to others is something Denise had never experienced when she worked in the business world. In that competitive world, in which her daily interaction was primarily with inanimate objects, namely computers, her personal life was discreetly kept out of sight. As a mother, however, she feels she does not have to monitor herself so carefully and she can breathe more freely.

Ann also reports feeling more comfortable with herself since becoming a mother, able to trust her "instincts" rather than meekly deferring to the authority of the "experts" in her chosen field. However, feelings of alienation from others continue to dominate her experience of herself in the world, and rather than finding in motherhood "the universal," she has carved out her own carefully protected niche, just big enough to include herself, her baby, and her husband. There she has discovered within herself deeply rooted feelings of loneliness.

Ann seems to have had a more ambivalent relationship to her work than Denise (though consciously her memories are uniformly negative), and consequently, Ann is more ambivalent about her decision to remain home. Ann vehemently denies having regrets about cutting herself off entirely from her career (interestingly, Denise does not protest as much), and yet, recurrent feelings of marginality and isolation from the mainstream culture mar her self-professed complacency. "I am separated from the community of my friends, who were my friends, but who are no longer my friends. . . . It's difficult for children and mothers to see where they fit in. . . . There is a great sense of loss when all of a sudden you are ripped apart from one side of your life, and you are isolated to a community of mothers."

Ann suffers as a mother because her attachment to the community of her friends has been severed—her life and aspirations no longer coincides with theirs. But perhaps even more significant is that with motherhood she has become disillusioned about the kind of a community she actually had. "It was not *who* I was but *what* I did that mattered," she remarked bitterly, and the loss of her friends is as much a source of anger as of sadness. Isolated from the social matrix in which she formerly participated, if only reluctantly, but alienated from the circle of mothers she now encounters in her everyday life, she has not yet found a new "home."

When a woman becomes a mother she finds herself catapulted into a new set of relationships, and changing circumstances force her to redefine the old ones. Her social identity has suddenly been altered, and this means that she sees herself differently in relation to others (the mother next door, her single friends, her work associates), and that they all see her differently as well, according to their own preconceptions, interests, and needs. Inevitably, the new mother is drawn closer to some people and farther away from others, as lives intersect and diverge in ways that they never did before.

"There is a woman in my building who literally did not see me until I had Brendan. . . . Now we talk, we share baby-sitters. . . . We had nothing in common before and now we do because we are mothers. It is as if I have entered the sorority and I have become a different person, and I both have and haven't." Susan's response to her neighbor's sudden realization that she existed was generally a positive one. She felt welcomed into the "club" and was happy to reciprocate her neighbor's overtures. However, it also made her sensitive to the fact that no matter how much *she* knows that she is fundamentally the same woman she always was, other people are going to treat her differently, perhaps even assume that she is a different kind of person, and she is not altogether comfortable with this. If all they see when they see her is that she is a mother, who then are they really seeing, and what aspects of her personality are cut out of the picture?

Susan was virtually invisible to her neighbor as long as she was childless and vice versa, but the converse is also quite common. Laura describes how the relationship she had with her boss, a single woman, was altered dramatically when she became pregnant, and how the changes in the relationship left Laura feeling invisible and distanced. "She was a good friend, but until recently, she never even asked me once about my son. During the pregnancy it was sort of like I wasn't pregnant, and I worked until the day I had him. A lot of this woman's social life was in the evening around work, but after the baby was born I was no longer as available to socialize week nights. There was no discussing this, and I believe that she never understood my dilemma."

Laura's conflict is not unique to her. Many women who continue to value their work and the relationships that evolve around their work identity feel both embarrassed and misunderstood when they no longer participate in the informal but routine social gatherings that take place after-hours. They feel that they are on the edge, whereas previously they were in the center of things; they do not like this feeling, but they are also unwilling to tear themselves away from home and family in order to continue as before.

If these were discrete, isolated incidents, their value would be simply anecdotal, but they are not. Situations such as these—in which one woman is suddenly included in her neighbor's life, and another woman is gradually excluded from her boss's social circle—illustrate the new social reality that mothers encounter at every turn, a reality that unavoidably colors their feelings about who they are, what they are valued for, and what they value for themselves.

It would be inaccurate, however, to speak only of "being included" or "being excluded," as if new mothers were the passive receptacles of other people's transient interests and desires. The changes in people's responses to women as they become mothers shadow the changes new mothers feel about themselves and their lives, and it is impractical if not impossible to say which comes first and which is the cause and which the effect. New relationships develop, and old relationships evolve or die out entirely (presumably because they are unable to adapt to the new atmospheric conditions), and there is a constant interplay between internal and external processes of change. A new mother senses a friend's indifference; a friend senses a new mother's preoccupation with things alien to her life; a colleague pretends that everything is the same as before the baby was born, or else assumes that nothing is the same, and withdraws without discovering whether or not this is the case and if it is forever after. Feelings get hurt, misunderstandings occur, and sometimes paths simply no longer cross.

Gina admits that she is less sympathetic to her best friend, whose problems with men feel far removed from her present-day life as a working mother. She recalls how she and her friend used to sit for hours poring over and analyzing each and every nuance of a conversation one or the other had with a boyfriend, a boss, or even Gina's husband. But now, all these intimacies seem far removed from the emotional tenor of her current life. Her evenings are packed full of domestic activities, and once the baby is finally asleep, Gina has little inclination to spend time talking on the telephone. She experiences herself and her friend as if they were of different generations, perhaps because as a mother she feels older, less carefree, distinctly a woman and not a girl.

However much Gina tries to pretend that everything is the same as it was before, that her affections are not inconstant, and that her loyalty to her friend has never been betrayed, she knows that her feelings about herself and her life have put a wedge between them. Though Gina tries to disguise her impatience with her friend, she suspects that her friend senses that things are not as they were; but what is also different is that they have not talked about these changes.

Perhaps Gina fears that were she to speak honestly with her friend she would open up a can of worms that she would rather keep tightly sealed. If they *really* started talking, she might have to acknowledge that she is, in fact, not all that sympathetic to her friend's concerns, and this could only lead to anger and hurt feelings. She would be forced then to hear her friend's criticisms of her and her life, and she worries whether she would be able to defend herself. At this point in her life, when so much of her energy is invested in her baby and her family, Gina prefers to gloss over the problems that beset her friendship with the hope that they may fade in significance with time.

Since time for socializing is increasingly scarce, many women find that as mothers they are more selective about how they spend the precious little free time they do have. Consequently, they can be less tolerant of their friends' shortcomings and less inclined to expend energy cultivating difficult friendships or ironing out conflicts as they emerge. Diane notes that a certain couple, with whom she and her husband used to socialize, frequently canceled engagements at the last moment. Although Diane had always found this kind of unreliability irritating, she accommodated herself to it and continued to appreciate their other qualities. However, since now their behavior affects not only her and her husband, but also their baby, and perhaps a baby-sitter, it has become intolerable—"I won't put up with that stuff anymore"—and the friendship has been allowed to lapse.

Even in more intimate relationships, new mothers find that they are unable to ignore qualities that may have always been present, but are only now experienced as abrasive. For example, Rachel has a close friend, Ella, whom she had known since high school and who, she realizes retrospectively, has always been rather self-absorbed, demanding, and infantile. Although their friendship was never a completely balanced one, Rachel being more often the listener and Ella being more often the talker, it had suited them both. Rachel had admittedly enjoyed nurturing, guiding, one might even say mothering her friend. But once she became a "real" mother to a real baby, this changed, and without any warning.

Rachel now spends more than enough of her time and emotional energy focusing on her baby's experience—listening vigilantly for any indication of distress, comforting him at all hours of the day and night, applauding his every accomplishment—so that she has little patience for the skewed relationship she has with her childhood friend. Rachel finds that she wants a little more nurturing herself in her adult friendships, and this is foreign to Ella. Whereas Rachel's needs and expectations for the friendship have changed since she became a mother, Ella's have not.

It became clear to Rachel why she was feeling so alienated from Ella when her friend visited her shortly after she came back from the hospital. Oblivious to Rachel's state of exhaustion and to her hesitation about having visitors so soon, Ella and her new husband descended upon the house, bringing with them Chinese take-out food for dinner, and leaving the mess for Rachel and her husband to clean up afterward. (Just like old times.) With this incident Rachel's feelings about her friend crystallized, and she no longer wished to spend time with her.

When Rachel confided in her mother her sense of outrage over her friend's behavior, she was taken aback when her mother pointed out to her that Ella had never been sensitive to Rachel's feelings, having always been too preoccupied with her own life problems to take notice of anybody else. Rachel had to agree, but the realization was somewhat disconcerting. It meant that *she*, Rachel, was the one who was challenging the status quo, and therefore it was she who was immediately responsible for the rupture in their fifteen-year-long friendship; how, she asked herself, could she blame Ella, when Ella was naively continuing to behave as she always had?

Other women describe generalized feelings of discomfort around nonmothers and wonder if these nonmothers are judging them and scrutinizing their relationship with their babies. "I think that other parents are big judges too, but when as a parent you see another kid screaming in the playground, there is always a part of you that knows that your kid has done the same at one time or another. I know personally that I was a harsher critic before I was a mother, and I assume that other people are the same way."

Sensitivity to criticism, real or presumed, is not uncommon. New mothers are acutely aware of their status as mothers, and when the difference between them and nonmothers becomes salient, the question arises as to whether this difference represents an insurmountable barrier to intimacy. This concern is not altogether unfounded. People generally like people who are similar to themselves (at least in certain dimensions that they deem important), and differences often lead to competitive feelings and mistrust—among neighbors and friends, as well as among nations.[2] And while some new mothers gird themselves against the possibility of criticism or rejection by either striking first or withdrawing, rejecting nonmothers before they can be rejected by them, others lean over backward and try to mask whatever differences exist. And by doing so they inadvertently create an artificial situation in which the possibility of real intimacy is precluded.

Deborah now works just one day a week as a mental health professional, and though she feels confident about herself as a mother, she admits to feeling inadequate, even empty-headed, when she is with people who do not have babies. "I try to think of things to say that are unrelated to kids, and I've actually run down in my head what to say beforehand so that people won't think I'm boring." Deborah is the kind of mother who has read all the popular "baby books," and who, as part of her professional training, is well versed in the psychological literature on early child development. Nevertheless, a reprimanding voice nags at her from within because she hasn't read the newspaper in weeks and therefore feels incapable of carrying on an intelligent conversation with anyone other than another mother. No matter how much Deborah wishes to remain intimate with women friends who are not mothers, her worries only stifle her spontaneity and infuse the atmosphere with tension. Her *efforts* to sustain the intimacy only subvert her desires to feel close, as she contorts herself and pretends to be what she is not in anticipation of her friends' disapproval.

The fear of being judged inadequate by friends who are not mothers is matched for many women by an equally intense fear of being envied by women who want to be mothers but who, for one reason or another, are not. Married friends with fertility problems and unmarried friends who have doubts about ever finding a suitable mate are a source of tremendous discomfort for many new mothers. Even, or perhaps particularly, when there are no overt signs of envy or jealousy, many mothers feel that they have to censor themselves lest they rub salt into already open wounds. They may feel obligated to down-play the joys of motherhood or focus exclusively on the anxieties. In either case, if they are monitoring themselves to protect their friends, the friendship cannot but suffer on account of it.

Elizabeth described how one friend, Kathy, who was having difficulty becoming pregnant herself, withdrew from her almost immediately after Elizabeth announced that she was pregnant. When she finally confronted Kathy toward the end of her pregnancy, she was accused of having been cruelly insensitive to Kathy's condition. Ret-rospectively, Elizabeth recalled that she had not subdued her spontaneous expressions of joy when she was with Kathy, and she began to feel guilty, though uncertain as to how to rectify matters. After a couple of attempts to make amends, Elizabeth reconciled herself to the fact that the friendship could not survive her pregnancy. Kathy seemed to experience Elizabeth's life as a personal assault, and no compromise was possible.

While in some instances a woman's hesitancy to share her experience as a mother may reflect her sensitivity to a friend's feelings, in other instances it may be more her own projection as a mother. If *she* would feel terrible if she had not had a baby, and if *she* would feel jealous of other women who had children when she had none, is it not plausible to assume that other women feel similarly even when in fact they do not? Whether her appraisals of other women's feelings toward her are accurate or exaggerated or grossly distorted, when a new mother anticipates nega-tive responses, the friendship in question is jeopardized, because she no longer feels she can be spontaneous.

Judith, who has also cut back on her professional com-mitments substantially since becoming a mother, admits that she is embarrassed and guilty when she feels forced to make lame excuses in declining her girlfriend Sharon's invitations to join her for week-night lectures on topics of mutual interest. When she first became a mother, Judith was adamant in her conviction that *she* was not going to lose touch with her colleagues, particularly Sharon, with whom she had developed a sisterly kind of relationship over the years, one in which she had happily deferred to Sharon, as she would to an idealized older sister. Gradually however, Judith began to admit to herself, if not to Sharon, that despite her insistence (was she protesting too much?), she really did not wish to spend her free evenings at lectures or seminars or other "educational" activities, at least not yet. This meant not only that she would not see her friend Sharon as frequently as she had in the past, but more significantly that she would no longer be able to play the role of Sharon's faithful protégée, a role that she now realized had bound them to one another. The "little sister" had grown up and was no longer her older sister's shadow, and relations were cordial but awkward.

With neither woman knowing quite how to resuscitate the dying relationship, they groped for a while, reminiscing and pretending that they were still like sisters—until the deception was too glaring and there was no reason to persist in it. Sharon had stopped informing Judith of evening events, and whenever they spoke of luncheon dates it was always tentatively, and with every postponement, the possibility of getting together became more remote.

In retrospect, what happened to their friendship seemed inevitable to Judith, but it was not without sadness that she watched her "big sister" slip from her life, wondering whether they would ever be able to reconnect on new terms. We know that Judith felt impotent to bridge the gap that now separated her from her friend. But we can well imagine that Sharon felt as powerless, if not more, since it was Judith, not she, who had initiated the changes in their relationship. Abandoned by her "little sister," Sharon may feel hurt, angry, and confused, and in all likelihood is unaware of the internal turmoil Judith has been experiencing with regard to their relationship. Only a future reconciliation will relieve both friends of the queasy sensation that comes when loose ends are left hanging, feelings are closeted away, and conflicts remain unresolved.

As mothers, women sometimes let down their guards, exposing aspects of their personalities that were previously well hidden, and, as it were, camouflaged by a carefully constructed social persona. When two friends enter motherhood at the same point in their lives, their nerves are raw, and every sensation, both positive and negative, is magnified tenfold, with either a warming or a cooling effect on their friendship. "There had been many dry spells in my twenty-year friendship with Fran, but since she had a baby not long after I had mine, we finally trust each other enough to be intimate. I think it is because we are both so proud of our babies that we no longer feel that we have to compete with each other about other things. I see a softer part of her because I think she feels more comfortable showing it to me."

By way of contrast, Elizabeth describes a friendship in which motherhood had the opposite effect. Her friendship with Claire began in college, and though they were always temperamentally different, Claire being the more reserved and Elizabeth the more expressive of the two, their differences, highlighting their different sociocultural backgrounds, were a source of mutual attraction. Elizabeth is Jewish, and Claire's family are descendants of the early English settlers in America. When Claire had her baby, they drifted apart for a while, but as soon as Claire's schedule became more flexible and there was more time to meet on common ground, their friendship was revitalized. However, since the birth of Elizabeth's daughter three years later, Elizabeth has felt a subtle but unsettling shift in her feelings about Claire, and senses that this is mutual, though the issue has never been broached. Elizabeth is confused about her feelings of estrangement, but knows that she does not feel close to Claire as a mother (in fact, in mothering she feels closer to another friend whom she had never felt very close to before), and that their differences inspire competition, rather than curiosity or even respect.

Elizabeth believes that she and Claire started to drift apart when she was still pregnant. Claire had had a difficult pregnancy, while Elizabeth had not; Claire had worked full-time up until she delivered, while Elizabeth's work schedule was considerably less demanding. Looking back, Elizabeth believes that these contrasting experiences posed a threat to their relationship and created feelings of resentment in Claire, which she nursed and never expressed. (How could she?) Moreover, Elizabeth wonders whether her confidence as a new mother did not grate upon Claire, who, being less sure of herself in this regard, tended to ruminate more than Elizabeth. Elizabeth rarely asked Claire for any advice, and admits that for some unidentified reason she has been particularly reluctant to turn to Claire for help, even though she senses that Claire would have enjoyed guiding and supporting her in the early stages of motherhood. In fact, when her newborn was crying inconsolably one evening and her husband was out of town, she felt more comfortable calling another, less intimate friend, than calling Claire. Turning to Claire at a time of need meant admitting defeat, though war had never been officially declared and the two women were ostensibly still friends and allies. Elizabeth is aware that she has distanced herself from Claire, but she feels that this is the result, not the cause, of Claire's resentment. However, as is often the case in such situations, it is impossible to locate definitively the origin of this cycle of suspicion and withdrawal.

From Elizabeth's point of view, Claire is an "overprotective mother," and Claire's elaborate, overly drawn-out bedtime rituals offended Elizabeth's need for order and limit-setting; she imagines that Claire finds her no-nonsense approach to bedtime equally offensive. What adds yet another dimension to this intricate web of competitive and friendly feelings is the marked contrast between their husbands. Claire and her husband share many of the responsibilities of child care quite equally, and at one point, when Claire's daughter began to express a preference for her father Claire backed away and assumed a more peripheral role. Not only have Elizabeth and her husband settled on a more traditional division of labor, but Elizabeth is disturbed when she hears Claire speak of her husband's involvement. When Claire's daughter cried at night she and her husband would *both* race up the stairs to comfort the baby, which is definitely not something Elizabeth's husband would be inclined to do. Although Elizabeth claims that she would never want her husband to encroach on her territory or compete with her for the role of primary parent, her irritation with Claire suggests that this issue may still represent an unsettled area of conflict.

Knowing that Claire is highly sensitive and easily wounded, Elizabeth is convinced that Claire is aware of her unspoken criticisms of her as a mother, but that being characteristically reticent, she keeps her distance rather than express her hurt feelings. Elizabeth has also become reticent, though for her this is new. She knows that somehow her hypercritical attitude is unfair, and rather than express her feelings directly she muffles them.

Social Comparisons

> *There exists in the human organism, a drive to evaluate his opinions and abilities. To the extent that nonsocial means are not available, people evaluate their opinions or abilities, by comparison respectively with the opinion or abilities of others.—Leon Festinger, 1954*

Women who have recently become mothers gravitate to other mothers for a number of reasons, some of which are merely practical. Mothers' schedules are more likely to overlap (who else, besides baby-sitters and mothers, is in the playground on a Tuesday morning at eleven o'clock?), and opportunities for social contact with nonmothers are few and far between, particularly during regular working hours. But there is something about the attraction to other mothers that goes beyond logistics. Women who return to full-time work have their antennae up and secretly scan the workplace for other mothers on the job. When they discover that they are not alone, they are tremendously relieved, as if this were proof that they are not imposters after all, and that they *do* belong in the conference room even if they have been changing diapers a few hours earlier. Surreptitiously, they begin to share baby stories.

New mothers seek each other out and voraciously soak up each others' tales of joy and woe because they are looking for an anchor in a sea of ambiguous meanings and emotions. Of course there are going to be exceptions to this general rule, and some women will even go out of their way to avoid extended contact with groups of new mothers, wanting to dissociate themselves as much as possible from their new group identity. This will be discussed at length later, but it is worth noting at this point that many new mothers are uncomfortable with the idea that their friendships are exclusively child-related, and even as they seek out other mothers and find themselves spending less and less time with single friends, they are aware of a countervailing impulse to reverse this trend. As they wrestle to keep their heads above water, they take little solace from people who have never been to sea or been tossed around by the waves. It is not only that other mothers are tolerant of endless stories about a baby's sleep patterns, his nursing habits, his bowel movements, or his diet, and that consequently, when they are with them they need not be self-conscious about their own peculiar fascination with such matters, but also that other mothers can and do reciprocate by relating their own experiences under similar circumstances, offering a basis for comparison. How else can women know what is normal and what is not? What are realistic expectations, and what are mere Hollywood fantasies? How else can women know when they should worry or feel guilty, or when they should relax and simply enjoy themselves? I am not suggesting that social comparisons *actually* provide absolute correct answers to these unanswerable questions, but only that new mothers rely on these comparisions to buttress their own at times faltering inclinations about how they should mother.

Roseanne, for example, regrets that she did not confide in other women when she was suffering along with her baby through the initial period of colic, and she reproaches her mother-in-law for waiting until the worst was all over to inform her that her husband also screamed for most of the first three months of his life. Isolated and confused during those early months, Roseanne did not know whether to feel worried, angry, or guilty when her baby (whose condition was further complicated by nerve damage during delivery) failed to respond to her efforts to soothe her. Her doctor's attention was understandably directed at her daughter's temporary paralysis of the arm, and something as mundane as colic was either not addressed during their frequent consultations or else was glossed over without adequate explanation.

Roseanne knew that she was exhausted and frustrated, and that this did not correspond to her image of what a "good" mother should be feeling, but what she did not know was whether her feelings or her daughter's behavior was "normal" or evidence that something was gravely wrong, with her, with her daughter, with their relationship. Feeling emotionally isolated, she paced her apartment with her daughter cradled in her arms and routinely circled the neighborhood several times a day, too worried about her baby to give herself a break, and too angry with herself and, worse yet, with her baby, to feel she deserved one.

Mothers are not unique in their drive to compare themselves and their experiences with like individuals. Psychologists have observed that when there are no objective or unambiguous standards of right or wrong, people rely on social comparisons to evaluate the accuracy of their judgments and the appropriateness of their feelings.[3] (In fact, it has been suggested that the need that people have to evaluate themselves and impose order on their otherwise chaotic experience is a major impetus for being with others.) Particularly under the sway of powerful emotions, when the capacity for objectivity has waned, people turn to others to confirm or disconfirm their view of reality.

A brief digression will help place women's experiences as new mothers within a more general psychological framework. Psychologist Stanley Schachter observed that when, under controlled experimental conditions, people are made to feel anxious, they are more likely to seek out other people, particularly people who are in the same situation.[4] Schachter suggests that this tendency to seek out others under the impact of anxiety reflects a basic human need to evaluate, through the process of social comparison, what is and what is not an appropriate emotional response to a given situation. In Schachter's classic experiment, participants were informed that as part of a scientific study they would receive a series of painful but not harmful electric shocks. Under these circumstances, they needed to evaluate against their peers whether they should panic, keep a "stiff upper lip," or feel proud to participate in a scientific study of this nature. They were not sure how to feel, and for better or for worse, they looked to others for guidance.[5]

New mothers also seek out "similar" others, and those they include in this category, and consequently those they compare themselves to, will influence how they mother and how they feel about what they do.

Motherhood as a Reference Group

As we see our face, figure, and dress in the glass,
and are interested in them because they are ours, and
pleased or otherwise with them according as they do or

> *do not answer to what we should like them to be; so in*
> *imagination we perceive in another's mind some thought*
> *of our appearance, manners, aims, deeds, character,*
> *friends, and so on, and are variously affected by it.*
> —*Charles Horton Cooley*, Human Nature and the
> Social Order, 1902

At the turn of the century, the sociologist Charles Horton Cooley developed the notion of the "looking-glass self" to convey the idea of the *self* as a social entity that lives and evolves in relation to others. Cooley was careful to point out, however, that it is not simply our reflections in the eyes of other people that color our feelings about who we are, but, more precisely, how we *imagine* other people judge these reflections. Since the judgments of others are various and, moreover, biased, the "looking-glass self" is vulnerable to the vicissitudes of fashion, prejudice, and custom.

A woman need not participate in any organized mother's group to experience the transition to motherhood as analogous to joining a club or becoming a member of a community. After the nine-month initiation period in which the mother-to-be is subject to the unique and dramatic transformations of pregnancy, labor, and childbirth, what woman could deny the bond that links her to every other mother? By having accomplished the "miraculous" (what, after all, could be more miraculous than reproducing life?), she has entered the realm of the completely ordinary, and any illusions that she harbored of being completely unique unto herself, a self-subsisting island isolated from the mainstream of society, are dispelled. People are loath to give up their illusions without being otherwise compensated, but, initially, the satisfaction many new mothers derive from their heightened sense of communion with others is compensation enough. Literally disillusioned, but in the most positive sense of the word, women tend to feel more mature, less lighthearted. As will soon become apparent to most women, however, mothers are a heterogeneous lot, and it is just another illusion to expect that the community of women is a completely harmonious one.

As soon as a woman identifies herself as a mother (even if she resists defining herself exclusively in those terms), she shares an essential aspect of her identity with other women who are also mothers. The alliance may at times be an uneasy one, as women struggle among each other to define what motherhood is and should be, but it is an alliance all the same. In the language of social psychology, the new mother has shifted her "reference group," the group with which the individual identifies or aspires to belong.[6]

Reference groups serve a number of functions for their members. They provide members with an organized worldview—that is, with norms, and values—and offer them a standard of comparison by which to evaluate feelings and opinions, opportunities and responsibilities, relationships and achievements. Whatever the basis is for the formation of a group—social, educational, or political— psychologists have found that in most groups subtle (and not so subtle) pressures are exerted upon members to conform to the implicit and explicit norms of behavior that constitute the group culture. Those who deviate, intentionally or not, mar the "illusion of unanimity" within the group and force other members to acknowledge that their way of doing things is not the *only* way, and indeed may not be the best way.[7]

As sociologist Charles Horton Cooley so aptly put it, "Thus every variant idea of conduct has to fight its way: as soon as any one attempts to do anything unexpected the world begins to cry, 'Get in the rut! Get in the rut! Get in the rut!' and shoves, stares, coaxes, and sneers until he does so—or until he makes good his position, and so by altering the standard in a measure, establishes a new basis of conformity.[8] Deviance from group norms can be particularly threatening if members experience every difference as a direct challenge to the group and a personal criticism of them and their lives. When a group feels under attack, the group defends itself, and deviants often meet with social rejection.

In the process of identifying with her new reference group, the new mother begins to assume and eventually internalize the attitudes and behaviors of other mothers, making every effort to adhere to the group norms particularly, but not exclusively, when in direct contact with other members. The culture of "the group" becomes a part of her just as she becomes a part of the culture. Translated into experiential terms, this means that the opinions and values of "the group," as it exists for her, will influence a woman's choices and feelings about everything ranging from her work, to her marriage, to how she handles her toddler's plea for an ice cream before leaving the park at five o'clock, to what she talks about and how she spends her leisure time.[9]

When a woman identifies with a circle of women who are also mothers, and she adopts the norms of the group, she may find that the ideas and values of her contemporaries clash not only with those of her mother, but also with those of her husband. Insofar as she has internalized her mother's values, and feels an allegiance to her husband and his way of thinking, she is liable to experience conflicts of loyalty. Moreover, when she is herself uncertain as to what is best for her, her marriage, and her child, she is particularly vulnerable to competing points of view.

Suppose, for example, her husband's notion of fathering is relatively traditional, and while all the other fathers in her circle of friends are willing to commit themselves to a certain number of hours per week taking care of their children, her husband is not. When arguments ensue between her and her recalcitrant husband, and they are likely to, who is to be the final arbiter of what is good or fair or necessary?

Or suppose a woman's friends encourage her to consider *her* needs as an individual and as a wife, needs for time alone and time alone with her husband, while her own mother, who rarely left her side before she was of school age, looks on, scandalized, when she broaches the possibility of a weekend away from the baby. What is she to think? Whose judgment should she trust?

Without any formal instruction, the new mother who frequents the neighborhood park learns quickly what kind of small talk is acceptable and what is not, what will foster feelings of belonging and facilitate her inclusion into the group of mothers who gather there regularly and what will mark her as an outsider. Depending on the particular group, she may be encouraged to talk at length about her baby's diaper rash, or ask for details about another baby's sleep pattern, or air her feelings of guilt and anxiety about leaving her baby with a baby-sitter for the first time. Commenting on the crisis of the homeless, who increasingly occupy the benches in the adjacent park, may even generate a positive response from the other women. But if she tries to initiate a conversation about the lead story on the front page of the daily newspaper, or a new exhibition at the art museum for which tickets need to be purchased well beforehand, she may very well meet with glazed expressions or polite nods, and this will inform her that these are *not* considered to be appropriate topics of playground discussion. There is no universal set of norms for new mothers (though within certain subcultures there is probably considerable homogeneity of opinions and values), but every group has norms, and each woman finds that she must strike a balance between joining the group and striking out on her own, at the risk of social ostracism.

Cheryl, whose case history was discussed at length in the previous chapter, felt both supported and subtly undermined by other mothers when she returned to her full-time position as a college professor a few months after the birth of her son. Cheryl was initiated into motherhood by the mothers in her neighborhood whom she encountered in the park, in her building, and in the supermarket during those first anxious months. These were women whom she would not ordinarily have met in her professional life or usual social circles, but they became intimates of sorts and her primary contact with other adults.

Pleasantly opinionated, with an ironic sense of humor, Cheryl exudes confidence in her role as a professional woman. Yet she approached motherhood tentatively. Left to herself, her tendency was to be overprotective of her son (as her mother had been of her when she was growing up), and it came as a relief when her contemporaries urged her to venture outside the house with her colicky son. Originally too embarrassed to nurse in public, she confined herself to her home during the first few weeks of her son's life—having committed herself to nurse him on demand until the time came for her to return to work. However, after seeing the other mothers nursing unselfconsciously in the local playground, she gradually worked up the courage to defy her mother's rules of decorum and follow their example; if she could not give herself license to nurse in public, the group gave it to her.

Cheryl was not accustomed to the self-imposed isolation of motherhood, but she needed validation for her impulses to be more daring, less constricted. To dare meant to depart from her own mother's strict set of rules and manners, and consequently, to risk failure. Realizing that she needed all the support she could muster in order to relax the overly harsh standards she imposed upon herself, she joined a play group that included five other women and their babies in order to give herself, as much as her baby, an opportunity to socialize on a regular basis.

As long as Cheryl's struggles and delights mirrored their own, the women in her group were always ready to offer her encouragement and support; but as soon as her path diverged significantly from theirs, as happened when, for example, she reaffirmed her commitment to her work, Cheryl sensed an almost imperceptible change in the atmosphere. They were no longer comrades in pursuit of a common cause; rather, feelings of competitiveness and mutual alienation began to surface. Suddenly, after feeling so grateful, so close to these women, Cheryl felt removed from them ("Who are these women to me anyway?").

Within this group of five women, Cheryl was the only one who was returning to full-time work, and without in any way intending it, she felt that she and her baby had come to represent a challenge to the group and its values. (Of course, none of this was ever made this explicit.) When Jesse, her son, had trouble separating in the morning before she went to work and on weekends when she and her husband occasionally engaged a baby-sitter, the other mothers in her group would say very nicely, "Oh, it is because he doesn't see you enough." Naturally, this made Cheryl question what she was doing: "I would believe it and it made me feel really bad. . . . At work, I never have these kinds of problems with other mothers; quite the opposite. There, I am the one who says that I don't see him enough, and they tell me not to worry." Depending upon whom she spoke to, her son's response was taken as evidence of incipient pathology or perceived as perfectly normal.[10]

Cheryl's individual decision had symbolic significance for all of the other women in her play group because it forced them to confront their own beliefs and feelings, which, in all likelihood, were not free of contradictions and ambivalaneces. What mother does *not* harbor some lingering doubts about how to combine her needs as an individual with her desire to be a good mother? And who among us does not wish, at times, to squelch all such doubts and proceed as if our path were the only path imaginable? Even the most satisfied woman in Cheryl's group might naturally ask herself, "How can it really be right for Cheryl and her baby if it is not right for me and my baby?" And then, "How can we be so different and both be right about how to mother and how to live our lives?" When the babies become the "proof of the pudding," comparisons within the community of mothers intensify feelings of competition and alienation, and the "deviant" (in this case Cheryl) may turn elsewhere for support and validation.

Judith's experience with a particular group of mothers who congregated in her neighborhood park and who functioned as a new "reference group" during the first several months of motherhood further illustrates how babies can become implicated in the competition that can develop between women when one member of a group deviates from the group's informal norms.

Judith describes herself as having spent a good portion of her free time during the first ten months of her baby's life in the neighborhood park (whose existence she hadn't known of before she had had her baby), and she had become a part of an informal circle of new mothers whose schedules were similar to her own. During the early months, she and the other mothers openly compared notes about labor, childbirth, and their babies' sleeping and eating patterns; they exchanged ideas about how to soothe the pain of teething, how to baby-proof their homes, and what to look for when buying a baby stroller. However, this is not to say that there weren't differences between them, and that these differences didn't lead to awkwardnesses or a subtle tensing when they emerged in the course of conversation. But the desire for communion and sisterly love overshadowed any feelings of competition or alienation.

For example, some of the women in the "group" conscientiously redesigned their living rooms and kitchens so that their toddlers would be able to roam the house without constantly being admonished not to touch this or open that, while others preferred to keep their living space pretty much as it always was and set verbal limits on their baby's activity when necessary. Of course each camp (and they *were* ideological camps) believed that theirs was undoubtedly the correct way to handle a toddler. ("A baby shouldn't be restricted so." "A baby needs to learn to live within structure.") But despite the differences, a peculiar kind of intimacy developed within this circle of women as each revealed, to the group of relative strangers, the details of her daily life with her baby.

Judith began to depend upon these women, and was convinced that they also depended upon her, for advice or simply for reassurance that whatever was happening within themselves and their babies was within the realm of the normal and nothing to worry about. For practical as well as emotional reasons, Judith ended up spending more time with these women than she did with her closest friends or even at times with her husband, and most of that time together was spent exchanging baby stories. Disagreements rarely surfaced, and when they did, they were automatically smoothed over, and criticism was reserved for women who were not in the immediate group; an atmosphere of camaraderie prevailed.

However, when Judith decided to return to work half-time, her decision set her apart from her new circle of friends, none of whom had yet committed herself to working outside the home quite that much. The change of schedule had an immediate impact on her relationship with "the group," since contact between the mothers had almost always been unpremeditated, pivoting around the overlapping schedules of the babies. Judith was anxious, however, not to lose touch entirely, and on occasion she would arrive breathlessly at the park at four o'clock in her "work clothes." As she awkwardly tried to negotiate with her soon-muddied baby, who implored her to go down the slide with her (just as all the other mothers were doing) high-heeled shoes and all, her friends greeted her in their jeans and T-shirts. She didn't know whether to feel proud that *she* was doing both—being a mother and a "career woman"—or sad that she and her baby had already missed the better part of the afternoon in the park.

Moreover, something fundamental had shifted within the group, or so she sensed. She was beginning to feel like an outsider, and, what was worse, in some intangible way she felt as if she had betrayed the others, and perhaps a part of herself as well. "Do they feel the same way about me, or is it my problem?" she would ask herself, as she relived the anxiety of her own early separation con-

flicts. As a child she had feared that by being different, by
becoming her own person, she was being disloyal to her
mother; as an adult she wondered whether her differences as a mother might not cost her her new-found
friendships.

One particular afternoon, her lingering uncertainies about
her decision to return to work resurfaced, with a vengeance, as she listened with one ear to a discussion about
a local nursery school that had lost a toddler in the subway a few months back. Judith asked herself whether she
was being selfish in wanting to return to work so soon,
and engaged in imaginary conversations with the other
mothers, accusing them of using their babies as an excuse
not to work, concluding, "They are just as selfish as I am
in their own way!" Judith read disapproval and suspi-
ciousness into the facial expressions of the women around
her, the very same women to whom she had turned, only
recently, for support and encouragement. She began to
wonder whether her baby really would be worse off two
years, five years, or twenty years hence, as the expressions on their faces seemed to imply.

And just as the smile on her baby's face had begun to
allay her anxiety, her baby crawled over to another unsuspecting ten-month-old (whose mother had *not* returned to
work) and bit her—an admittedly not uncommon occur-
rence among babies of this age. Worse yet was that her
baby showed absolutely no remorse for her act of aggression, and instead protested ferociously when Judith, apol-
ogizing to everyone within earshot, tried to pull her away.
(Of course, Judith *knew* from her books on child development that a ten-month-old baby couldn't possibly feel
guilt, but in the heat of the moment, this didn't seem to
matter—what if no one else understood this? And why
hadn't anyone else's baby bitten someone that afternoon?)

Under these circumstances, it was particularly difficult
for Judith not to experience a hint of reproach as her
friend rushed over to protect her own "innocent" baby.
Judith began to wonder, "Could this bite be related to my

recent change in schedule? Is that what 'those women' are thinking? Are they critical of my decision to go back to work? Are they right to be critical, if indeed they are?" And on and on, until her baby did something so captivating that the idea that there was anything to worry about faded into oblivion.

"Mirror, Mirror on the Wall . . ."

> *We are ashamed to seem evasive in the presence of a straightforward man, cowardly in the presence of a brave one, gross in the eyes of a refined one, and so on. We always imagine, and in imagining share, the judgements of the other mind. A man will boast to one person of an action—say some sharp transaction in trade—which he would be ashamed to own to another.*
> —*Charles Horton Cooley*, Human Nature and the Social Order, 1902

Comparisons are inevitable and can be either encouraging or demoralizing, depending upon whom a person is comparing himself to, and how he feels about who he is and what he is doing in the first place. If a new mother is filled with doubt about her choices or even questions her ability to choose correctly, she will, in all likelihood, be more easily swayed by the opinions of others.[11] If, moreover, this doubt is associated with generally low self-esteem, a woman may find herself vacillating at every juncture and every time she encounters someone who has a different opinion. Insecurity feeds upon itself, and the more such a mother looks outside herself for "solutions" to her problems, the more she flounders and the less she trusts her own judgment. In order to avoid the confusion and the anxiety of social comparisons, an insecure woman may become quite rigid in her approach to mothering, vigilantly screening out all competing points of view. (Freud's notion that opposites often reflect underlying similarities

is relevant here.) Terrified of disturbing her own tenuously
held psychic equilibrium, she will have little "tolerance of
ambiguity" and will not be able to admit controversy.
What is right and what is wrong will correspond to discrete and indisputably self-evident categories, and the opinions and behavior of other mothers will be rendered
irrelevant. She maintains her stability at the expense of
psychic complexity.

Self-confidence is an important factor in determining
how a woman responds when she experiences subtle pressures to conform to group norms, but it is also important
to identify the particular subgroup of mothers she turns to
(in reality or in her imagination) when she is trying to
evaluate herself as a mother. This reference group, which
may consist of one, two, or ten thousand other women,
will influence her opinions and feelings along with any
other groups she continues to identify with apart from the
group of mothers.

Behavior that is normative from the point of view of one
group is deviant from the point of view of another, and
when a woman is caught between two very different
reference groups (a group of nonworking mothers and a
group of women and men who share her professional
interests, for example), her allegiance to one may constitutes a betrayal of the other. Consider the following
example.

In contrast to Cheryl and Judith, Deborah feels awkward in the company of other mothers as well as former
colleagues on account of her decision *not* to return to work
more than one day a week. Most of the other mothers she
knows with babies over a year old are already working at
least two days a week, if not more, and in order to avoid
what she experiences as embarrassing questions, she admits to lying about her own schedule on occasion. While
the decision to be an "almost full-time mother" was hers,
and while she maintains that she would not have had it
any other way, it has nevertheless been difficult for her to
screen out the responses of others with whom she still

identifies professionally. Being a full-time mother, she says, is "not the image I want to project in the world."

Deborah acknowledges that she was never completely confident or happy when she was working and attributes her insecurity to the fact that in her own family her sister was incontrovertibly seen as the "intelligent one." According to the family lore, Deborah's strength lay in her social finesse, and therefore it is not surprising that she felt immediately more secure in her ability to mother than in her ability to perform as a professional. Although she is resolute in her decision to remain home nearly full-time until her children are at least school age, concerns about her capabilities outside the domestic sphere continue to plague her. She has not entirely relinquished her desire to usurp her sister's position and be the "intellectual" of the family; and if Deborah is only completely comfortable disclosing her abbreviated work schedule to other mothers who do *not* work outside the home at all (as she reports), it is because she has not managed to dissociate herself psychologically from those women who do.

Where one woman encounters disapproving or sympathetic glances when she decides to return to work, and another woman encounters the same kinds of responses when she doesn't, many women encounter *both* positive and negative reactions to every decision they make about their babies and their lives as mothers. Being betwixt and between is psychologically exhausting, and gradually, without premeditation, mothers tend to forge alliances that insulate them from those women whose values are incompatible with theirs, and whose life choices pose a threat to their psychic equilibrium.[12] In this process the "universal community of mothers" is fragmented.

Precisely because motherhood brings women together as members of a social group in pursuit of a common cause, it can also create a gulf between women who are mothers that, once formed, is difficult if not impossible to bridge. As new mothers, women come to depend upon other women for validation and encouragement, but if

this group identification increases the potential for intimacy, it also increases the potential for conflict and disappointment when such support is not forthcoming—as we
saw from the experiences of Cheryl and Judith. Sharing
the experiences of mothering, an experience as intimate as
any can be, accentuates for each women how similar *and*
how different she is from every other woman, and it is
this uneasy combination of being so similar and yet so
different that generates the most intense approach-
avoidance conflicts.[13]

Rebecca joined an informal mother's group shortly after
her son was born, and she spoke enthusiastically about
the sense of community that had developed within this
heterogeneous group of five mothers. All the women in
the group had had their babies at approximately the same
time, and though they were relative strangers (they had
all met in the preparation-for-childbirth class sponsored
by the hospital), they soon developed into a cohesive and
supportive group, meeting consistently for more than a
year, with plans to continue meeting indefinitely. Rebecca
marveled at the differences between the babies, and because each seemed to have its own unique strength (one
was more verbal, another more friendly, and another more
physically agile), the atmosphere was remarkably free of
competitive feelings. The group was a haven for Rebecca.

However, over the course of the year, Rebecca noticed
that she was not being altogether frank about her responses to Elise, one of the other mothers, and this was
contrary to the implicit norm of openness and honesty
that prevailed within the group. She began to feel uncomfortable about her secretiveness but was nevertheless reluctant to express her true feelings either to Elise or the
the group at large.

Rebecca's discomfort crystallized one afternoon when
Elise, without the slightest hint of self-consciousness, reported a method she used to instruct her one-year-old
son. (It had never occurred to Rebecca to be so methodical
at this early age.) Elise described how she would repeat to

her son each morning an identical phrase, such as "Here is a toothbrush," and that over the course of several months her son was able to understand one hundred "concepts." Rebecca did not feel comfortable questioning Elise's method of instruction, though it offended her sensibility and contradicted what she had learned in developmental psychology. Moreover, she felt it would be a betrayal of the group ethos to poll the other group members for their reactions behind Elise's back. Without condoning Elise's instructional techniques Rebecca admitted that for a fleeting instance it had occurred to her that perhaps *her* son was developmentally delayed in comparison with Elise's child prodigy and that therefore she would be wise to keep her criticisms and doubts to herself.

Ultimately, however, Rebecca became convinced that her comrade-in-motherhood was turning her son into a robot. Feelings of competition gave way to feelings of alienation, as it became apparent that Elise's approach to being a mother was blatantly obnoxious to her, and that their differences transcended the particulars and were irreconcilable. Now that the seeds of dissension had been planted, Rebecca no longer felt quite so inspired by the group as a whole. Unwilling not to be judgmental when she felt a judgment was warranted, Rebecca gave up her dream of unconditional acceptance and began to wonder when the group would cease to function as a haven in the midst of a competitive and divided world.

Ironically, similarities as well as differences between women can generate a host of inner conflicts, for they can lead women to see their own "worst qualities" (qualities they had hoped to stifle) reflected back at them. Many women who are attracted to other mothers because they are looking for validation and support for who they are and what they feel are simultaneously repelled by other mothers because they fear the loss of their independence and the weakening of their will. Being accepted, flaws and all, can be reassuring *and* disconcerting, and there may be a boomerang effect. The phenomenon might be compared to Groucho Marx's sentiments when he said, "I wouldn't want to be a member of a club that would have me as a member." Particularly when a woman feels that her creativity or her image of herself as an intelligent, worthwhile human being is jeopardized by her affiliation with the group (whether this is necessarily true or not), she will resist the impulse to belong, and may even deny any allegiance to the group as such. In such cases, any attraction the group holds for her is overshadowed by her impulse to dissociate herself from it.

Elizabeth was confronted with this dilemma as a new mother when she found that other mothers were at times unflattering reminders of what she did not want to be but felt she was in danger of becoming. Elizabeth's internal conflicts about who she is and who she wants to be manifest themselves in her resistance to joining in conversation with other mothers she encounters in the local playground. "I do not want to talk about possessions— baby strollers, high chairs, all the materialistic aspects of mothering. I worry too much about these things in the privacy of my home." In her attempt to vanquish the enemy within herself, Elizabeth has avoided its counterpart in the external world. Curious about the women she sees, she has preferred to keep her distance, maintaining one-to-one contact with a few women but refusing to allow herself to melt into the group. It is as if by mingling with the other mothers en masse Elizabeth fears that she will wake up to find that she has been seduced into becoming the kind of woman she consciously repudiates but unconsciously identifies with.

However much a woman resists affiliating herself with mothers as a social category, such affiliation is inevitable, whether *she* chooses to recognizes it or not. A woman's experiences are rarely unique to her, and she, along with every other woman who is a mother, must learn to manage the irrational at home and in the outside world. Doctors, artists, and secretaries, the pragmatists and the spiritually inclined, must all learn to live with their baby's neediness, their two-year-old's opposition, and their three-year-old's insatiable appetite to know everything even when explanations are infinitely time-consuming and maybe even impossible.

Moreover, regardless of the kind of work they do or the differences in their personalities, most mothers find that the burden of juggling family and career falls on their shoulders. Husbands may be "liberated" and employers supportive, but generally neither are all that flexible themselves—and certain rules just don't bend. The legacy of sex roles is something all mothers share, and as it unites them, it also creates enmity among them. The image in the mirror is not always so pleasing.

As babies and young children, we learn about who we are from the reflections in the mirrors of our parents' eyes; by the time we are adults, most of us have organized these reflected images into a more or less stable identity. Yet even so, we continue to live among others and to depend upon the external world to confirm the reality of our images of who we are and what we can be.

Motherhood thrusts a woman into new forms of relationship and shuts the door upon the old, and the effects are felt at the deepest levels of personality. As a mother, a woman sees herself reflected from different angles and set in new surroundings. Aspects of herself that were previously obscured become visible, and features that were prominent no longer occupy center stage. As the background changes, the figure in the foreground no longer appears the same. As new internal images coalesce, the new mother projects these images in her relations with others; and they are reflected back to her once again, and the cycle recommences. A new mother's sense of herself as an individual is in continual flux; she is the same, but then she is not, and the reflections that stare back at her confirm but also disconfirm the new images she holds of herself. Her reflection in the mirror is subject to distortion, filtered as it is through the imperfect eyes of those who see her.

5

Values in Collision:
The "Perfect" Mother,
the "Perfect" Woman, and
the Imperfect Self

Goddesses, Gods, and Other Mythological Beings

*I blame myself if the toy I buy my daughter turns out
not to be the toy she's most interested in. For weeks I
was obsessive over the fact that the table I had built for
her wasn't exactly the right height for her comfort—she
wasn't using it as blissfully as I wanted her to use it. It
is all because I make demands on myself that I should
be exactly right on the mark.—Elizabeth, thirty-seven,
mother of an eighteen-month-old daughter*

*I've just read T. Berry Brazelton, who says that when
you come home from work you should rock your child
and read to him. But when I come home from work I
generally feel really tired, and when Jesse asks me to
put on Sesame Street I do. There have been times
when I have even fallen asleep on the couch watching it
with him. Then I wake up and feel very guilty, and I
wonder if I'm doing right by him.—Cheryl, thirty-
nine, mother of a two-and-a-half-year-old boy.*

*The glorified self becomes not only a phantom to be
pursued; it also becomes a measuring rod with which to
measure [a person's] actual being. And this actual
being is such an embarrassing sight when viewed from
the perspective of a godlike perfection . . .—Karen
Horney,* Neurosis and Human Growth, *1950*

148

Imperfect creatures in an imperfect world, we dream of gods and goddesses and paradise and conjure up images of perfection—the ideal mother who is always patient, the ideal woman who is always passionate, the ideal person who is always creative, and the ideal family whose members are always loving. These "phantoms" inspire us to transcend our limitations (they are strong where we are weak), seduce us into believing that we can do the impossible (they know no boundaries, while we are made of flesh and blood), and torment us when we are forced to admit that we are indeed flawed.

The drive for perfection appears to be a universal one. What culture does not have its gods, and what person does not have a secret, idealized image of what he would like to be?[1] But the desire to soar beyond one's limitations has negative as well as positive implications. It propels us forward—but at the risk of falling flat on our faces, ashamed and guilty. Moreover, when we impose our standards of perfection on others, whom we see as extensions of ourselves, and "make relentless demands as to *their* perfection," we deflate their value as human beings as much as we inflate it by pretending they are gods.[2]

All this is further complicated by the fact that each individual within a given culture is confronted with a variety of ideals from which to choose, and some of these appear to be in direct contradiction: Is it "better" to be assertive or modest? Competitive or cooperative? Autonomous or interdependent? Masculine or feminine? Traditionally the answers to each of these questions have varied along sex lines—what is considered "good" for a man is not necessarily considered "good" for a woman, and vice versa.

Thus, the conflicts that emerge when a woman strives to be simultaneously the ideal mother, the ideal woman, and the ideal person are of two kinds. On the one hand, there is the conflict between what she actually is and what she wants to be ("I wish I were more patient"; "I wish I didn't buckle under when my two-year-old has a temper tantrum"). On the other hand, there is the dilemma of selecting her own particular set of ideals from the different versions of perfection offered in the culture. Each version promises a different solution to the problem of human limitation; each represents fundamentally different value systems.

Women question how important it is for them to climb the ladder in the career of their choice, or make a significant contribution to the society as a whole; and they wonder how important it is to them and to their child that they see his first step, watch him play with his friends in the park, soothe his angry tears, and just be by his side when he is sick. In trying to answer these questions women find that they must ask themselves how much value they attach to status, money, intellectual achievements, and independence—their own and their child's. What makes these questions particularly problematic for women is that some values are traditionally "feminine" and others represent a break with tradition.

Images of the ideal mother permeate the culture, and like the gods and goddesses of Greek mythology, they assume human forms and meddle in the affairs of mortals. Contemporary goddesses do not identify themselves as such—we are, after all, a secular society—but they appear to us on the television, in the movies, in museums, in women's magazines, or as projected images superimposed on unfamiliar women seen from a distance. Representing themselves as women, just like you and me, they easily delude us into believing that if we only tried harder, we too could be nearly perfect (as they apparently are).

Since the media not only reflect but also shape our ideals of womanhood, it is not surprising that the message we hear today through the media is a mixed one. The modern woman, as portrayed in the movies or on the television, should be both traditional *and* untraditional. She should be sexy, aggressive, and independent, and she should do creative work outside as well as inside the home. This image bears little resemblance to the Norman Rockwell posters featuring matronly women with aprons serving their family a traditional dinner, complete with apple pie. But beware the consequence should the contemporary woman neglect her "feminine" side and fail to temper her sexuality with due regard for her domestic responsibilities.[3]

Women's magazines advise women on asserting themselves on the job and moving up the corporate ladder, as well as how to "dress for success," look ten years younger, lose weight, turn an ordinary meal into a creative masterpiece, and make Halloween costumes from odds and ends in the house. The resounding message is "to know no boundaries"; the fulfilled woman does it all, has it all, and you should too.[4] From this vantage point, it is "natural" for mothers, who, in the final analysis, are only flesh and blood, to feel blameworthy, at times even inadequate, first as mothers and then as human beings.

Although both men and women struggle to bridge the gulf between their actual and their ideal selves, and although there is no reason to suspect that one sex is more burdened by this struggle than the other, it seems that women are more likely than men to experience an intensification of this conflict in the context of their role as parents. In our culture, motherhood has been the central feature of a woman's identity, at least over the past hundred years or more, and therefore a woman's evaluation of herself as a person has been inextricably linked with her evaluation of herself as a mother.[5] Even for the so-called career woman, motherhood is rarely peripheral to her estimation of her worthiness, which rises and falls with the vicissitudes of her child's development.

A man may pride himself on his financial acumen or his intellectual achievements, berate himself for every minor setback in his career, and yet not blink an eye when his two-year-old son has a temper tantrum in front of dinner guests, or give it a second thought if he explodes at his three-year-old daughter when she accidentally spills her milk at breakfast. Most fathers seem to be able to dismiss these imperfections in their children and in themselves as inconsequential (if indeed they register them in their minds as imperfections at all) simply because they do not perceive them as evidence of their own flawed character. There may be feelings of irritation or hints of remorse, but there is no immediate threat to their self-esteem.

By contrast, a woman's self-esteem is directly implicated in her perception of herself as a mother, even when being an astute businesswoman or a talented artist or a sexually attractive wife is also a very central aspect of her identity. Consequently, a woman often feels ashamed and guilty when her child has a temper tantrum in front of guests or even in front of strangers in the local playground and may berate herself mercilessly for having been impatient with him for dawdling over his cereal when she is trying to get out of the house for an early morning meeting at work. She may very well ask herself what *she* did wrong to produce a child who could protest so ferociously at having his teeth brushed, or she might engage in an extensive debate with herself about the incident at breakfast—was she being insensitive to her child or was she justified in setting reasonable limits? Everything that is remotely related to mothering has a bearing on her feelings about herself, so she is less comfortable than her husband with the idea that she may be flawed as a parent and that her child may be behaving poorly or feeling badly.

There can be little doubt that at least some of these differences between men's and women's experiences as parents are cultural in origin. In earlier times, women were restricted to only a few occupations, which were deemed appropriate to the biological and psychological characteristics they were presumed to have; thus women were largely confined to the world of babies, children, and other domestic concerns, and this was considered only reasonable and natural. Today, however, few scientists try to justify rigid sex roles, and in theory at least, the world beyond the home is viewed as a woman's world too, and the right, perhaps even the obligation, of women to participate in it as full partners in the human enterprise is now recognized.[6]

Inevitably, as women have come to perceive themselves and to be perceived as fundamentally more similar to men than they are different—*as subjects* of history, in and of themselves, and not merely the mysterious *Other* Simone de Beauvoir speaks of in *The Second Sex*—the ideals associated with womanhood have shifted to accommodate these changes.[7] One important shift is that, for the most part, women recognize that they need not make motherhood their entire identity. In fact, within certain social circles the pendulum has swung in the opposite direction, and a woman who does not aspire to be anything other than a devoted mother and wife is looked upon with suspicion, curiosity, or concern. But whether women feel that they *should* or *should not* allow mothering to dominate their lives, being a "good" mother (whatever that happens to mean to a particular woman) continues to be extremely important to a woman's image of herself once she has a baby. (And often this comes as a surprise to new mothers who perceive themselves as "modern women.") Women are continually asking themselves if they are too involved or too distant, too indulgent or too strict, too critical or not demanding enough.

So, for example, while Deborah is prone to worry about being overly enmeshed with her one-and-a-half-year-old daughter, who seems to cling to her more than her cousin's child clings to her cousin, Diane is prone to worry that she is not sufficiently playful with her two-year-old son; moreover, she admits that she was terribly bored during her two-month leave of absence from work and wondered whether there was something seriously wrong with her for feeling that way. Deborah is reassured when she reads books on child development and learns that her daughter's behavior is "normal" for her age, but this does not alleviate her doubts entirely when invidious comparisons between her child and other children are made again and again. Diane is reassured when she compares herself to her parents and other parents of their generation who rarely, if ever, got down on the floor to play with their children, but she still feels twinges of self-condemnation when she sees other new mothers playing enthusiastically with their two-year-olds the games two-year-olds like to play. The content of the anxiety is different for each woman, but most women, like Deborah and Diane, are concerned with how well they are mothering and whether their personality traits are doing irreparable damage to their babies. They seem to be asking themselves whether a Higher Authority on Mothering would find grounds to accuse them of being the toxic kind of mother who is the butt of so much criticism in our culture.

Self-criticism comes in endless varieties and is not always internally consistent. One woman criticizes herself for being too bored to stay home with her son full-time (she *should* love every second of mothering), and then turns around and criticizes herself for leaving her job early to get home by six o'clock (she should *not* allow the quality of her work to suffer now that she is a mother). Another woman berates herself for simply wishing to get away from her colicky baby (she *should* always want to be there to soothe and comfort), and yet worries that her overprotectiveness is stifling her and her baby (she should *not* foster a dependency that is ultimately inhibiting). And a third fears that in her effort to be the perfect mother (she *should* always be attuned to her toddler's inner experience), she has inadvertently created a naricissistic monster who continually challenges her authority until she finally explodes at him with rage. Whatever the form it takes, the "tyranny of the should," to borrow a phrase from Karen Horney, rests on the assumption that perfection is a possibility and that human limitation is deplorable.

Recent changes in the cultural ideals associated with womanhood have created some new dilemmas for women who are mothers: the dilemma of having to choose between competing values, and the related problem of whether a woman can or should want to "have it all," which is a variant of the problem of feeling that perfection is attainable. A woman today might well ask herself, now that she actually has more freedom to consider various alternatives: "What is more important and what is more valuable—shaping public policy, infiltrating the corporation, creating a poem, having money for private school or a vacation, or spending time with a toddler, building sand castles, running errands, telling stories, and just being there?" And in real life there is rarely closure on any of these questions. But then, when do the scales tip in one direction or another? When a mother begins to panic that her professional identity is slipping from her fingers, and it is? When her husband wants to go back to school to further his career and the bills begin to mount? When Johnny seems old enough and hardy enough to withstand the upheaval of separation? Or when Christopher is having problems getting off to nursery school each morning?

Ultimately, the scales tip when the anxiety or the guilt or the frustration becomes too intense (and every member of every family has his or her own boiling point), when competing interests can no longer be ignored. At these junctures, there is a reshuffling of priorities, until a new sense of equilibrium is found.

Life was simpler, though considerably more confining, when gender roles were rigidly defined and women were either deprived of the freedom to choose or else were convinced (as one who follows a posthypnotic suggestion is convinced) that the only paths they ever really wanted to take were the traditional ones.

The Idealization of Mothers: Angels and Vipers

> *As for the mother, her very name stands for loving unselfishness and self-abnegation and in any society fit*

*to exist, it is fraught with associations which render it
holy.—President Theodore Roosevelt, in his address
before the National Congress of Mothers, 1905*

*Megaloid momworship has got completely out of hand.
Our land, subjectively mapped, would have more silver
cords and apron strings crisscrossing it than railroads
and telephone wires.—Philip Wylie,* Generation of
Vipers, *1942*

As long as the institution of motherhood continues to
be viewed through an aura of holiness, we can expect to
hear of saints and witches, disciples and heretics, deeds of
sacrifice and deeds of sacrilege. Although to some extent
this has been the case at least since the advent of Christi-
anity, there have always been epochs in which motherhood has been idealized to a greater or lesser extent. In
America, over the last hundred years or so, motherhood
has been regarded as an emblem of feminine virtue, and
mothers have been ascribed special powers to uplift themselves, their children, and the nation as a whole.[8] The
idealized mother came to represent the spiritual side of
life and served as a necessary antidote to the competitive
and materialistic world outside the home.

The good mother, as she was conceived at the beginning of the twentieth century, was self-sacrificing and
nurturing, and her selfless devotion to her family was her
greatest source of happiness.[9] There was never any question of conflict between a woman's needs as a person
and her role as mother, because ministering to the needs
of others was considered an expression of the female
character. A woman "naturally" found fulfillment in
culvitating the potentialities of her children.

Women of the day were educated about their "natural"
propensities through child-rearing manuals, sermons, and
popular literature. In fact, much of women's formal education was expressly designed to prepare them for their
nurturing functions. Courses in home economics and cook-

ing are only the most obvious examples. G. Stanley Hall, a prominent psychologist at the turn of the century, warned against the corrupting influence of higher education for women, and condoned it only when it could be seen as useful in preparing women for their maternal role.[10]

But the idealization of motherhood had a paradoxical effect, as idealizations generally do, and over the years, mothers were vilified as well as praised, condemned for loving too much as well as too little, accused of fostering dependency and guilt after having been urged to place their children at the very center of their emotional universe. The logic was circular, and seemed to go something like this: if *good* mothering is critical to the development of human potential (as it had been argued), then *bad* mothering must be responsible for the psychological and moral failures we see all around us on an individual as well as on a global level. In fact, when this argument was taken to an extreme but logical conclusion, any evidence of human failing could be used as proof that some mother somewhere was not mothering as she should have!

This is not as far fetched an argument as it might appear to sophisticated audiences today. In 1928, John Watson, a prominent behavioral psychologist, published an infant and child-rearing manual in which he warned against the danger of mother love, which he believed was responsible for producing weak and dependent children: "The fact . . . that we rarely see a happy child is proof that women are failing in their mission."[11] Though most people today (and perhaps even in his day) would probably dismiss such an argument as overly simplistic, if not blatantly misleading, its legacy lives on when women secretly, and against their better judgment, blame themselves unreasonably for their children's sadnesses and live in terror of their children's anger. When Susan reports that her three-year-old son's anger pierces through her like a knife, or when Judith describes the irritation and guilt she feels when her three-year-old daughter "regresses" and insists that she is a baby, each mother is responding to more than just anger and regression. They are personalizing their children's behavior and experiencing it as a reproach.

Psychologically, the oscillation between the idealization and devaluation of mothers is not surprising. Idealization often leads to disappointment when reality seeps in, and those whom we believed to be giants are brought down to human scale. All of us experience this kind of disillusionment in relation to our parents whom, as young children, we perceived as omnipotent and ominiscient. If, however, despite our disappointment, we refuse to give up our illusions and insist, even more vehemently perhaps, that our dreams are reality, and conversely that reality *should* conform to our dreams, then we leave ourselves vulnerable to bitter disappointment as each idealized figure inevitably fails us again and again. Thus, the very process of idealization creates the psychological conditions for vilification. Insofar as our young children idealize us they also are wont to rage against us for not being perfect. Thus our cultural ideals of motherhood as well as our modern-day witches may be seen as deriving from the prototypic mother-child relationship.

Theories of child care and child development have changed over the course of the century, and the image of the good mother has been modified to reflect these changes, but, up until recently, one crucial element has remained constant: the ideal mother molds herself and shapes her life according to the needs of her children and her family. For her, there can be no serious conflict between *her* needs and *their* needs, simply because her children's fulfillment is her greatest fulfillment—the two coincide; there is complete harmony. This of course is "the best of all possible worlds," to borrow Voltaire's ironic view of naïve idealism, and psychoanalysts know that this is also every child's fantasy. It can be difficult for mothers to accept that this is a fantasy they cannot and should not fulfill, however much their children protest (and they do!). After all, we harbored such fantasies of unbounded and unconditional love when we were growing up, and our children's protests resonate with our own.

Translated into everyday life, this means that a mother should not only be attuned to her children's needs for tenderness, encouragement, autonomy, and limit-setting twenty-four hours a day, but should also be able and willing to respond appropriately and selflessly. On the other hand, if the authorities inform her that this kind of ministering to her child's desires only undermines a child's independence of spirit, weakens his will, and subverts his autonomy, then she should resist her "instincts" and follow a more "scientific" approach (as mothers were advised to do during the 1930s and 1940s). According to this dogma, she should faithfully adhere to schedules and enforce special diets; she should resist the temptation to jump in and rescue a child in distress; she should act on "reason," not on feeling, even if it pains her; her failure to restrain herself may do irreparable damage to her child. But, whether *regularity* and *scheduling* or *attachment* and *bonding* are the key words, the ideal mother should always be available to ensure that the ideal program is carried out.

In contrast to the idealization of motherhood, D. W. Winnicott's conception of the "good enough" mother humanizes mothering by relieving mothers of the burden of always having to be perfectly attuned to their children in order to raise reasonably healthy adults. In fact, according to Winnicott, part of a mother's responsibility is to *disillusion* her child just enough so that he can learn to live comfortably in reality.[12] Protecting a child from every disappointment and every frustration is ultimately not good mothering, he would argue, because in doing so the parent renders the child impotent to cope with real life and real people. A healthy adult has to learn to live with his and other people's anger and frustration, and he can only learn this if as a child he is given a chance to see that he and his mother and their relationship survive periodic rages and disappointments. But still, practically speaking, the notion of the "good enough mother" begs the question. What is "good enough"? And how much "illusion" is necessary? And when?

"Masculinity" and "Femininity" and the World Outside

> *But do not forget that I have only been describing women in so far as their nature is determined by their sexual function. It is true that that influence extends very far; but we do not overlook the fact that* an individual woman may be a human being *in other respects as well.*—Sigmund Freud, "Femininity," in New Introductory Lectures on Psychoanalysis, 1933 (*Italics mine*)

> *Young woman often ask whether they can "have an identity" before they know whom they will marry, and for whom they will make a home. Granted that something in the young woman's identity must keep itself open for the peculiarities of the man to be joined and the children to be brought up, I think much of a young woman's identity is already defined in her kind of attractiveness and in the selectivity of her search for the man (or men) by whom she wishes to be sought.*—Erik Erikson, Identity, Youth and Crisis 1968

Traditionally theory held that a woman's identity took shape within the context of being a mother and a wife. Sociologists have spoken in terms of social status and social roles, and have pointed out that a woman's status in the world is derived indirectly from her husband's occupational position.[13] Psychoanalysts, on the other hand, have spoken in terms of personality characteristics, suggesting that a woman's personality and self-concept are inextricably linked to her biological functions and normally crystallize only in her relationship to a husband and children. (Though Freud would not have argued that a man's personality is any less determined by anatomy and biological functions than a woman's personality, it has never been suggested that a man's identity "must keep itself open for the peculiarities of the [wo]man to be joined and the children to be brought up.") Sociological and psychological theories thus complement each other, and describe woman as she was in mid-twentieth-century America.

But, over the past few decades, the reality of the two-income household has affected more and more American families. Divorce and single parenting are also not uncommon occurences, and women with children are entering the labor force in increasing numbers and at earlier ages.[14] Whether the demographic changes are the result or the cause of fundamental changes in women's conceptions of themselves—as individuals and in relation to others—the traditional ideals associated with motherhood have lost much of their appeal for many women, even on the level of fantasy.[15]

Change generates more change, and as women participate more fully in the world outside the home, they become aware of aspects of themselves and their personalities that would otherwise have been submerged or would not have been recognized by them or by others. The diplomacy and managerial skills women have always had to cultivate as mothers and as housewives were rarely identified as such. And, being invisible to the world, these characteristics were not integrated into women's self-concepts. Moreover, women's desires to excel and be held in esteem were disguised, transposed onto their children, whose achievements they promoted, applauded, and sometimes appropriated for themselves. Hence the origin of the overintrusive, suffocating mother.

As the conditions of women's lives change, they find that they have capabilities their mothers and grandmothers never dreamed they had themselves. Moreover, they realize that they have interests of their own that are unrelated to domestic life. They enjoy making money, exercising power, and simply negotiating as adults in the "real" world. They find that, like men, they are gratified when their work yields a discrete and finished product that justifies their efforts and confers meaning on their lives. Most significantly perhaps, they discover that they are not as different from men as they had been led to believe, and that in fact, the generic "he" includes them after all.[16] This is a radical change.

Clara Thompson, a psychoanalyst who attempted to integrate cultural influences into traditional Freudian theory of female personality development, notes that as they entered "a domain that had been in the possession of men, in which the so-called masculine traits of decisiveness, daring, and aggression were usually far more effective than the customarily ascribed feminine traits such as gentleness and submissiveness . . . women could not but help to change the personality traits acquired from their former cultural setting."[17] Having revised their concepts of themselves, women are spurred on in the pursuit of nontraditional goals, and new conceptions of the ideal woman have emerged.

The women's movement, and the movement within the field of psychology that identified "self-actualization" rather than "adjustment" as the ideal standard of mental health, provided the raw material for the development of new ideals of womanhood incorporating many of the ideals traditionally associated with "masculinity." Sometimes, however, the baby was thrown out with the bath water, so to speak, and all that was traditionally "feminine" was devalued by women as much as by men—until such time as it became clear that motherhood needed to be integrated into this new picture of womanhood and that the "masculine" ideal was not the antidote to the "feminine mystique" after all."[18]

Independence, Relatedness, and Values of Living

It is easier for me to decide how to handle the family as

*a group than it is for me to figure out what to do for
myself. I'm giving Teddy all the attention I thought I
missed, but have lost some sense of my own individual
identity, something I created for myself in my twenties
mainly through my professional life. . . . Now I'd like
to do more for me.—Charlotte, thirty-three, mother of
a nearly three-year-old son*

*Sensitivity to the needs of others and the assumption
of responsibility for taking care lead women to attend to
voices other than their own and to include in their
judgment other points of view. Women's moral weakness, manifest in an apparent diffusion and confusion
of judgment, is thus inseparable from women's moral
strength, an overriding concern with relationships and
responsibilities.—Carol Gilligan,* In a Different Voice,
1982

The traditional ideals, values, and characteristics associated with being a good mother, a good wife, and a good
woman are often incompatible with the ideals and values
of the world of work, a world that up until recently was
perceived as primarily a male domain, into which women
were admitted only out of duress.[19] If womanly virtues
bear some resemblance to the Christian virtues both men
and women aspired to at the beginning of the century,
they were certainly not the values of the marketplace,
where men spent their days and dreamed the American
dream, nor are they the values of the "rugged individualist," who is the all-American hero whether he is a cowboy, an entrepreneur, or a Nobel laureate.

As long as men and women inhabited two different
spheres, it seemed only reasonable to assume that they
were essentially different kinds of people, and that what
was a good quality in a man was not necessarily a good
quality in a woman. It posed no contradiction that men
but not women should be independent, adventurous, and
domineering, because these qualities were, by definition,
"masculine." And if women (but not men) were supposed

to be emotional, supportive, enabling, and facilitating (features that Jesse Bernard, a prominent sociologist, once referred to as women's "stroking function"), this also made sense, because these qualities were incontrovertibly "feminine."[20] "Masculinity" and "femininity" were conceived of as opposite ends along a continuum, and so it followed that the more feminine a person was the less masculine he or she could be and vice versa.

The characters of Mr. and Mrs. Ramsay in Virginia Woolf's novel *To the Lighthouse* embody the masculine and the feminine element, as it has been traditionally conceived in our culture, and the fictionalized relationship between this husband and wife is paradigmatic of the complementary but strained relations between the sexes. Mr. Ramsay is a philosopher, a man of ideas who strives for "truth" and justice. He is a man who measures himself against these standards and has little tolerance of the irrational in himself or others. As he tramples on his children's feelings, he is unaware of the pain he is inflicting and, moreover, is incapable of seeing the value in treading more delicately. Mrs. Ramsay is as powerful a figure as her husband, but her mission is to "surround and protect" others, even if by doing so "there was scarcely a shell of herself left for her to know herself by." She hopes to serve as everyone's buffer against the pain of the world, and if in the process of soothing an aching ego— her husband's or her son's or a dinner guest's—she dissimulates and sacrifices the "truth" as her husband would define it, it is only in pursuit of a higher "truth" upon which the very fabric of civilization and social harmony rests.

Mr. and Mrs. Ramsay are in awe of each other, yet Mr. Ramsay characterizes his wife as "irrational" when, at the beginning of the novel, she reassures their son that despite the ominous weather conditions they might yet be able to visit the lighthouse the next day. And Mrs. Ramsay characterizes her husband as unfeeling: "To pursue truth with such astonishing lack of consideration for other people's feelings, to rend the thin veils of civilization so wantonly, so brutally, was to her so horrible an outrage of human decency that without replying, dazed and blinded, she bent her head as if to let the pelt of jagged hail, the drench of dirty water, bespatter her unrebuked." Mrs. Ramsay's response to her husband's truth-telling mirrors her children's responses to their father—her son has fantasies of bludgeoning his father with an axe when he ruthlessly insists that there will be no trip to the lighthouse the next day. Mrs. Ramsay epitomizes the woman who is mother to the world and who consequently cannot help but see her husband through the eyes of her children, the eyes of her dinner guests, as well as through her own eyes. He knows one perspective, she knows many.

The differences between men and women that Virginia Woolf evokes in her characterization of Mr. and Mrs. Ramsay reflect fundamental differences in values. Mr. Ramsay, as the archetypal male, is in solitary pursuit of truth and meaning. If he is to succeed in reaching his goal he must not allow anyone to divert him from his path. Society is a distraction; feelings, his own or other's, are apt to cloud his vision; and small talk is intolerable. In psychological terms, he strives for ever-greater differentiation and autonomy.

Mrs. Ramsay, as the archetypal female, also seeks meaning in life, abhors chaos and untempered nature. But for her, success is inextricably linked with her relations with the people in her life and their relations with each other. If a dinner guest is squirming uncomfortably she feels it, and it is a signal for her to restore outer harmony and inner peace. If her husband has qualms about his position in history, her truth is not to evaluate what his status actually will be but to relieve him of his psychic burdens. In psychological terms, she strives for ever-greater relatedness and harmony.

While some feminists may dismiss these archetypal figures as caricatures that only mislead us by reinforcing stereotypes about the nature of men and women, Carol

Gilligan sees it somewhat differently. In *In a Different Voice* she argues that as groups men and women do each indeed tend to emphasize different values: the value of individual rights and the value of concern and care for others respectively. "Each sex sees a danger which the other does not see—men in connection, women in separation." The ethic of self-sacrifice, which Gilligan associates with the value women place on connectedness, has made it difficult for women to define their rights and identify their own "voices"; the ethic of individual rights, which Gilligan associates with the value men place on autonomy, has made it difficult for men to empathize with others and become intimate. Rather than extolling the virtues of one principle over another, Gilligan favors an integration of the two and a reexamination of the cultural climate in which the traditionally female perspective is not validated or valued.[21]

Whether our stereotypes about women and men have some basis in reality, or whether they are merely necessary fictions we have invented to uphold the way things are or the way we want them to be, stereotypes continue to exist and influence our understanding of what it means to be feminine or masculine, a "real" woman or a "real" man.[22] They become self-fulfilling prophecies as we strive to be what we believe we "naturally" should be and what our mothers and fathers felt they should be for generations before us.

As long as women were defined primarily in terms of their mothering and caretaking, "femininity" was naturally associated with traits comprising an "expressiveness-warmth" cluster. Women tend to be perceived as more socially sensitive, more nurturing, more easily hurt, and more childlike than men, who tend to be perceived as more rational, more independent, more adventurous, and more dominant than women. And, as in the case of all stereotypes, what is implied is that these characteristics are inherent and immutable.[23]

Whether the qualities ascribed to women are ultimately valued as much as the qualities ascribed to men (and many would argue that they are not), it seems obvious that successful navigation in the modern "world" requires a good measure of "masculinity" (as it has been defined), which in effect puts women in an awkward and handicapped position. If certain activities are naturally "feminine" and others are naturally "masculine," then women who behave in a "masculine" manner and men who behave in a "feminine" manner are "unnatural," or in modern parlance, pathological. In fact, as women have ventured beyond the boundaries of the home and have begun to compete with men on their own terms, they have been accused of penis-envy, masculinity complexes, and unresolved sexual conflicts, among other things, as if the desire to do what men typically have done is synonymous with the desire to be a man.

Reflecting in 1942 on trends within the culture as well as within psychoanalytic circles of the day, psychoanalyst Clara Thompson put it this way: "Not many years ago a woman's decision to follow a profession—medicine, for example—was considered even by some analysts to be evidence of a masculinity complex. This rose from the belief that all work outside the home, especially if it called for exercise of leadership, was masculine, and anyone attempting it, therefore, was trying to be a man."[24]

It is only relatively recently that we, as a culture, have begun to question the inviolability of the narrow definitions of masculinity and femininity that have governed the lives of men as much as women and encouraged all of us to become rather lopsided and partial human beings. Whether this skepticism about the varying "nature" of men and women is warranted or not, the result is that the boundary between masculinity and femininity has been blurred, and consequently there is greater latitude for women to "act like men," and men to "act like women" than existed in previous generations.[25] Men can be sensitive and still be manly; women can be strong-minded and still be womanly; both can be competitive as well as yielding. At least in theory.

But, if anatomy is destiny *only* up to a point, and nobody can tell us more specifically at what point nature leaves off and nurture begins, then the relationship between womanliness and motherliness is more complicated and ambiguous than was previously thought. It is precisely our uncertainty about how much "motherliness" is "natural" and therefore good for everyone involved, including the mother, and how much is stifling and therefore bad for everyone involved, including the mother, that creates such conflict for the modern woman. When a woman becomes pregnant and then becomes a mother, her natural, biological nurturing and relational functions are suddenly spotlighted (in her mind and in the minds of others), and at that critical juncture, who can blithely deny that there are differences between the sexes, whatever their origin—even as we all agree that women are unquestionably people too?

Ideals in Conflict and the Woman in the Middle

> *I met a former classmate and she told me she is a thoracic surgeon. I haven't achieved anything. . . . It's true I have two lovely daughters, but that doesn't sound like much, and when I saw her I felt badly.*
> —Helen, thirty-eight, mother of two

> *I thought how much harder it is now than it must have been even a century ago to say which of these employments is higher, the more necessary. Is it better to be a coal-heaver or a nursemaid; is the charwoman who has brought up eight children of less value to the world than the barrister who has made a hundred thousand pounds? It is useless to ask such questions for nobody can answer them. Not only do the comparative values of charwomen and lawyers rise and fall from decade to decade, but we have no rods with which to measure*

them even as they are at the moment.—Virginia Woolf,
A Room of One's Own, *1929*

What gives life meaning? What is success? How does an individual man or woman best meet his or her potential? What is the lived life? Big questions, certainly unanswerable in the abstract. Each of us grapples with these questions in one form or another beginning in adolescence as we grope to create a cohesive identity through which to express our individuality and command the respect and appreciation of our fellow man. In becoming mothers women realize that what seemed to be the obvious solution to the problem of identity and relatedness no longer is. Today there are more choices, and women are forced to rethink who they are and what they value in life. The conflict, which is particularly a woman's conflict, can be formulated as follows: If a woman aspires to be a respected and accomplished person, a "success" in the eyes of the world, must she fall short as a wife and a mother (in her own eyes as well as in the eyes of others), and ultimately compromise her "womanliness" and her sexuality?[26] And there is yet another conflict, this more generic to the human condition: How do we balance our needs for individual fulfillment with our needs for connectedness and interpersonal relatedness without sacrificing one for the other?

It is presumptuous of course even to imagine that there could be answers to these questions that would satisfy everyone, let alone one individual over the course of an entire life, but once our basic needs are satisfied and we are relatively secure with ourselves, we have the luxury of asking ourselves these questions and considering varying solutions. The price we pay for this luxury is indecision and a certain amount of inner conflict.

The ideology of self-fulfillment has swept across the country over the last few decades, but ironically it has been associated with both spiritual and material expansiveness (the so-called me generation in pursuit of "success" of every form), optimism about the nature of human beings—and a deep pessimism about the future of humanity as a whole.

Abraham Maslow, a psychologist and humanist, popularized the term "self-actualization" during the 1970s, asserting that psychological health is not merely the absence of pathology or good adjustment to the conditions of life. According to Maslow, the ideally healthy person strives to achieve higher spiritual values and "peak experiences" of beauty, truth, aliveness, and order. In the process of transcending the mundane, the individual becomes all he or she can be.[27] Though Maslow's values are the antithesis of materialism, and he makes a clear distinction between self-actualization and individual "success" in worldly terms of status, money, and power, his focus is on the individual's quest for spiritual growth and fulfillment.

In contrast to Maslow, historian Christopher Lasch describes a darker side of the trend toward self-fulfillment. He suggests that as a culture, we have become disillusioned with traditional values and attempt to fill the void by creating a "culture of narcissism" in which the "me" is the focus of an inordinate amount of attention. Within this culture our goals are limited to the gratification of the individual.

> Even when therapists speak of the need for "meaning" and "love," they define love and meaning simply as the fulfillment of the patient's emotional requirements. It hardly occurs to them—nor is there any reason it should, given the nature of the therapeutic enterprise—to encourage the subject to subordinate his needs and interests to those of others, to someone or some cause or tradition outside himself. "Love" as self-sacrifice or self-abasement, "meaning" as submission to a higher loyalty—these sublimations strike the therapeutic sensibility as intolerably oppressive, offensive to common sense and injuri-

ous to personal health and well-being. . . . Mental
health means the overthrow of inhibitions and the
immediate gratification of every impulse.[28]

The qualities associated with motherhood—empathy,
sensitivity to others, patience, flexibility, a willingness to
compromise, nurturance, and self-sacrifice—could not be
more at odds with the qualities associated with the me
generation, a name that speaks for itself. New mothers
describe an overriding sense of connectedness and intimacy unlike any they have ever experienced with any
other human being. They also find themselves immersed
in the details of life's basics—eating, sleeping, defecating,
walking, climbing, seeing, smelling, and breathing. All
this sensuousness is what early mothering is mainly about.
But, it is difficult to reconcile the idea self-actualization as
it has been typically conceived with this sense of being
bound up to another and immersed in the details of
his life. Is mothering then something apart from self-
actualization? Does the one threaten to undermine the
other? Is there hope for peaceful coexistence?

Combining Motherhood and Work: When "Having It All" Is Impossible and Not Having Either Is Simply Not Enough

Women are reluctant to abandon the ideal of self-
fulfillment—particularly since today, self-abnegation in
mothers (or in anybody else for that matter) commands
little admiration. The self-sacrificing mother is patronized
and is more often the target of derision than of praise.
Moreover, today's women are unwilling, unlike those in
past generations, to be relegated to the lowest-paying and
least desirable jobs as if this were their fate, one they
should embrace wholeheartedly. But the large majority of
women want to become mothers all the same. As mothers
they are aware that they need to plan for the future

actively, but they are nonetheless immersed in the realities of the present. This dual consciousness forces women to reckon with certain conflicts of values that men can more easily avoid because of their substantially different parental role. Women face a conflict between their goals as individuals and their goals as members of a family, and a related conflict between present and future perspectives.[29]

To live fully in the present, savoring experience for itself rather than as a means to an end, is one value (often *de*valued, as we tend to emphasize products, not processes). To live always with an eye to the future, so that dreams can become realities and the present but one step along an imaginary path leading to a better future, is another.

When Rebecca, for example, lets herself relax and enjoy her Fridays at home with her one-year-old son, she is living fully in the present. Only when she feels no internal pressure to *do*, to accomplish, can she marvel at his developing personality, which, it turns out, is quite different from her own. Only then can she allow the day to unfold without undue premeditation or review. On the other hand, when Rebecca is evaluating her position at the university where she works in terms of her past achievements and her long-term aspirations, she is living with an eye to the future. Her satisfaction with what she is doing today is inextricably linked with what it will lead to next year or five years from now and whether she anticipates being happy or unhappy at some distant point in the future. Who can say which perspective is ultimately more fulfilling? More admirable? More valuable to the human enterprise?

Today many women seem to be asking themselves whether they can encompass both sets of values, the stereotypically masculine *and* the stereotypically feminine. And if they can't "have it all," can't they have a taste of everything? Or is that mixture ultimately unsatisfying, leaving them with nothing at all on which to hang their hats? Although the average mother does not articulate these questions, they are implicit in the quandaries mothers express about their work, their babies, and their future.

Most women and men never question the necessity of working sixty-hour weeks in order to achieve success in their careers. It is understood that these are the rules of the "game," and if they want to play they will have to conform to them or else risk being accused by the other players of being unmotivated or uncommitted.

On the other hand, some women postpone their individual life goals to make room for motherhood: "Moving ahead in the company will have to wait for later, I just don't want to work sixty hours a week now;" "I see other women with families and it's forgivable to take things slower and finish my dissertation when I can." Other women redefine their goals and reconsider their values: "The goals I had were more external—degrees, status— but there's nothing materialistic about my goals now. . . . I feel in touch with life and *that* is what life is all about;" "It is more important that the child get my attention than a Calvin Klein sweater;""I've spent a lot of time on the professional side of my life, and now I'm reorienting my life toward the family."

And still others learn to live with the guilt, the gratification, and the doubt that come from refusing to take sides in the perennial tug of war between opposing values: "Clients always ask me about the baby, and the older men at work give me their sympathy and tell me that it is really too bad that I have to be at the office. It doesn't make me angry, because I know to a certain extent I'm thinking the same thing. Guilt feelings are there for sure but I just learn to live with them. . . . Everybody in life has to give up something."

Elizabeth describes what is for her a "monotonous, continually recurring conflict": the conflict between her desire to work more and her desire to be with her daughter. "Sometimes I look back on the days when I could stay at work as long as I wanted to, and I think, 'Wouldn't it be nice to have a cup of tea at five, and then go back and work some more, meet someone for dinner at eight, and get back home by eleven.' " But even if Elizabeth could, in theory, structure her life to do just that, she is unwilling to do so. She does not want to lose that time with the family in the evening and prefers to lament the loss of her freedom rather than to recapture it. If Elizabeth wishes that her work held a greater attraction for her than it does at present, there is nothing to be done, because it just doesn't. What she wants in the abstract does not coincide with her inner reality. She has made her choices.

Nancy, who returned to full-time work when her baby was two months old weighs (two months later) the value of work against the value of staying home with her baby and questions whether her choice to work is the more or the less selfish one to have made. On the one hand, she admits, somewhat guiltily, that she enjoys her work as well as enjoying the standard of living it allows her and her family to maintain. And while Nancy believes that giving her baby time and attention is more "important than buying her a lot of clothes," she would be more than a little reluctant to sell the family house they recently purchased, which is what they would have to do were she to leave her present position in order to spend more time at home with the baby. On the other hand, Nancy also thinks eighteen years ahead to when her daughter will be ready for college and wonders whether it wouldn't be even more selfish of her to quit her job now, devote herself full-time to mothering (a fantasy she claims is not altogether unappealing), and in the process neglect to put aside money for her daughter's education. "I've always been a scattered person and have gotten drawn into things I enjoy. Now I know I have to focus and prioritize." Sensitivity to the needs of others has suddenly become an important consideration to her, and she would have difficulty feeling good about herself if she thought that she was selfishly pursuing only her own pleasures.

If what Nancy says seems contradictory and confused, it is because she continues to struggle with the choices she has made. What she thinks she knows "intellectually"

—that women should consider their own needs as well as others'—is difficult to translate into real life; emotionally she exists not only as a separate individual but also in relation to her family. She wants to give to her baby, to her husband, as well as to herself, but how best to satisfy all three is not always self-evident, and "giving" takes many different forms. Since the value of unselfishness has become more salient for Nancy, she has become suspicious of her pleasures, on the job or at home. To enjoy anything, be it work or motherhood, at someone else's expense is by definition selfish, and so she hesitates before settling into what is immediately most comfortable for her. She is willing to sacrifice spontaneity for self-respect.

The individual woman's conflict of values expresses her unique personality, but also the hierarchy of values she unconsciously assimilated growing up in her particular family, as well as in the broader social context in which she lives. In our social interactions we learn to measure a person's merit, dignity, and worthiness, and arrive at our conclusions as to what qualities and achievements deserve the attention and respect of others. The characteristics associated with good mothering—patience, the ability to compromise, and sensitivity to the needs and opinions of others—are qualities that by their very nature are mostly unrecognized. They are taken for granted precisely because they are the very qualities that allow life to proceed smoothly and create the necessary illusion of effortlessness. The good mother is by definition unobtrusive, and by definition seeks no applause. Since the work of mothering is mostly invisible, there are no bonuses, no promotions, no congratulations after the first few months, and little prestige. The fuss we make over Mother's Day is the exception that proves the rule.

Many women don't like to think that external rewards such as status, money, power, and recognition influence their feelings about themselves and what they do, even though the ability to work and assume responsibility for oneself is the hallmark of adulthood for women as well as for men. After all, traditionally it has not been considered "feminine" to be concerned with such matters; a woman's rewards are spiritual and internal. Today, however, it is unrealistic and a touch grandiose for women to suppose that they can transcend such worldly concerns when men cannot. Unworldliness is a "feminine" virtue conceived at another time, born of necessity; it is a virtue that denies the all-too-human desire for external validation and is an encumbrance when a woman tries to navigate in the world outside the family.

But if some women continue to insist that they have no interest whatsoever in status, prestige, money, or social power, and other women unabashedly embrace the traditionally "masculine" values of the workplace, it seems that many women today feel caught betwixt and between, aware that both perspectives are painfully limiting and that the devaluation of the "feminine," for want of a better term, is as false to their experience as its idealization was to the experience of their mothers and grandmothers.

Ann disparages the business world she left behind her when she became a full-time mother and yet acknowledges that she is uncomfortable spending money when she is not earning any herself. Her husband manages the finances now, and she does not like the feeling that she has lost some control. Roseanne vehemently denies any interest in climbing the corporate ladder (something she had been intent on doing before she had the baby), but she is also bored staying home all day and cherishes her one half-day at work. She worries that were she to return to work she might find the pull irresistible—"I might have difficulty keeping my priorities straight." To avoid confusion, she has temporarily removed herself from any possible source of temptation.

On the other hand, motherhood has served as an added impetus for Diane to advance her career and increase her earning capacity, which she proceeded to do as soon as she returned to her job after a three-month maternity leave. Faced with the responsibility of having to pay for child care (there was no question in her mind that she would be returning to her full-time job as a hospital administrator), she asked her superiors for more responsibility as well as a raise, and got both. Diane feels that she has to plan for the future, now more than ever, and for her this means reaffirming her commitment to her career, rather than moving away from it. "I'm more conscious of what savings we need and for the first time we realize that we need to make out wills. . . . I don't know what would have happened at work if I hadn't had the baby." Psychologically, Diane's career goals and her parenting goals coalesce; each fuels the other as together they propel her forward in the direction she was headed before she became a mother.

Rebecca, unwilling to forgo the pleasures of work, but with a heightened awareness that there are other sides to her personality, and other forms of pleasure, falls somewhere in the middle. She is very conscious of how much she enjoyed the prestige, the power, and the fast pace that accompanied her position as chief investigator in a city-run research project, but she traded in some of the power and status for a more flexible work situation that would allow her to spend more time with her family. Although she had qualms about surrendering a position she had worked so hard and so long to attain, she has discovered aspects of herself she had long buried—she can be playful, emotional, spontaneous, and connected to many different kinds of people—and this gives her something else.

Any value conflicts a woman might have simply as a result of living in this culture at this point in history are compounded when qualities of "motherliness" are associated in a woman's mind with self-abasement, unhappiness, or abuse by reason of her particular upbringing. Under these circumstances she will struggle with her desire to be a "good mother" and her fear that as such she may lose her self-respect and the respect of others. Judith, whose conflicts around her daughter's temper tantrums were discussed at length in an earlier chapter, describes her own mother as having been patient, loving, and even-tempered, qualities that balanced out her father's volatility and nervousness. But her mother was also overly deferential and, according to Judith, suffered from low self-esteem. Moreover, her "motherly" virtues were taken as evidence of her inferiority in a household where the ability to argue vociferously was considered the measure of intelligence. As a mother herself, Judith repeatedly struggles with her temper, and though she consciously wants to be more patient than she is, she fails, because it is only in failing that she successfully dissociates herself from a quality she unconsciously learned to devalue.

Challenging the "Forbidden," Acknowledging the "Impossible": The Three-Dimensional Mother

If, as psychoanalyst Joyce MacDougall states, "There is little doubt that in our unconscious fantasies we are all omnipotent, bisexual, eternally young, and immortal," then motherhood is inevitably a humbling experience, because as mothers we cannot help but acknowledge our human limitations. In our relations with our dependent yet extraordinarily willful children we come face to face with the naked realities of existence—emotions that are raw and various (ours as well as theirs), attachments that are enduring and mysterious, beginnings that are followed by losses and then new beginnings. We witness the awesome progression from innocence to maturity (ours and theirs) and become conscious of the aging process, the preciousness of life, and the inevitability of death.

Though motherhood highlights for women their strengths as well as their specialness (they find that they can be depended upon to do more than they thought they could, and that they are very, very special to their babies and young children), as mothers women also realize anew how impossible it is to be everything to everyone, or for that matter everything that they would like themselves to be. (Is this maturity?) Nobody, man or woman, can be perfectly attuned to the needs of others and wholly committed to the contemplative life of the mind. Nobody can be single-minded in their devotion to career *and* single-minded in their devotion to their family, just as nobody can lead the cosmopolitan life of the city and the pastoral life of the country at the same time. For women, motherhood is a turning point wherein values need to be clarified and choices have to be made

Many women today are challenging what has been forbidden them in previous generations. (Why should either sex have a monopoly on empathy, adventure, or ambition? And why must the capacity to mother disqualify women from participating in the human enterprise?) In doing so, however, they sometimes fault themselves for not being able to do the impossible—to be everything and to know no limits. As long as our ideal images of motherhood are acknowledged as ideals, products of the imagination, they can inspire us just as we are inspired by a beautiful poem or statue. Otherwise they interfere with our making our way as best we can and torment us when we fail to be as perfect as they.

6

The Subjective Self

Conceptions of the Self

It is a little bit of an identification crisis for me. . . . I had this naïve view that I would organize everything and just go back to my regular schedule. I never anticipated wanting to be with the baby as much as I do. He brings out a different part of me which I wasn't really in touch with much before—an emotional, playful part. —Rebecca, thirty-seven, mother of a one-year-old son, working three-quarters time and pregnant at the time of the interview

It has been a total upheaval. Like dying and being born again. To me there is a definite mark that separates this part of my life from what came before. I was geared to having a career, being successful, being out in the world, and then all of a sudden I found myself at home with a baby doing baby things, not having any real intellectual stimulation, and wondering where I go from here.—Roseanne, thirty-four, mother of a two-and-a-half-year-old girl, working one day a week outside the home

"Who are you?" said the Caterpillar.
This was not an encouraging opening for a conversation. Alice replied, rather shyly. "I—I hardly know, Sir, just at the present—at least I know who I was when I got up this morning, but I think I must have been changed several times since then."—Lewis Carroll, Alice in Wonderland

180

Our sense of self is paradoxically an experience of continuity and discontinuity, being and becoming simultaneously. You need only look at a series of photographs of yourself from age three to age twenty-five or even age forty to become convinced beyond a doubt that even as you change you are always unmistakenly the same person you always were. At certain critical points in a person's development, however, the balance between the experience of continuity and the experience of discontinuity tips, and the discontinuities temporarily overshadow the essential sameness. Because of the dramatic physical, emotional, and cognitive changes that accompany puberty, adolescence is one point at which this kind of disequilibrium typically occurs. Motherhood may be another such turning point in development, as new needs come into focus, requiring new forms of satisfaction. At these junctures, when the thread connecting past, present, and future selves is camouflaged by the ever more complex skein of existence, there is a crisis in identity.[1] In the process of resolving this crisis, new images of the self coalesce and a new equilibrium is established.

As mothers, women catch glimpses of themselves—their physical and emotional characteristics—that were previously obscured or else selectively not attended to.[2] They realize potentialities (both positive and negative) that had been lying dormant, only awaiting the opportunity to emerge from the shadows and assert their existence. The potential for unselfish devotion to another human being and the potential to feel momentarily carried away by waves of impotent rage are just a couple of examples. But the particular experiences a woman has as a mother not only *reflect* the deepest levels of her personality, but also, in the process, *color* her perceptions of who she is as a human being apart from her child. They confirm but also challenge a woman's beliefs about her values or her character; they may enhance or pose a threat to her self-esteem.

As a mother, a woman gives herself freer reign to follow her "intuition"—and with good results. At another point she explodes with frustration and gets no results at all. She feels in control and she feels out of control, on top of the world and at the mercy of everybody, even a "helpless" dependent baby, immeasurably special and very ordinary. She finds herself rushing from the office to get home early only to be greeted by her baby's screams and her husband's irritation that dinner is not yet ready and also finds herself rushing from home to make it to the office on time only to realize that she should have prepared more extensively for a meeting the night before. Suddenly she feels inadequate precisely at the point at which she is trying harder than ever. She feels alternately loved and unappreciated, loving and bitterly resentful; she is acting in ways that make her proud and ashamed, angry and guilty, confident and confused. All these new perceptions of herself, in action and in limbo, lead to subtle shifts in her sense of her capabilities, her interests, her strengths, and her weaknesses.

A woman's sense of her self undergoes a metamorphosis as she gradually integrates her identity as a mother into her identity as a person. Despite the expectations of many modern women, who pride themselves in being able to separate their personal from their professional lives as men have traditionally been able to do, mothering is not an experience that is easily compartmentalized. The intense emotional, physical, and fantasied involvement most new mothers have with their babies does not exist as a thing in itself outside the mother. It emerges out of the deepest layers of her personality and thus reflects her own rational and irrational wishes and fears as well as her baby's. As these wishes, fears, and associated images of the self are unearthed and exposed to the light of day, they alter her perceptions of who she *really* is, and what she is capable of doing, now and in the future. Subjectively she has changed as a result of her experience, even when life after the baby resumes its "normal" course and she returns to the world outside the home two months, one year, or five years later.

On the outside, it may not be long before a woman appears just as she did before becoming a mother—she may hold the same job, talk about the same things over lunch with her coworkers, enjoy the same movies, and she may even fit into the same size clothing. But there will be another layer to her understanding of herself and her understanding of herself as a woman in relation to men and in relation to the larger world. Toxic wastes, working overtime, the holiday season, God (His existence or non-existence), and government policies regarding education, abortion, and national defense are among the many aspects of life that are seen through a new lens, which now includes a child in the picture.

Certain fundamental characteristics of motherhood challenge a woman's established sense of her identity as a distinct and completely familiar person unto herself. The first nine months after conception, the baby is literally inside a woman's body, a relationship between the self and another human being that is completely unique and has ramifications for the evolving relationship. After the baby is born, separation—physical as well as psychological—is a developmental task for mothers as well as for their babies. Of course, once the umbilical cord is cut, the baby is undeniably not the mother and the mother is not the baby, but as we have seen in an earlier chapter, what is physically self-evident is not always psychically real, for the baby or for its mother. Identification and overidentification are two points along a continuum.

Although there are a range of normal responses to the question of how soon and how much separation is desirable for the mother and for the baby during the first year or more, mothers who by all other standards would not be considered psychotic or out of touch with reality often respond as if their babies are extensions of themselves and that they are an extension of their babies, and in a manner of speaking they are. Their moods often fluctuate with their babies' joys and miseries, and many women are convinced, as well they might be, that the reverse is also the case—that their babies are acutely attuned to their moods in a kind of parallel fashion. After all, the baby is utterly dependent upon its mother or mothering figure for its physical and emotional well-being, and fluctuations in a mother's mood inevitably have a transforming effect on the baby.[3] Inevitably questions arise: "Is the baby anxious, upset, or angry because I am anxious, upset, or angry? Or do I only perceive her as anxious, upset, or angry because I think I would be feeling that way if I were in her shoes? Do I know instinctively how she feels because I am her mother and am closest to her? Or do I mistakenly think I know how she feels for precisely the same reason?"

To be sure, many women today are vaguely aware that there is a danger in responding to their children as if they were extensions of themselves. It is bad for them as well as for their children. However, being alert to the possibility of such danger does not guarantee immunity, and the line between being attuned (which is "good") and being enmeshed (which is "bad") is not always so clear when one is a participant rather than an observer.[4]

The experience of overlapping identities is not without some objective basis in reality, since from the point of view of the baby, the mother or a mothering figure is absolutely essential for survival. The baby simply cannot exist without someone to mediate between him and the world outside. He cannot protect himself from harm, or gratify his needs for food or affection; he cannot even identify what his needs are. Someone has to be there to anticipate them for him, to interpret the meaning and significance of his cries, and to hold him secure when he feels that he is disintegrating. D. W. Winnicott speaks of the mother as providing the infant with a "holding environment." Most of the time the mother, who has already served as protector and nurturer for nine months, continues in this capacity. Her term of office is indefinite, her responsibilities ambiguous.

Although few would dispute the importance of attachment and bonding between mother and infant, we have only begun to understand the nature and extent of the bond that develops during the early months of life. And, of course, the baby's experience is even more difficult to decipher than the mother's. But this is exactly what a good mother must do—she must try to understand and interpret her baby's messages, and imagine what his experience and needs might be, though his language is imprecise, her senses are imperfect, and her projections may lead her astray. In short, she must enter his phenomenological world without losing herself in it.

The process of disentangling a mother's identity from her baby's is further complicated by the fact that a mother's influence on her infant is often inadvertent and unconscious, and occurs even while the baby is still in utero.[5] A mother's voice—and perhaps at some point in the future we will find that even her unconscious feelings of joy and tenderness, fear or sadness—can penetrate the amniotic membrane along with caffeine and nicotine, iron and calcium, and other substances both toxic and nourishing. Moreover, researchers are discovering that infants are able to distinguish their mothers from everyone else far earlier than was previously suspected (by voice tone and by smell), which only confirms what many women know intuitively: that meaningful communication between a mother and her baby is never limited to spoken language. But precisely because communication is largely nonverbal and messages are sent and received without even being thought, feeling not reason forms the basis of their mutual connection.[6] Psychoanalyst Christopher Bollas refers to this preverbal mode of communication and understanding as the "unthought known."[7]

Yet if the interpenetration of a mother's and a baby's subjectivity threatens to envelop new mothers in a world of sensation and diffuse meanings, renowned psychiatrist and infant researcher Daniel Stern reassures us that at least for the infant psychological separation begins very early on. By two months infants "seem to approach inter-personal relatedness with an organizing perspective that makes it feel as if there is now an integrated sense of themselves as distinct and coherent bodies, with control over their actions, ownership of their own affectivity, a sense of continuity, and a sense of other people as distinct and separate interactants."[8] In other words, Dr. Stern is suggesting that almost immediately after birth, the baby begins to catch glimpses of himself as an entity apart from his mother. And, what begins as a faint glimmer of what it means to be a separate individual develops over the next few years into a sense of a self existing apart from but among other selves.

But whether the infant is actually incapable of dif-ferentiating himself from his mother, or whether in fact the experience of merging with the mother is a later construction—the anxious and wishful fantasies of an older child—it is the *mother's* subjective experience of her baby and their relationship that is of primary concern here.[9] After all, it is her *perception* of her baby's helplessness and his autonomy that will determine her response to their interdependency; it is her *perception* of how similar he is to her that will determine the strength of her positive and negative identification with him. She cannot help but bring her own preconceptions and prejudices to bear.

A mother may interpret her baby's bedtime tears as an intentional manipulation, a natural desire for prolonged contact that need not be gratified, or as an expression of profound neediness which should be ministered to indefi-nitely, depending upon her understanding of who she was as a baby, what she needed from her mother, as well as her memories of her mother's responses to her. She cannot get inside her baby's mind to discover the "true" meaning of the outburst—if such a thing exists. And the baby certainly cannot argue its case conclusively—its per-spective is too limited, it does not always understand the difference between wish and need, and it does not have the language capacity to communicate this difference if it did understand. But even if it did have the words available, the baby is too easily swayed by its mother's perspective to know for sure what his own perspective is; her interpretation of reality is too convincing, and inevitably it colors his understanding of himself and their relationship.

In the process of serving as interpreter and mediator for her baby, many a woman finds that she must reassert time and again, to herself and others, that which she ordinarily would take for granted—her separateness, her individuality, and her human limitations (including her limitations as interpreter and mediator for her child). Nobody but a baby can reasonably expect her to read minds, or see into the future, or perform miracles, but as a mother she may begin to feel that she should be able to do all these things for her baby. Each woman's failures in self-assertion reflect her own needs and the needs of others— her baby, her husband, and any other co-conspirators—to deny her these realities: that she is indeed a separate individual, and that she, like everyone else, is painfully limited despite her baby's illusions to the contrary.

We have digressed into what may seem to be murky waters only to illustrate how and why the psychological distance between a mother and her baby is too small, the feelings too intense, and the boundaries separating her identity from her baby's too permeable, at least in the beginning, for most women to emerge from the early months of mothering unchanged. Even the woman who is committed to remaining just as she always was must work harder to stay in one place, to limit herself to one body, to one emotional universe, and this in itself makes her different. During the early months, when the seeds of change are being planted, many women are hardly aware that, microscopic as they are, they are germinating. But then months, sometimes years, later they acknowledge, often with some ambivalence, that not only are their lives different now that they are mothers but that *they* themselves are different as well.

Although some women experience the changes in the self as existential—that is, as so profound as to touch upon the very essence of their personalities—other women experience the changes as more subtle and find it difficult to pinpoint what exactly feels different, though they sense that some internal shifts have occurred. Realizing that the self is not a fixed entity but one that is continually evolving in response to changing internal and external realities can be disturbing as well as comforting. And while some women pat themselves on the back for the accommodations they have made, never anticipating that they could find it in themselves to be as patient or as self-sacrificing as they have come to be, others resist, sometimes violently, the idea that they are in any way affected by the fact that they are mothers, as if to admit this would be a sign of weakness or poor character, or a betrayal of feminism. They mistake rigidity for strength, and identify flexibility with surrender—a common misunderstanding in our culture.[10]

Roseanne, who experienced motherhood as a major disturbance to her psychic equilibrium, looks back at the person she was before she had her baby with amazement and disbelief. The work she did, the goals she had for herself, and the relationship she had to the world at large all feel alien to the person she is now. She was going to be a success, and that meant being a successful career woman. She was to be the anomaly in her working-class Irish-Catholic family. Roseanne looks back to the days before motherhood with wonder more than with nostalgia, but she exudes a sense of uneasiness in her present state, which still remains one of limbo. If her past and present selves look so radically different even to her, she has to question the stability of her current identity as a full-time wife and mother. What, she asks herself, can she reliably expect to be like in the future? She attempts to sort out who she was then from who she is now without losing hold of what is essential to being Roseanne.

Rebecca, whose characterization of her "identity crisis"

is far less dramatic than Roseanne's, finds herself questioning her assumptions about herself as a master-planner and an intellectual. While she enjoys her newly discovered capacity to "play," she worries about what this means in terms of the larger picture of herself and her life. Surely she had submerged this playful, emotional aspect of her personality for so many years for a good reason. She wonders whether she will still have the discipline to accomplish the "serious" work that she had always set out to do now that she has finally "let herself go." Waves of panic are short-lived (she is, after all, as capable as ever of committing herself to her work when and if she chooses to), but nevertheless they mar her self-assurance.

And finally, there is Julie, who denies any significant changes in her feelings about herself and focuses exclusively on what has changed around her. People see her differently now that she is a mother (she's not as much fun), the rhythm of her daily life is not what it was (she's harried and irritable), and her baby-sitter and her husband control her comings and goings. Nevertheless, she insists that *her* feelings about herself have not been affected, and she shrugs off the possibility as if it were something foreign to her way of thinking. And who can argue with her subjective experience? Apparently, whatever changes have occurred have only grazed the surface and she has not allowed them to penetrate into the deeper layers of her personality.

Whether a woman is struck by her essential sameness or by the unexpected differences in her feelings about her self (and the balance between a sense of continuity and discontinuity of self is forever tipping, first in one direction and then in the other), most of the time she can identify specific changes in her body image, her sexuality, her identity in the outside world, and her feelings of self-confidence. Most of the time, the central text is as it was, with revisions and more revisions.

Sexuality, Femininity, and Other Mind-Body Conundrums

> *I have greater respect for my body and its capabili-
> ties. . . . Having a baby is such a female thing; and it
> feels very feminine to be so attuned to my body.—Laura,
> thirty-five, mother of a three-year-old boy, and preg-
> nant at the time of the interview*

> *When I was breast-feeding the first few months I felt
> like I was a baby machine, not a sexual object in any
> way.—Julie, thirty-two, mother of a ten-month-old boy*

> *Being pregnant was very difficult, seeing my body
> changing, getting fatter and fatter. I feel less sexual
> because my husband was there when they cut me open
> and you lose all sense of the mystery. On the other
> hand, I feel more feminine because having a baby is the
> most female thing you can do—the ultimate in being a
> woman.—Kate, thirty-three, mother of a fifteen-month-
> old girl*

Having a baby is a quintessentially female experience. To state the obvious, becoming a mother is incontrovert-ible evidence of femaleness, but this is only on the level of biological reality. Psychic reality is never so unambiguous, and the relationship between feeling female and feeling sexual, feminine, creative, and the object of desire is by no means self-evident. The subjective experience of being pregnant, giving birth, being a mother (whatever image that evokes in an individual woman's mind), having a mother's body, doing motherly activities, reflects biologi-cal realities to be sure, but only as they are refracted through the prism of individual and cultural symbolism.

Asking a woman about the impact of becoming a mother on her feelings of femininity is like giving a Rorschach test. Unwittingly, each woman projects her own ideas and images of what it means to *her* to be a feminine woman and then responds according to these terms. This is because femininity is a psychological construct, and as such does not exist as a thing in the real world, but only in the imagination. If some women say they feel less feminine since becoming mothers, while others report the opposite experience, this often reflects their varying definitions of femininity more than anything else. Regardless of how a woman defines femininity, and there are bound to be infinite variations, most women experience subtle or not so subtle pressures from within themselves to be feminine (whatever that means to them) simply because they are female and quite naturally want to fulfill as best they can their destinies as manifest in the culture.[11]

To some women being feminine means being nurturing, patient, graceful, intuitive, and self-sacrificing. These personality characteristics coincide with cultural ideals of motherhood, and as some women begin to incorporate these qualities into their personalities when they are mothers, they feel more feminine. Ann, for example, notices that since becoming a mother she experiences an inner contentment, a quiet gracefulness, and she associates these qualities with femininity. In her mind, competitiveness, time-pressure, and a diffuse sense of discontent with oneself and with the world are part of a masculine sensibility. She hopes to rid herself of these "masculine" qualities now that she is at home with her baby, and though she feels she has succeeded more or less, remnants from the days she was active in the world of publishing continue to plague her. (Recall Ann's impatience with her toddler's delays and her persistent concerns about wasting time discussed in an earlier chapter.)

Rebecca, who continues to work outside the home but no longer sees herself as on the "fast track" professionally, also feels unquestionably more feminine and describes how in the process of nursing her baby she was put in touch with her "nurturing side." And Susan, who acknowledges long-standing conflicts about assuming a stereotypically female identity (it was not an accident that she waited until she was forty to have her first child), also claims that motherhood has made her feel more "female," more "normal" ("normal" being defined in terms of what the majority of people in a particular culture do), and more feminine; for her the three are inextricably interwoven. It is as if by taking the plunge and becoming a mother Susan was giving herself the go-ahead to relax her defenses as a woman and a human being. In the context of motherhood she could allow herself as well as others— her husband, her friends, even strangers—access to areas of her psyche that were previously off-limits. Feeling more open, more part of a community, and more in tune with her own dependency needs adds up in her mind to feeling more comfortable with herself as a person, but also as a woman, and this seems more feminine.

When femininity is defined in terms of personality characteristics, women may oscillate between feeling at times more and at other times less feminine than before they became mothers precisely because their moods are so volatile and they alternate between feeling positively angelic and positively demonic. Judith, for example, describes herself feeling *very* feminine when she is loving and patient with her baby and her husband, when she thoroughly enjoys an outing to the park or zoo, and when she feels at ease with herself and confident that what she is doing (at home and outside the home) is valuable and creative. This is because she associates femininity with inner harmony and generosity of spirit. However, when she feels claustrophobic and irritable, which she does not recall having felt quite so frequently before she embarked on motherhood, and when on a Sunday afternoon *en famille* she wonders whether she will ever be able to sit down and read a book without constantly being interrupted, she feels distinctly unfeminine. This is because she is resisting doing what women have always done throughout the ages and what the Mrs. Ramsays of the world have always done graciously without a trace of ambivalence.

Many women, however, associate feeling feminine with

certain physical and emotional characteristics that make them desirable to men and are distinctly not part of their experience of themselves as mothers. In their minds, the feminine woman is girlish, delicate, sweet-smelling, freshly made-up, and even a bit pampered. She is concerned with her appearance, takes the time to make herself look and feel attractive, and indulges herself with visits to the beauty parlor, pretty negligées or expensive perfumes, all with this end in mind. She does not smell of baby ointment or spit-up, or wear clothes designed to hide, more or less, the inevitable peanut butter-and-jelly or ice cream stains she is likely to absorb over the course of the day. She does not have circles under her eyes or varicose veins, or carry fifteen extra pounds. If there is any question about what this version of the feminine woman looks like, you can find her on any magazine cover or in any "lifestyle" advertisement. And so, though these women also find themselves to be more nurturing, more patient, less selfish, and perhaps more mature now that they are mothers, they feel generally less rather than more feminine.

Gina describes growing up in a culture in which the boundary between mothers and nonmothers, women and girls, was clearly drawn and reflected graphically in their physical appearance. Girls had long hair and wore sexy dresses; their virginity was their treasure. Women were matronly, they gained weight, and their clothes were drab; the house was their domain. Women who did not fit into the category of either girl or mother behaved motherly or else risked being ostracized, pitied, or dismissed as eccentric—literally outside the inner circle.

In reflecting on her own experience, Gina finds that she feels more mature, and more self-confident since becoming a mother, but also less feminine. She has gained weight, and when not at work, she rarely gets out of jeans and an oversized shirt. She spends most of her free time close to home. Gina is a woman who says she has redefined many of her goals since having had a baby, meaning that she has decided that such "externals" as degrees, titles, and salary do not count quite as much as they used to. Apparently, cultivating what she has defined as her "feminine" side has also become less of a priority.

Elizabeth also makes the distinction between motherliness and femininity explicit. For her, femininity conjures up images of carefree frivolity and self-adornment, and she has little time or inclination for either now that she is a mother. Organizing elegant dinner parties, cooking gourmet meals, and dressing to fit the part of hostess are in her mind feminine aspects of her self that have receded into the background. Moreover, in contrast to Susan, who feels that as a mother she is more receptive to other people, Elizabeth finds that she is *less* open to possible intrusions from friends and strangers, and more "self-protective." Having so little time and space for herself, she keeps careful guard over her privacy. This insularity feels less feminine to her.

While a heightened sense of femininity is generally associated with positive experiences of the self, a diminished sense of femininity is not unequivocally experienced as a loss—though some women continue to express nostalgia for the days when they themselves were protected and coddled and were not always protecting and coddling somebody else. This willingness to let go of the "feminine" probably reflects the ambivalence many women feel about our cultural stereotypes.

Traditionally, femininity has been associated with passive receptivity, dependency, indirection, and deferentiality, as well as womanliness, lovableness, spirituality, and privilege. In a culture that frequently measures women in terms of what they look like and not in terms of what they can do and in which women's bodies seem to exist largely for the purpose of attracting men, it is not surprising that some new mothers experience a sense of freedom when they realize how irrelevant clothes, makeup, and weight are to their relationship with their baby.

The baby desires its mother's body, but the baby needs her body for nourishment and comfort; the baby requires that its mother attend to its needs, but its needs are to be held, to be played with, to be fed, and to be kept clean. In this relationship with her baby, a new mother begins to see her body in a different light. Its value lies not only in its sexuality or physical attractiveness, but also in its ability to nurture, to absorb raw experience—labor, birth, sleepless nights, colic, and all forms of bodily excretions—and to endure.

To be desired and loved as a mother is not glamorous or romantic or sexual, but for some women this comes as a kind of relief. As mothers, they feel justified in turning their attention to other, more important things—at least temporarily. If this means that they feel less feminine, it does not seem to be too great a sacrifice, because they feel more authentic, more serious about life and about themselves. When femininity is experienced more as a burden than as a source of strength, motherhood grants women a reprieve. The feminine straitjacket can be loosened, and if some people don't like what bursts forth as a result, women have at their disposal new sources of power and worthiness more suitable to their present reality.

Whether a woman feels more or less feminine during the early years of motherhood—and this seems to depend largely on how femininity is being defined—many women observe that they are far less focused on their appearance, and more specifically, that they are less concerned about being physically attractive to men. In Diane's words, "I feel equally attractive, but I'm not equally interested in being attractive. I've withdrawn from that part of life and it is totally irrelevant to me."

Diane is not alone in her professed indifference to being attractive to men, though perhaps she is more adamantly unambivalent about it, which is simply characteristic of her personality. Rebecca also indicates a shift in her sense of herself as an attractive female and is certain that she communicates her unavailability subliminally when she encounters men on the street, at work, or in the context of social events. As with Diane, there is no evidence that she is concerned over the subtle change she experiences in her relations with men, and this may be because she feels that she has initiated it.

Kate admits that she feels less attractive to men, and though she bemoans the fact that she has gained weight, she makes it clear that she wants to get back into shape for herself and not in order to be more attractive to men. She is explicit about why she cares less about being attractive to men: "I don't need them, because I have a baby, a career, and a husband." Apparently Kate is not concerned that her weight gain poses a threat to her relationship with her husband, Rick. Their bond has deepened in the process of becoming parents together and in having weathered all kinds of minor crises together. Whether she is five or ten pounds heavier than she was on their wedding day has faded in significance. She no longer feels that her sexual attractiveness is the basis for their mutual attachment.

Deborah feels that she exudes motherhood wherever she goes, even when her baby is not with her, and imagines that were she to go into a singles' bar the men would pick up the signals immediately and without her having to say a word would understand that she is a mother and not a potential sexual object. Whether or not the men she encounters actually perceive her as she perceives herself, it is clear that for her the sexual charge is largely absent in her relations with men. Although Deborah acknowledges that her sexual interest in other men began to wane when she got married, she never before experienced herself as palpably different and perceptibly unavailable. But rather than expressing regrets or nostalgia for the days when sexuality was a constant preoccupation, Deborah seems to relish the change that motherhood brought, enjoying her new, more matronly status. Apparently, as long as the baby is an important arbiter of a woman's value, the cult of femininity and beauty loses some of its appeal, and its power over women's feelings about themselves and their relationship to the world is diluted.

Of course it is naïve to suppose that the feminine ideals

no longer exert any influence over women's feelings about themselves once they have become mothers and turn their attention to other matters. And in fact a problem can arise when these ideals pull women in one direction and the demands of motherhood pull them in another. Women who have always prided themselves on their figures and their physical attractiveness are understandably disturbed when they can no longer fit into their premotherhood clothes and no longer have the luxury of taking the time to look their best. Similarly, women who have prided themselves on their willingness to give of themselves emotionally are disturbed when they find themselves bickering with their husbands over who should put the baby to bed and who should relax, tune out, and read the newspaper.

Breaking out of the familiar but confining cocoon of femininity can be "liberating"—a rite of passage from girlhood into womanhood—but it can also precipitate a serious crisis of identity when a new mother feels that her mature woman's body is less attractive, or even ugly, and that her needs as an individual who happens also to be a mother are reprehensible and unfeminine, a betrayal of her sex.

Lydia, a thirty-eight-year-old mother of a nine-year-old girl, became actively bulimic shortly after her daughter was born. Since adolescence Lydia had been unrealistically concerned with her weight, and though she had always been very slender, she chronically worried that she was not thin enough. During her pregnancy she allowed herself to eat normally for the first time in years, and she gained forty pounds, which was not unusual, given her height and frame. Her relaxed attitude about her body was short-lived, however, and Lydia became terrified that she would be unable to shed the extra weight and return to the way she was before she became a mother—slender, stylish, a woman who was in control of her life and in the process of building a successful career in the fashion world. Consequently, she put herself on a starvation diet, rapidly lost all the weight she had gained and more, so that over the course of the next few years she became seriously underweight. Desperate to free herself from her self-imposed diet regimen, Lydia began to binge complusively, purging herself of the forbidden food afterward through the abuse of laxatives. While Lydia's distorted body image and conflicts around eating and weight predated her becoming a mother, the loosening of her customary defenses during pregnancy and its aftermath frightened her so much that she felt obliged to withdraw even deeper into the protective but suffocating cocoon she had only begun to emerge from in the process of becoming a mother.

Lydia's symptomatic behavior is certainly not attributable to motherhood per se, and perhaps she would have become anorectic and then bulimic even if she had not experienced the changes in her body associated with pregnancy and motherhood. However, her symptoms graphically and dramatically express some of the conflicts many women experience, but never express overtly, when they see their bodies changing and realize that time does not stand still even for them. The dream of returning to an age of carefree, girlish innocence is shattered when, as mothers, women find that they must not only surrender their claim for protection and care, but also their right to focus their attention on taking care of themselves. Lydia's eating disorder was her way of trying to turn back the clock.

As is evident from Lydia's rather extreme reaction, it can be anxiety-provoking for a woman to see this kind of change in her body and in her disposition, particularly if she believes that her feminine charms are the basis of her power and security. If a woman feels that her sense of worthiness is dependent upon looking and acting a certain way, she may resist the changes in her body and her personality that motherhood brings. Her resistance need not take the form of self-starvation, but she may attempt to squeeze herself literally and figuratively into her former shape and suppress feelings that do not fit neatly into her picture of the "feminine woman."

Roseanne's conflicts did not revolve around the changes she observed in her body, though, like Lydia, she had gained a lot of weight during her pregnancy. Instead, her conflicts pivoted around the changes she observed in her disposition—she felt moody, drained, and needy—and her sense that motherhood signaled the end of the honeymoon period she was enjoying so thoroughly in her marriage. According to Roseanne, before the baby arrived her relationship with her husband was quite romantic; during their courtship, her husband wined and dined her and played the part of the gallant gentleman. Although she worked up until her delivery, she felt protected, revered, and pleasantly indulged. She was her husband's little girl, and he was her mentor and her knight in shining armor rolled into one.

Roseanne's unconscious expectations of motherhood were that it would be a continuation of the romanticized world of her early marriage, only more so because as a mother she would be defining herself more exclusively in feminine terms. Through motherhood she hoped to separate herself from the masculine world of work, ambition, and competition. Convinced, after spending several years climbing the corporate ladder, that being a businesswoman did not satisfy her or suit her personality, Roseanne decided to pour herself into the business of becoming an irreproachably good mother.

After the birth of her baby, with her immediate and long-term career plans in a state of limbo, Roseanne felt that she had to prove to herself and to everyone else that she could be the quintessential mother, and motherhood and the cultivation of the "feminine" virtues she associated with it became her vocation. Naturally the reality of caring for a baby bore little resemblance to her fantasy images, and to her dismay, the delicate, feminine lady she aspired to become never materialized; in fact she receded farther than ever before into the horizon. In what was a misguided attempt to preserve her girlish illusions about herself, her husband, and her baby, Roseanne tried first to deny and then to suppress her feelings of frustration, anger, and exhaustion at round-the-clock mothering. These messy and ungenerous feelings were only evidence to her of her unworthiness as a woman and as a human being now that motherhood was her full-time occupation. So when Roseanne failed to be the selfless, calm, and cheerful mother she thought she should be, (and she failed repeatedly despite her earnest wishes), and when her previously chivalrous husband began to criticize her for being irritable, selfish, and anxious (unlike her previous sweet self), her guilt became overwhelming. But rather than forcing her to change her course and revise her fantasy goals for herself, Roseanne's guilt only spurred her on in her quest to become the pure, selfless mother of her dreams. The more tired and frustrated she became, the more she berated herself for feeling this way, and the more she tried to make herself over. It took two years before she was able to relinquish the idealized image she had created in her mind long before she had actually become a mother. Only then, feeling less feminine but more "real" and more "earthy," was she able to extricate herself from the cycle of frustration and self-recrimination, and work sympathetically with herself, "warts and all."

As might be anticipated, there is no one-to-one correspondence between feeling feminine and feeling sexual, and women who experience motherhood as a confirmation of their femaleness and even of their femininity seem to see no contradiction in the fact that they also often feel less sexual since becoming mothers. A brief digression into the larger cultural expressions of this phenomenon may be helpful before examining some individual women's experiences.

There is a long tradition in our culture, dating back at

least two thousand years, in which motherhood has been separated from sexuality, and the figure of the matronly woman is juxtaposed against the figure of the sexual temptress. The most obvious instance in which this splitting of the two realms occurs is with the Virgin Mary, the Mother of Christ. She is a paradigm of the mother cleansed, as it were, of any sexual experience or desire. Though it can be argued that this polarity is part of an entire worldview in which the spirit and the flesh represent the irreconcilable forces of good and evil, this does not explain why fatherhood has seldom been conceived as antithetical to male sexuality. To the contrary, in the world of the imagination as well as in real life, a man's becoming a father is often taken as concrete evidence of his virility, and in some circles is cause for pride and off-color humor.

Both men and women sometimes experience domesticity and sexuality as being in opposition to each other. While many women continue to feel feminine and womanly without feeling sexual, however, most men's sense of masculinity and manliness is inextricably linked with their sexuality. Therefore, when a man feels that his sexuality is being threatened by his and his wife's parental responsibilities, the threat is to the core of his very being (which does not appear to be the experience of most women), and he will resist the domestic influence as he would resist any other threats to his very identity as a man. Whereas a man might feel emasculated were he to allow his parental role to interfere in any way with his sexual potency, a diminishment in a woman's sexual desire does not appear to pose such a threat, and in this culture, at least, may even enhance her sense of herself as feminine and womanly.

Even when female sexuality after motherhood is acknowledged as it was by the Greeks, it is expressed outside the domestic sphere. Aphrodite, the goddess of love, is married to Hephaestus, who is the only one of the Olympic gods who is physically deformed (he is lame) and unattractive. However, she expresses the sexuality for which she is famous in her extramarital affair with Ares, the god of war. Of course Greek goddesses were allowed their extramarital affairs, and thus were able to be both mothers and sexual beings. Historically, women have not been given such license, and their sexual life (though not men's) has generally been confined to the marital relationship. Inasmuch as domesticity and sexuality have been seen as antithetical tendencies, women (but not men) have been forced to sacrifice the one for the other. Artemis, the chaste goddess of the hunt who shuns the sexual approaches of men, is also, ironically, the goddess who is responsible for protecting women in childbirth. So even among the Greek deities it is recognized that for us mortals the spheres of motherhood and female sexuality are kept apart, and Chastity, personified in the goddess Artemis, attends at the bedside of new mothers!

The split between a woman's sexuality and her motherly and wifely functions is a theme that runs through nineteenth-century Romantic novels, from *Madame Bovary* to *Anna Karenina*. In both these novels, the female protagonist abandons marriage and family for sexual passion and ultimately takes her own life as a result of these contradictions. It is interesting to note that Anna Karenina's brother, Stepan Arkadeyevich Oblonsky, a chronic philanderer despite being a father of numerous children, does not meet such a tragic end. His conflicts are practical—his wife temporarily turns him out—but they are never existential, and in the end he need not relinquish his sexuality in order to continue to function as a father and husband, or vice versa. Of course, in fiction, as well as in real life, the opposing experiences of men and women can present a problem when a woman's sexual interest diminishes upon becoming a mother and her husband's does not, and in the case of Oblonsky it could be argued that this was a significant factor in his philandering.

Even in Freud's formulation, in the "normal" course of development a woman's desire for a penis is replaced by the desire for a child, and thus her sexuality finds its greatest fulfillment in motherhood. Following this argument to its logical conclusion, a mature woman's sexuality is subsumed in motherhood and expressed through her love of her baby. This being the case, it might be expected that her desire would diminish upon becoming a mother. Again, as with the Greeks and the Romantics, sexuality and motherhood are not successfully integrated, because they do not coexist. Freud does not split sexuality and motherhood but instead fuses them into one and the same process.

It seems clear that historically we have found it difficult to integrate images of motherhood with images of sexuality, yet it is not altogether clear how much this reflects the reality of women's sexual experience as mothers (they feel less desire as the baby becomes the primary focus of their emotional energy), and how much it shapes that reality (they no longer perceive themselves or are perceived as sexual, so the baby becomes the primary focus of their emotional energy). In all likelihood both processes are operating, and the contradictions women experience as they alternate between their identities as mothers and their identities as sexual partners are an expression of the particular cultural tradition from which we have emerged at least as much as the culture is an expression of these contradictions.

Many women are aware of changes in their feelings about their sexuality and report less sexual contact and less desire since having become mothers. This is in spite of the fact that the contemporary mother is often portrayed in the media as sexy and girlish, paying homage to the sexual revolution, Masters and Johnson, and the "discovery" of the female orgasm. Although a diminishment in sexual feelings is by no means a universal experience, and some new mothers find that they feel more sexual than ever before, a decrease in desire seems to be common enough to suggest that an explanation lies beyond the individual psychologies of the women in question. It has something to do with the meaning of sexuality for women in this culture.

Women who say that they feel less sexual as mothers often attribute the change to fatigue, lack of time, and the difficulty of acting spontaneously when there is an infant or young child in the other room who might awaken and interrupt the lovemaking at any moment. Since mothers, more often than fathers, are primed to respond to their babies' moment-to-moment needs, women are more likely than men to anticipate disruptions and to be distracted even when, momentarily, there are none. Nobody can argue with these practical and very real changes in the lives of men and women; they are bound to affect their sexual behavior. But this is the surface, not to be dismissed, but not to be mistaken for the entire story. If we listen carefully to how many women talk about their sexuality, we can hear echoes of a culture in which women's sexuality has largely been conceived as an offering, a treasured gift, even a surrendering of will, rather than an expression and an enhancement of the self. From this perspective it is not surprising that new mothers would resist one further *demand* (if this is in fact how it is experienced) on their bodies and their emotions.[12]

Unwittingly, Deborah articulates this view of sexuality when she tries to explain why she feels "definitely less sexual" since becoming a mother. She begins by talking about fatigue, schedules, and other obvious impediments to sexual passion. But then she shifts to another level of explanation. "I have this child that's attached to me all day long, and the last thing I want is somebody pawing me at night. When Sarah's in bed I feel that that is my personal time. To have to think then of somebody else needing me in a sexual way is too difficult."

She is but one among the many women who express the old stereotype of sexual relations between women and men. The typical scenario involves a man who wants sex all the time and a woman who gives in conditionally and only with misgivings. If it is a comedy, the woman receives love, marriage, and a family in return for her sexual favors, and the scales are balanced between the sexes. If it is a melodrama, the sexual liaison threatens to undermine the woman's self-respect, and in her surrender to desire, she ultimately feels as if she has betrayed herself. In either case, sexuality is depicted as something not for her or for them but for him.

The scenario is part of a larger configuration in which, paradoxically, women's sexuality has been simultaneously overemphasized and minimized. Women have traditionally been thought of as the *objects* of male desire rather than the subjects who desire. In more poetic terms, women are generally cast in the role of the beloved, not the lover. The multimillion-dollar beauty industry is testimony to this model of sexual relations, in which women work very hard to please, entice, and thereby reign victorious. Women's sexuality is a means to an end, not an end in itself, more a form of power by which to seduce a man, than a source of mutual pleasure and shared expression. It is only recently that we as a culture have even acknowledged that women, too, have sexual needs and that their satisfaction is not simply vicariously achieved in satisfying a man.[13] Insofar as these ideas have insinuated themselves into women's unconscious experience of their own sexuality—and it is difficult to imagine that anybody could be entirely immune to a cultural tradition dating back thousands of years—and they feel that as sexual partners they tend to give (up) more than they receive, then motherhood will represent a turning point.

The relationship a woman has with her baby or young child is inherently an unbalanced one, even when both mother and infant derive pleasure from it. A mother is there to give whatever needs to be given, emotionally or physically; this is her child's right and her responsibility. If she is gratified in the process, so much the better, but it is not her due. There is no quid pro quo for mothers, and, in fact, when a mother expects the kind of reciprocity from her child that she expects from adults ("I just read to

you; now let me read peacefully for fifteen minutes"), it
can be a source of enormous frustration. Against this
backdrop, any experience, sexual or otherwise, in which a
woman feels she is giving more than she is receiving,
ministering to someone else's needs rather than attending
to her own, becomes magnified. Her needs to nurture and
to inspire have been well sated through the activity of
mothering. And inasmuch as these needs have fueled her
sexual desires in the past, they no longer press for gratification outside the baby in the present.

If, moreover, a woman feels confident that she has
given more than enough of herself in her relationship
with her baby, she may feel justified taking more for
herself outside that relationship. This may mean that she
will begin to make more sexual demands on her husband
and feel unsatisfied with what previously felt like a satisfactory sexual life. Or, if she feels depleted by her mothering, it may mean that she will be less hesitant about
putting limits on the "demands" of others for her to
perform. Sexual desires do not appear so urgent when
compared with a baby's demands for attention, food, or
comfort, and a woman may feel that she can postpone her
own and her husband's gratification more easily than she
can postpone her baby's. She has gained confidence in
her right to do so—in becoming a mother she has become
an "adult," and it is her perogative.

Of course, being sexual does not necessarily mean giving in to demands, or ministering to another's needs; this
is but one rather unfortunate construction of female sexuality. Some women find that sexual relations are more
important to them than ever before precisely because their
relationship with their child is so unbalanced and their
sexuality offers them a channel through which they can
express their own adult needs and be replenished. "Physical intimacy with my husband is so different than being
with the baby that I definitely enjoy it more now," says
Roseanne, who also admitted that she feels less feminine

and less concerned over her attractiveness. It is as if, having been freed of the encumbrances of the "feminine" role, Roseanne has been able to enjoy her sexuality on a more equal plane.

Laura's sexuality has also taken on a new form since becoming a mother. Like Roseanne, she feels less concerned about whether men find her an attractive woman, and has turned her gaze inward. She feels more attuned to her body after having gone through labor and delivery, more confident of her capabilities, and also more sexual. Motherhood has enhanced her feelings of sexuality because her body has become a source of pride and no longer assumes a purely decorative function in relation to others. Sexuality is more, not less, hers to enjoy now that she feels physically more powerful and less passive.

Motherhood brings to the fore beliefs, feelings, and conflicts that women have about their sexuality, their femininity, and their bodies because all are implicated in the process of having a baby. When a woman defines her sexuality in terms of male desire and defines her femininity in terms of girlish innocence and lacy undergarments, motherhood comes as a shock to the system, an experience that feels antithetical to being sexy and being feminine. Some women experience relief that now that they are mothers they no longer have to be as dependent upon men to confer upon them a sense of worthiness and are pleased that they can turn their attention to pursuits other than the pursuit of beauty. Others panic, however, and frantically try to reconstitute the identity as a sexual and attractive woman that they fear they are in the process of losing.

Whether a woman feels pleased or anxious at having "let herself go" depends of course on whether she feels more or less in control of herself, more or less true to herself, as a result of having let go. Were the strictures she previously imposed on herself uplifting, or burdensome? Did they stifle her sexuality, or inspire it? Were they necessary for her self-esteem, or did they merely reinforce her insecurities about herself? How a woman answers these questions for herself will determine the significance for her of "letting go" of old forms and images of the self.

It seems, however, that the tension that may exist between being a sexual and feminine woman and being a mother is not inevitable—even if it is common and deeply rooted in our cultural tradition. A woman need not sacrifice sexuality for maternal tenderness, nor must she be deliquent in her parental responsibilities in order to satisfy her sexual passion (as if the two forms of relating to another human being were incompatible). And she need not merge the sexual and the maternal aspects of her identity together, only to relate to men as if they were children and to equate sexual desires with children's desires for love and attention. These compromises are the stuff of tragedy: Anna Karenina's led to her suicide, and generations of women quietly resigned themselves to varying degrees of sexual anesthesia. But what is needed is a redefinition of terms.

When a woman's sexuality is recognized as a natural expression of her self and her womanly capabilities and is no longer perceived as essentially passive or demeaning—a means to an end—then women will experience sexual relations as gratifying and restorative, even when as mothers they are no longer quite so concerned with being an object of male desire. Sex will not be extraneous or burdensome now that there is a baby to attend to, but a welcome complement to the mother-child relationship in which, by virtue of her greater maturity, a woman must subordinate her needs to her child's. Only then will it be clear that motherhood and sexuality are neither mutually exclusive nor interchangeable aspects of a woman's identity.

"To Love and to Work": Who Are You and What Do You Do?

> *I realize that for a while at least, I'm going to have a job rather than a career, and sometimes that is difficult to adjust to. I wonder sometimes if I'm really serious about fulfilling myself professionally or if I am just trying to make a couple of bucks and have something else to do besides play with this little one. I look at other women and think "Can I do more?"—Rebecca, thirty-seven, mother of a one-year-old boy, working three-quarters time*

> *I feel I wasted so much of my life working. When I worked in business, nothing felt grounded or like it had any integrity; so much was just greed. . . . I have no desire to go back to that kind of work. . . . If my husband said I had to go back to work we'd be divorced by now.—Ann, thirty-seven, mother of a two-and-a-half-year-old boy, home full-time*

> *I'm more committed to my work now that I have the baby because I feel if my work is going to take me away from her it better not be a waste of my time. But I'm also less committed in the sense that if this job does not work out, I have a child at home whom I would happily stay home with. . . . The job is just not that important.— Nancy, twenty-nine, mother of a four-month-old girl, working full-time*

Erik Erikson relays the following story. When Freud was asked to describe what a "normal person" is capable of doing, his reply was surprisingly succinct: "To love and to work."[14] But his answer is deceptive in its apparent simplicity. Though Freud was surely not thinking about women or the conflicts they experience as they try to integrate work, motherhood, and sexuality into their sense of themselves, his comment is apropos. If, according to Freud, a goodly proportion of us fall short of his definition of normality in one way or another, this is only testimony to the fact that it is exceedingly difficult to love without allowing our passions to interfere with our productivity and to work without allowing our work to inhibit our tender and sexual feelings.

Mothers are certainly not unique in their efforts to construct a viable work identity through which they can feel productive and loving. This is a challenge for every human being, and the difficulties we encounter stem from the fundamental psychological conflict between the desire for intimacy and connection and the desire for separateness and autonomy. According to Freud, life is a continual, unremitting struggle to reconcile our individual desires with the needs and desires of those with whom we live. Compromise is an inevitable, if somewhat tragic aspect of human existence, and if we are realistic, we can only hope to forge relatively satisfactory compromises.

But if this is the human condition, becoming a mother forces the issue for women. Motherhood demands that choices be made and concrete steps be taken. Time to reflect comes after the fact, and when there is time to reflect and take stock of what has come to pass, it becomes clear to many women that their relationship to work has undergone a metamorphosis that is not easily reversed and is inextricably linked with the positive and negative feelings they have about themselves as mothers.

"To work or not to work?" does not appear to be the question that troubles most contemporary women. The majority of mothers today will work outside the home at some point in their lives.[15] They will work because they want to work, because they have to for financial reasons, and because they have unconsciously assimilated the lessons of the women's movement, which warned women of the various ills that would befall them and their children if they were to fail to venture outside the world of the home and family. The overprotective, "castrating" mother, and the depressed, middle-aged woman suffering from the "empty nest syndrome" are but a couple of the apparitions we have learned to watch out for lest we fall prey to them.

But if most women now assume that work outside the home is and should be an integral part of their lives and their identities—some are even convinced, prior to having had a baby, that their relationship to work is not measurably different from their husband's—motherhood challenges that assumption. Motherhood demands that each individual woman reassert her commitment to extra-familial activities and involvements (a commitment many other people are only too willing to relieve her of), or else come to terms with the idea that she has been changed.

While fatherhood goads men on to achieve ever greater "success" and financial security, motherhood functions, for good or ill, as a deterent to worldly achievement. This can take both a positive and a negative form. Motherhood still offers women a legitimate alternative to success via the marketplace and provides them with the opportunity to bow out of a career graciously if they so choose.[16] Depending upon your point of view this is liberating, seductive, or blatantly undermining.

As Nancy noted, if she discovers that her work as a financial consultant is more draining and less rewarding than she would like, and that her commissions do not begin to compensate for what she has to pay in the form of stress, it *feels* less catastrophic now that she has a baby. The baby allows her to consider alternatives to pushing herself forward at all costs; after all, there are a great many people she knows who would applaud and congratulate her were she to temper her ambitions and play the more traditional role of wife and mother. Even though she continues to work pretty much as before she had the baby, this internal shift has altered her psychological relationship to work, and if on a daily basis she is not less conscientious, in the larger picture she *is* less dedicated.

Diane also tends to panic less on the job when pressures appear insurmountable, although she maintains that she is more committed than ever to her career as a hospital administrator. She is able to respond with greater equanimity because her perspective on what constitutes a crisis has changed after having lived through months of sleepless nights when her son had colic. Moreover, when she found that most of the items on her desk were still waiting for her, untouched, when she returned from her three-month maternity leave, Diane realized that little is as urgent as she used to think it was. Life goes on, deadlines are usually met or extended, and henceforth she will reserve her anxiety attacks for real life-and-death matters.

But if motherhood gives women greater freedom than men to opt out of a difficult or stressful job situation and to put work in the larger perspective of their lives, it also denies women the freedom to continue uninterrupted whatever they were doing before the baby arrived. Once a mother, it is no longer possible for a woman to take for granted the work she does outside the home—even when routines are more or less reestablished and everything appears to be the same on the outside. Rather than pressing her forward to ever greater success, motherhood forces a woman to reconsider her commitment to her job and reevaluate its place in her life as a whole. If a woman is to work and to mother, *she* has to create the conditions to make this possible; they are not a given in this society.

Whether a woman ultimately renews her commitment to her career ("I'm committed to having something for myself outside the family . . ."), modifies her expectations for "success" (". . . but I'm also clear that I don't want to be a workaholic"), or postpones her ambitions indefinitely ("I've learned to take it day by day"), in the very process of weighing and reflecting upon her needs, her baby's needs, and her family's needs, a subtle transformation occurs, and her work identity is altered. Latent conflicts emerge with full force.

Even before Ann became a mother she felt alienated in her work as a commercial editor. She never identified herself with her position at work, but rather felt constrained and artificial in it. Motherhood only crystallized her feelings of marginality in relation to her work and gave her permission finally to turn her back upon this aspect of her identity. As her son turns two and a half and she realizes that he is beginning to need to have time away from her, she still has no plans to return to work of any kind: "I'm sick of the greed and sick of watching American business do business."

This kind of wholesale rejection of work and the identity associated with work does not appear to be common, at least not among middle-class women. This is because the "freedom" motherhood confers upon women to get out of the rat race, to slow down, to forget about the Nobel Prize, or the partnership, or the extra commission, is also paradoxically a curtailment of freedom, insofar as it implicitly discourages women from pursuing the pleasures of public life—power, recognition, money, prestige, and intellectual achievement. In this fashion, motherhood poses a threat to a woman's identity as a productive, participating member of society. Even Ann, who consciously champions full-time mothering and vehemently disparages the business world she left behind, admits as much. She claims that because she does not work outside the home she feels as if she is no longer "a contributing member of society." If Ann's sense of alienation is characteristic of her personality, and it seems to be, her life as a nonworking mother only casts her further out onto the periphery, reinforcing any pre-existing tendencies to feel marginal.

Deborah, who works only one day a week since having a baby, feels psychologically disconnected to her work more than ever and questions seriously whether she should change fields entirely. Although motherhood did not create the crisis in Deborah's work identity—she had never felt altogether comfortable working in the field of mental health, because the money was poor and she was not entirely confident of her abilities—it brought the crisis to a head. As a mother of an eighteen-month-old girl, planning to have a second child in the not-too-distant future, Deborah has indefinitely postponed making a decision. Her ambivalence about her work has been chronic, and she is unlikely to act precipitously now. She checks her impulse to chuck her career entirely and start something altogether new when her children (one yet to be conceived) are of school age. But she knows that motherhood could easily push her over the fence she has been straddling for several years. For now she resists the seduction—she doesn't like to think that she would use motherhood to avoid confronting her insecurities. But it is unclear how long she will continue to struggle with them now that she has a clear and respectable alternative.

Charlotte's reluctance to push her son into an organized child-care situation in order to pursue her own professional goals was behind her decision to leave her agency job and work as a consultant with more flexible hours. Her abbreviated work schedule, coupled with the isolation that comes with working out of her home, left her feeling fragmented and uninspired about her work. "Since I'm not giving enough professionally I'm not getting enough either," she observes, aware that this is a self-perpetuating cycle. While Charlotte is certain that being a mother is an essential aspect of her identity, her recent working experiences lead her to question the substantiality of her professional identity and its value to her and to other people.

Even women who have returned to their normal work schedules notice that their relationship to work has changed—they are working fewer hours, spending less time with colleagues after-hours, and watching the clock when meetings run late—and are clearly uneasy about it. They see themselves being pulled away from something they have always valued, and though they feel justified, they also question their own integrity as workers, and wonder if others are questioning this as well.

And well they might! Sociologists have noted that though women are "normatively required to give priority to their family" (and it is a rare mother who would admit to feeling otherwise), they are also expected, at least if they are professionals, to be committed to their careers "just like men."[17] And so, as women realize that their attention is divided and that their devotion to their work is not all that it was or could be were it not for competing interests, they worry lest they become dilettantes who dabble with this or that and ultimately fail to make a serious commitment to anything. Some women bend over backward to ensure that they and their work are taken seriously; others gradually withdraw from the field.

Rebecca expressed concern that despite years of education and training her work had become "just a job" and not a "future-looking career" now that she had gotten off the fast track in order to have a more flexible schedule. Rachel also finds herself vaguely anxious as she sees the consequences of having cut back on her hours at work. She runs a business with her husband, and prior to having had the baby all decisions were made jointly; now that she is not at the office as much as before, she is not always consulted, even though she is only a phone call away. Although Rachel is certain that she does not wish to extend her hours just yet (she enjoys her time at home with her nine-month-old son, and, moreover, has difficulty leaving him with strangers), she does not want to be forgotten or left out. Nor does she like feeling guilty for abandoning the business, which, until the birth of the baby, was as much her responsibility and priority as her husband's.

All of these women have wrestled to accommodate work and mothering into an identity that they can live with. Insofar as motherhood is an experience of interdependency and connectedness, it becomes the arena in which each woman confronts her needs to define herself as an individual unto herself. It is difficult, however, for a mother to set limits and erect boundaries in the emotional context of the home, where the needs of others are paramount.

Work then becomes the channel through which many women assert their separateness and independence. The struggle to maintain an identity as someone who works outside the home, therefore, has symbolic as well as practical significance. Just as the family is a refuge from the impersonality of the workplace, the workplace functions as a psychological and physical refuge from the intricate web of feelings and relationships that threaten at times to obscure a woman's individual characteristics and capabilities.

Self-Confidence

I feel absolutely more confident now that I'm a mother because I follow my instincts and listen to my body. . . . I run my house and my home and I'm more in control than I ever was working in business. I finally feel like an adult. . . . On the other hand, sometimes when I'm sitting in the park I wonder where my life is and where my life is going. . . . I feel that as a mother I'm not a contributing member of this society.— Ann, thirty-seven, mother of a two-and-a-half-year-old boy

Most of my adult life I based my self-confidence on my ability to be attractive to men as well as my ability to function well as a professional. But now I feel fat and unsure about where I'm going professionally. I think I've gained an understanding of what I want from life in the long run, but on a day-to-day basis my emotional life is a real roller-coaster.—Charlotte, thirty-three, mother of a three-year-old boy

As long as the colic lasted, I thought I wouldn't ever be able to make a decision again. But as it turns out I've managed to combine a full-time job and have even gotten myself a promotion. Because I see myself handling more than I did before I had a baby, I have more confidence in myself and my capabilities.—Diane, forty-two, mother of a two-year-old boy

Self-confidence is not a static quality that we acquire once and for all, for better or for worse. Nor does self-confidence exist in a vacuum, invulnerable to the successes and failures we encounter in our everyday lives; rather, it expands and contracts in the process of our relating to people and problems. When we see ourselves taking risks, solving problems, creating beauty, or even just managing to survive a crisis without crumbling under, this naturally bolsters our sense of ourselves as capable and effectual human beings. When we feel attractive and sexual, respected and appreciated by those around us, this is an additional boost. However, when we see ourselves floundering for solutions, grasping at straws, imagining little, and venturing even less, we begin to doubt whether we are in fact capable of mastering life and negotiating in the world. If, moreover, we come to depend upon others for positive feedback because we feel we can't measure for ourselves when we are doing well and when we are not, and these others are not only inconsistent—adoring us one moment and ignoring or condemning us the next—but also loudly proclaim how we have failed, and rarely congratulate us for our virtues, this is yet another blow.

In her analysis of feminine psychology, Karen Horney argues that women's lives, which have traditionally pivoted around being mothers and wives, create the conditions in which feelings of insecurity can proliferate. According to Horney, when, on account of custom or circumstance, a person depends exclusively upon his or her ability to love and be loved for a sense of self-worth, he or she will inevitably be prone to insecurities and loss of confidence. "A sound and secure self-confidence draws upon a broad basis of human qualities, such as initiative, courage, independence, talents, erotic values, capacity to master situations. . . . If, however, one's self-confidence is dependent on giving or receiving love, then one builds on a foundation which is too small and too shaky—too small because it leaves out too many personality values,

and too shaky because it is dependent on too many external factors."[18]

If we agree with Horney that there are certain universal
self experiences that are prerequisites for a solid sense of
self-confidence, then it follows that motherhood, insofar
as it is associated with changes in these self experiences,
will play a significant role, positive or negative, in boost-
ing or deflating women's self-confidence. Depending on
how a woman's experience as a mother alters her feelings
about her sexuality, her femininity, her physical strength,
her maturity, and her image of herself as a productive
participant in the world at large, motherhood will feed her
sense of confidence or undermine it. In many cases it
functions in both ways simultaneously.

Continually placed in the position where she has to
make decisions—big ones, such as who should care for
her baby when she is away at work for thirty hours a
week, and small ones, such as which brand of stroller she
should buy—Rebecca is proud to see that she does not
obsess endlessly as she characteristically did as a student
and then as a professional woman. There is simply no
time now for this kind of indulgence. And although on
occasion life feels out of control, as it never did before (she
had always been a systematizer), Rebecca congratulates
herself because despite all her responsibilities she still
manages to remain on top, more or less. Even when her
son awoke one morning with an ear infection, she was
able to get him to the pediatrician, make new arrangements with the babysitter, and arrive at her office before
lunchtime, confident that all emergencies had been resolved. Moreover, now that Rebecca has much more responsibility than before having the baby, she is less
self-critical. "I have a kid, I work, I feel more deserving; I
can ask for a break and give myself a break too."

On the other hand, Rebecca is not used to being as
goofy as she is with her baby, and in her mind it feels less
mature to her, less dignified, to be gurgling and cooing on

an afternoon than to be working in an office with other adults, books, and numbers. She has always been a very verbal and articulate woman whose self-esteem has been based in large part on her intellectual achievements, and why not? Aren't these the abilities that gain her recognition and respect outside the playground, and aren't they the tools she has at her disposal to make an impact on the world outside her immediate family?

Charlotte also feels both the positive and the negative impact of motherhood on her self-esteem and sense of equilibrium. She observes that in the process of caring for her son she has had to stretch her patience and her imagination and as a consequence has become more aware of her strength as a human being. During the first couple of years of her son's life his sleep problems left her feeling physically exhausted and emotionally drained, but this did not prevent her from playing with him endlessly on rainy days, and she never felt that she seriously compromised her values in order to make *her* life easier. (Television was limited; her involvement was not.) Although Charlotte has fallen victim to self-doubt, wondering whether she is at times overly indulgent or at other times frighteningly explosive, she has never collapsed under the weight of all the additional pressures, and ultimately this gives her reason to feel proud. Yet because Charlotte has not focused as much as she had on her professional goals, they feel distant and diffuse, and when she feels depleted or overwhelmed with anger, or "stretched too thin," she eats too much and spends too much and feels overweight and out of control. Insofar as her sexual attractiveness and professional achievements have been implicated in her self-esteem, and she admits that they have, her experience of early motherhood has taken some of the wind out of her sails.

The power of motherhood to take away with one hand and give back with another is the experience of many women. Diane watched herself desperately and unsuccessfully try to soothe her baby's cries during his colic; she felt inadequate, but more than that, she felt guilty at being angry when she thought she should be understanding and sympathetic. An ambitious and capable woman, she was not used to failing, but when she tried to placate her wailing baby she could not help but feel that she was failing again and again. However, this too passed, and not only did she survive her first three months of mothering without turning into a witch, but her baby and her marriage are intact. Moreover, she has secured for herself a promotion and a raise since returning to her job after a three-month leave of absence, and her doubts about herself have faded into the past. From this vantage point (she has been back at work for nearly two years now), Diane feels stronger, more patient, and more, not less, certain that she can shape her life and her self to meet her changing needs.

For Judith, motherhood initiated a process of self-revelation that initially shook up her feelings of self-confidence but ultimately left her feeling more sure of herself, if humbler. Never having anticipated that she could seriously feel angry at a small and comparatively helpless creature, let alone one whom she loved so much, it was with shame, confusion, and self-condemnation that she witnessed herself struggling to contain her own irrational responses to her daughter's irrational temper tantrums. With time, however, Judith realized not only that she is not the unflappable and ever-empathic woman she deceived herself into thinking she was (the messy emotions she recalls having felt during childhood and adolescence were apparently still smoldering underground), but also that despite her deficiencies of character, her daughter is a happy, friendly child and their relationship is a very good one.

Self-revelations are not always flattering, but they are unavoidable in the process of mothering. Our frailties are exposed where once they were carefully disguised, and

our supposed best qualities temporarily fade in significance. But self-confidence based upon only a partial understanding of who we are is illusory, precarious, and in
the long run unstable, more bluster than substance. As
Freud noted, "When the wayfarer whistles in the dark, he
may be disavowing his timidity, but he does not see any
the more clearly for doing so."[19] As mothers, whistling in
the dark sometimes can help, but when we can no longer
bring ourselves to whistle, we have the opportunity to
confront our insecurities head on, to face the unvarnished
truth about who we are.

In addition to mentioning specific experiences in which
women do or do not exercise their "initiative, courage,
independence, talents" once they become mothers, it is
important to examine how the characteristics of babies
and young children are in themselves inherently threatening to a new mother's self-confidence. As Gina so aptly
observed, our babies adore us and we are the center of
their universe. This feels good, and even makes us feel
powerful, allows us to feel generous with our affections
and confident that we are good people. Ironically, however, it is this adulation that seduces women into feeling
that they should be able to do the impossible, as their
babies assume they can, and ultimately sets the stage for
their toddlers' unreasonable demands and irrational rages
when their mothers turn out not to be omniscient and
omnipotent. This is a normal aspect of development, painful as it may be for the mother who is the target of such
"abuse," but as family therapist and psychiatrist Salvador
Minuchin notes, "Children cannot grow and become indi-
viduated without rejecting and attacking."[20]

What mother has not felt impotent and frustrated when
her baby implores her to do something, anything, to make
things better—even when she knows not what to do and
could not do it even if she did? And who has not been the
target of the unparalleled rages of a two- or three-year-old
who has been thwarted "for his own good"? And when
the developmentally normal narcissism of the three-year-

old, which makes a child of that age so captivating, is expressed in the form of surliness and arrogance, what mother cannot help but feel sometimes that she is being treated by her loved one as if she were a scullery maid whose sole purpose is to wait on the little prince or princess? The assaults on a woman's dignity, her sense of herself as one who is respected and loved, take all shapes and forms; the naked emotion, the neediness, the narcissism, the sense of entitlement are not normally encountered in relations with adults. As adults we are generally more discreet, and to our horror our beloved babies and young children brazenly express the most reviled aspects of our unconscious.

Denise misses the "good reviews" she used to receive when she did a good job at work. She doesn't get them (nor should she expect to) from her two-and-a-half-year-old; she is taken for granted, as a good mother should be. Denise doesn't talk about how she responds to her daughter's "bad reviews" of her performance as a mother—and mothers inevitably get these bad reviews when they insist upon hats, or baths, or sharing of toys. Perhaps Denise is so confident that she is doing a good job as a mother that she is able to brush aside her daughter's reproaches, her expressions of disappointment, her accusations. Her reticence leaves this an open question.

Susan, however, is not so sanguine, and her three-year-old son's talent for playing her off against her husband and hitting her where it hurts the most "sets off a rocket inside her" as her anger intermingles with self-doubt. Susan reassures herself that her son is only trying to assert his masculinity, identify with his father, and separate from the baby-mother relationship he associates in his mind with her (she has taken some course in developmental psychology). Yet, when someone you love shouts insults containing a grain of truth at you, it is bound to be disconcerting, if not deflating. This is one of the liabilities of becoming a mother.

There are divergent opinions about the psychological benefits and disadvantages of combining work and motherhood. On the negative side, psychologists and sociologists have pointed out that women experience strain as they try to juggle schedules and create a balance between their loyalty to their family and their loyalty to their work. And then there are the sex-role stereotypes, which, by defining competitive, aggressive, and autonomous behavior as "masculine," generate a host of internal conflicts when women choose to behave in a competitive, aggressive, and autonomous fashion on the job and then worry lest they lose their "femininity" and with it their capacity to be good mothers. And finally, there are the interpersonal conflicts between husband and wife that surface when each, after having worked a full day on the job, feels that the other should be shouldering more of the domestic responsibilities.

On the positive side, however, it has been argued that work serves as a kind of psychological buffer, enabling women to derive satisfaction outside their family, so that they need not put all their eggs in one basket. This "buffer" has always been available to married men, who have been able to turn to their work as a way of compensating for the frustrations and disappointments that are bound to come up in the context of marriage and the family. In the language of sociology, women with "multiple roles" have more opportunities for "status enhancement" and "ego-gratification." As sociologist S. D. Sieber notes, "An individual with a wide array of role partners . . . is able to compensate for failure in any particular social sphere or relationship by falling back on other relationships."[21]

In support of this position, we should note that despite the potential for "overload" and conflicting allegiances, there is some evidence that involvement outside the home functions as a protection against depression. Depressed working women have been found to recover more quickly from their depression than housewives; that is, they are able to resume their normal level of social functioning more rapidly. Moreover, this effect seems to hold even when women work out of necessity rather than for "self-fulfillment."[22] One explanation for this finding may be that work provides women with an alternate source of social identity, from which they can derive their self-esteem. Going back to Horney's formulation, work would be expected to bolster a woman's self-confidence if in that context she is able to exercise initiative, creativity, and assert her independence.

While many nonworking mothers feel more confident than ever before about trusting their "instincts," and with time even become more tolerant of their shortcomings as mothers and as human beings, they are also frequently less secure about their status in the world, their ability to compete and excel in the workplace, and even their capacity to engage in intelligent conversation among strangers. Sandra, the lone "housewife" at a high school reunion filled with lawyers, doctors, writers, and designers, smiles bravely, and, armed with photographs of her children, listens intently to tales of worldly success. She speaks with just a hint of hesitation; the other housewives just didn't show up.

Whether this loss of confidence will be a transient experience, or one that will function as a self-fulfilling prophecy, unnecessarily inhibiting women from venturing forth once their children have grown, is difficult to know. Probably it will depend on a myriad of factors, most importantly the woman's needs and anxieties prior to having become a mother. What we can say, however, is that such changes in a woman's image of herself as an intelligent and capable human being reflect the conditions of full-time motherhood in this time and place, as much as the actual qualities of the individual women involved. Self-confidence in a man or a woman, a mother or a nonmother, needs to be nourished, updated, and tested again and again against new life challenges. Insofar as full-time mothers have limited opportunities to do just that, they may underestimate their capabilities and find, moreover, that nobody, not even the most well-intentioned, is able to argue convincingly otherwise.

Motherhood changes women's perceptions of themselves and in the process changes them as well. Our subjective experience is our reality, and the baby is part of our subjectivity as we are a large part of his. The crisis of identity precipitated by motherhood is resolved when the new picture of the self is experienced as more Me than any of the earlier versions, and when this feels right, at least for the time being.

7

The Marital Relationship

The Paradoxical Bonds of Parenting

The fact that parenthood is "normal" does not eliminate crisis. Death is also "normal" but continues to be a crisis event for most families.—E. E. LeMasters, Parenthood as Crisis, 1957

Having a baby has a contradictory effect on the marital relationship. It draws a husband and wife closer together but also frequently casts them into adversarial roles, as each struggles to assert his or her individual perspective on what they share in common. As parents, the bond between a husband and wife is irreversible and suddenly very tangible. Whereas marriage vows can be broken, and "I love you's" can be qualified and conditional, parenthood is (in most cases) unambiguous and not subject to renegotiation. When a husband gets a bonus at work, it is *his* bonus even if he shares it with his wife; when a wife gets a higher degree, it is *her* diploma even if the husband partakes of her pleasure. But the baby is *their* baby, not hers or his alone, and this kind of sharing is something qualitatively different. With the birth of a baby, the marital relationship is no longer exclusively a two-person affair. The baby is a source of mutual pride, joy, and anxiety; the baby is also the vehicle through which husbands and wives express feelings of tenderness, jealousy, competitiveness, and deprivation.

And yet, even though having a baby affirms as it expresses the intimacy existing between husband and wife, it also poses a threat to this intimacy. The "I" of singlehood and the "you and I" of marriage resist being submerged into the "we" of parenthood, even as the baby is embraced wholeheartedly. So while many men and women find it possible to let each other "live and let live," to be together and be separate too as long as they are simply husbands and wives, they lock horns as soon as they become fathers and mothers too.

Before the birth of the baby, energy, and love seemed to be in ample supply, at least retrospectively, but no more. As one woman put it, "I'm probably fulfilling less of all my husband's needs since the baby was born, because there is less time, I have less patience, and when there is a limited amount of energy and I have to choose whether to spend it on myself or on him I choose myself. Before there was enough, and I didn't have to make those choices." Another woman points out, however, that in her experience, it is not her husband's needs that are neglected, as much as hers. As is the case for many women, Rebecca has always taken it upon herself to be concerned over whether other people are comfortable and well taken care of. And while she does not perceive herself as an extraordinarily sensitive woman, she is aware that most of the men she has known, including her husband, are comparatively deficient in this regard. So in times of scarcity, her personal needs and pleasures are the ones most likely to be postponed or muffled or simply left unsatisfied.

When nerves are raw, emotional reserves are depleted, and self-confidence is faltering, seemingly trivial conflicts (should two-year-old Jennifer be allowed to decide who gives her a bath or shouldn't she?) assume monumental significance. Husband and wife attempt to accommodate the baby and one another without compromising their sense of personal integrity. But sometimes being accommodating and understanding with regard to a baby or a spouse feels less like cooperation and more like surrender, and then self-respect becomes implicated. Simple disagreements become complicated and unreasonably tumultuous affairs.

As the couple becomes a threesome, and the lives and feelings of husbands and wives are more tightly inter-woven than ever before, cherished illusions having to do with individual autonomy, marital harmony, and sexual equality are shattered. Moreover, romantic love and ratio-nal forms of discourse become anachronisms from a not-so-distant past just at the point when they are most needed as a reprieve from the raw emotions and dulling routiniza-tion of parenting. As tensions build, so pressures build to deny that there are any problems, and when the denial fails, as it must, there is the added guilt because of the possibility that problems within the marital relationship may ultimately affect the baby. Marital stability and har-monious relations, more important now than ever, are ironically more than ever under fire.

As we shall see in the discussion of triangular relation-ships and symbolic interactions that follows, when problems within the marriage are too threatening to acknowledge, they can be disguised and displaced onto other relation-ships, and unfortunately the baby or child sometimes serves in this capacity. When this happens, marital prob-lems are redefined as problems with Susie or Johnny—she's too timid, he's too aggressive; she needs more encouragement, he needs more limits. At a deeper level the "he's" and "she's" secretly stand in for both the adults and their children as wife and husband ask each other for more encouragement or more structure—in code.

While many women acknowledge that the marital rela-tionship suffers during the early stages of motherhood, for reasons we will soon discuss at length, it is also com-mon for women to feel more committed than ever to resolving whatever conflicts arise between them and their husbands. Having a baby is a jolt into adulthood, and though at various points most women vigorously protest their loss of innocence and whimsy and "regress" in bursts of temper or despair, they also realize that they are no longer playing at being grown-ups and that what they do now is serious business. From this perspective, their relationship to their husband matters more than ever.

Nancy claims to have fewer arguments with her husband since becoming a mother, and attributes this to her greater willingness to consider and then give in to her husband's requests. Before the baby, they frequently came to an impasse when her husband objected to her staying out late with friends after work. But now, not only does Nancy want to come home to be with her husband and new baby, but she reports feeling generally "less combative." Having left her adolescence behind with motherhood, she does not feel the need to constantly assert her autonomy at the expense of her relationship with her husband. She feels more mature—and it simply is not worth it any more. "Before you have children, when you are just going out with somebody, you can walk out on the relationship at any time. When you get married it is more difficult to walk out, so the arguments get very intense because you feel you have to live with this person for the rest of your life. But when you've had children, you have really made the decision that you plan to stay in this relationship. Therefore, why let the arguments get out of control, particularly over stupid things?" Similarly, Laura also consciously resists becoming embroiled in conflicts with her husband, noting that her son is a constant reminder that the bickering is not constructive.

If Nancy and Laura desist from fighting because they feel more mature and more committed to their marriages, other women find that they are more critical and more argumentative than ever—but for similar reasons. Being responsible for the well-being of a helpless and dependent child leads some women to feel that is it all the more crucial that their relationships with their husbands are the way they "should" be and that imperfections, theirs as well as their husband's, be ironed out if not eliminated entirely. They are less, not more, likely to "turn the other cheek," or dismiss minor annoyances as unimportant. If the bonds of marriage feel more permanent now that there is a baby, it is more critical than ever that they be comfortable and not oppressive.

Gina, for example, maintains that she and her husband argue more frequently and with greater intensity since the arrival of the baby—but she perceives this as an improvement in their relationship, rather than a sign of its decline. She and her husband have characteristically dreaded confrontation, but when Gina became pregnant unexpectedly they found it as difficult to remain silent about their ambivalent feelings as it was difficult to speak openly with each other. In speaking honestly they ran the risk of hurting and being hurt, but if they had remained silent, they would have sentenced themselves and their unborn baby to long-term disillusionment and alienation. Fearing that the unspoken would come back to haunt them (an interpersonal form of the "return of the repressed") and would eventually contaminate the entire family atmosphere, Gina and her husband decided to go into marital counseling. Whether it was the counseling or the realities of parenting or a combination of both, they are more comfortable voicing their feelings and opinions to one another now that they are parents. For them, this translates into more naked and heated conflict, but Gina is willing to pay this price. She has exchanged the illusion of perfect harmony for a stronger emotional connection to her husband, and because her husband also feels more connected to her, the specter of marital conflict is less frightening, avoidance of conflict less appealing.

Elizabeth admits that her husband finds her "horribly critical" of him as a father, and yet she reports this with a gleam in her eye as if it were testimony to the strength of their relationship rather than its tenuousness. From her description, her critical attitude does not reflect a fundamental rupture in their feelings for each other, for if it did she would not be so sanguine about her complaints and her husband's characterization of them. What it does reflect is her unwillingness to tolerate certain of her husband's shortcomings—his carelessness, his glazed expression when his mind is on his work and not on what she is talking to him about—when they may affect not only her but also their vulnerable baby. Because her investment in the marriage is greater, her expectations are higher, too. She feels justified in asking for more and secure enough in her husband's commitment to the marriage to do so.

The additional pressure many new parents feel to make their marriage work can also backfire, when, for example, in panic a husband begins to drink heavily upon finding out that his wife is expecting a baby, or a wife interprets every minor criticism from her husband as a potential betrayal, evidence of incompatibility, and a harbinger of future disaster. When there is no exit (who can walk out in the middle of an argument when there is a baby in the next room waiting to be bathed?), and yelling at the baby's father (or mother) in front of him (or her) feels too much like child abuse, anger builds up and every blemish in the marriage partner may stand out even more than ever, and every obstacle to marital harmony appears momentarily insurmountable.

Alicia's husband, Raymond, who had always felt uncomfortable because Alicia had more diplomas and earned more money than he, experienced fatherhood as one more challenge to his masculinity. Parenthood was the stage on which he felt he had to prove himself to be a man and his wife's equal. But the burden of proof was too great for Raymond, and after a brief period in which he refused to shoulder any of the domestic responsibilities in what appeared to be a feeble claim to masculine privilege, he provoked Alicia into a fury, then retreated to his mother's house in order not to be defeated by her head-on.

Alicia might have been more sympthetic to her husband's insecurities were it not for the baby and her own uncharacteristic need for emotional as well as practical support. (Prior to having the baby, Alicia had no problem playing "mother" to her impetuous "adolescent" husband.) Precisely because the stakes were so high, Raymond's betrayals were too painful to tolerate, his abdication of responsibility was too enraging, and the marriage could not withstand the pressure now that there was a real baby involved.

The Legacy of Sex Roles

Scene: A neighborhood playground.
Characters: A couple in their mid-thirties and their ten-month-old-baby boy.

Take 1: Mother mounts the slide with baby in tow. Father stands below, applauding their progress and urging them on to ever greater feats of courage. Baby looks uncertain, mother mirrors baby's expression, father continues to encourage.

Take 2: Mother, having descended from the slide with no major mishaps, straddles a rocking horse with the baby. Father, seated on a nearby bench, suggests that mother bring their son over to the sand so that he can play with the other children.

Take 3: Mother crouches in the sand with their son, gently pulling him away from the other children's sand castles, which he is intent on smashing. Father smiles, and from his seat on the bench takes a picture.

Take 4: Baby begins to scream with fury at having been thwarted in his efforts to smash sand castles, and mother attempts unsuccessfully to comfort him, glancing back toward her husband, who remains seated. Father asks why the baby is crying, and continues to watch.

Take 5: Mother holds crying baby, attempts to distract him, and talks to another mother, who tries to reassure her that a nap may just what is needed (her own gurgling baby had a long nap just before coming to the park). The women exchange knowing smiles. Father begins to read the paper.

Take 6: Baby continues to fuss, mother makes her excuses to her sandbox companion and informs father that it is time to return home. They gather up their belongings and exit (baby still crying in mother's arms). Mother looks furious, but masks her frustration with smiles, and does not ask her husband to hold the baby even while she strains to put on her shoes with the baby squirming in her arms. Father does not offer to help, but gathers together stroller. He appears unruffled and oblivious to all that has transpired.

In becoming parents, a husband and wife are inevitably confronted with new experiences and new role expectations. Some of these are shared, and as such they heighten feelings of intimacy and connectedness. In contrast, other experiences create a gulf between a husband and wife where none previously existed, as, for example, when a mother changes her work schedule and her husband's schedule remains essentially the same. Then feelings of alienation, resentment, and jealously infiltrate the marital relationship. "How can he understand my experience when he is only with the baby an hour or two in the evenings and on weekends?" "How can she understand my experience when her focus has changed and the baby consumes so much of her time and interest?"

The legacy of sex-role stereotypes casts its shadow on even the most modern marriages, to the horror *and* satisfaction of new parents. Though many women consciously repudiate traditional ideas about what it means to be a woman and what it means to be a man and are indignant and enraged when their husbands suddenly revert to their own fathers' style of parenting from the sidelines, many also harbor ambivalent feelings about leaving the past behind, because the past, with all its stereotypes and restrictions, includes their parents, their childhood experiences (good as well as bad), and their cultural heritage. Sometimes there is even nostalgia for a time when sex-role boundaries were clearer and life was apparently simpler.

But the past cannot be recaptured (nor would most women want to be in their mother's or grandmother's shoes for long), and women who are ecstatic at finally being mothers are also sensitive to infringements on their "inalienable rights" to liberty, justice, and the pursuit of happiness, even within the privacy of their own families. And so, with these two competing strains, internal and interpersonal conflicts about sex roles and parenting are rampant for women, if not for men.

For example, Deborah, who formerly worked full-time but has cut down to one day a week since having the baby, envies her husband's business lunches at comfortable restaurants and his freedom to walk down the street unencumbered on his way to work. At the same time, however, she acknowledges that she would be intensely jealous of him if they were to trade places and he were to be home with the baby instead of her. And although Charlotte insists that she misses her professional involvements (having also cut back from full-time to part-time work since the baby was born), yearns for time away from the family, and looks forward to the time when her son is in school five days a week and she will feel comfortable committing herself more fully to her career, she also admits that now that she is a mother, "old-fashioned" ideas of the family take hold of her imagination and she finds herself wanting to "be taken care of by a man" and resenting what she describes as her husband's "egalitarianism"—particularly since his ideas of equality are limited to the marketplace and she, not her husband, ends up doing most of the household chores.

Nancy, who has worked full-time since her daughter was two months old, rails against the women's liberation movement, which, she believes, deceived women into thinking that they had nothing to lose but their shackles. "You cannot have it all, and though you do give something up if you stop working, there is something to be said for being there to watch that child develop, and receive the love it wants to give." And yet, protests aside, Nancy has no plans to leave her job and lose the money, the status, and the excitement it brings to her life, nor would her husband want her to.

Nancy describes her husband as extremely attached to their daughter, but because he cannot or will not adjust his customary rhythm (the rhythm of a workaholic), he is incapable of caring for her more than a few hours at a time. He expresses his affection by buying things for her, making things for her, and "helping out" with child care when Nancy is in a pinch, and basically conforms to the traditional model of the devoted but peripheral baby-ignorant father. Despite his old-fashioned fatherly behavior, however, Nancy's husband is quite modern when it comes to the issue of whether Nancy should work full-time. He does not quarrel with the fact that they need the money she earns as much as they need the money he earns, and under such circumstances, he would never suggest that she quit her job and devote herself full-time to motherhood. Although there is no question in either of their minds that her job is indispensable, neither is there any question who is the primary parent—it is incontrovertibly Nancy. The convergence of tradition and modernity that Nancy describes epitomizes contemporary sex-role contradictions within marriage.

Traditionally the roles of mother and father were distinct and clearly defined—the father was responsible for earning the money, and the mother was responsible for caring for the children and maintaining the home. Although certain kinds of marital conflicts may have been and may still be avoided by adhering to this rigid division of labor, ultimately such an arrangement may widen the gulf between a husband and wife as each is relegated to a separate sphere of existence. This is graphically illustrated in social gatherings when women have generally tended to gravitate toward other women and men have tended to gravitate toward other men. Often men and women hold parallel conversations across the dinner table. Women talk women's talk and converge around the kitchen, and men talk men's talk in the yard, the den, or sprawled out in the living room. And why not? Since their lives have been radically different, they have very different interests and concerns. For those couples whose marriages conform more or less to this traditional model, becoming parents only crystallizes the presumed differences between men and women.

Today, however, many couples approach parenting without a clear blueprint to guide them or divide them. The past is of little help; wives work, often up until the last weeks of pregnancy, and it is assumed that they will work again at some point or another. Moreover, the doctrine of "separate but equal" is less convincing than in prior generations. Boundaries between a husband's and a wife's role as parent are fuzzy and overlapping, and the responsibilities and rights of the father and mother are subject to negotiation. Although both husband and wife may subscribe to an ideology of sexual equality and view their parents' relationship as antiquated, they are not really put to the test until the baby arrives. There was no problem being "equal"—or not equal, for that matter—because there were fewer responsibilities to be divided.

As parents, husbands and wives compete for time and space and recognition, and whether the person who takes primary responsibility for the child should also be the one who is primarily responsible for vacuuming, cooking, and marketing can become a subject of heated debate, laden with symbolic and ideological significance. The intensity of the emotions these debates engender should not be underestimated. Time spent mothering is not time spent making money or making a name or making history, but is a mother's "free" time therefore less valuable, more rightfully filled up with domestic chores? Is her need for freedom, leisure, or personal pursuits to be taken as seriously as her husband's? Does forgoing certain amenities necessarily go with the job description? Must a woman pay dearly for getting her heart's desire?

Democracy, within a nation or within a marriage, is always fertile ground for dissent, and today, patriarchal notions of marriage and the family are on the decline.[1] Sex-role stereotypes once used to justify and buttress traditional family structures are no longer sanctified by science, and even our religious institutions are reconsidering traditional distinctions between men's and women's social and spiritual functions. (Witness the growing numbers of female ministers and rabbis.) In this period of transition, in which there is little consensus and change leads to reaction and then reaction against the reaction, the potential for marital discord is greater than in previous generations.

In the present cultural climate men are generally willing and often even eager to "help" their wives bathe, feed, soothe, and play with their babies and young children, and many new mothers applaud their husband's loving devotion to their babies, expressing surprise and pleasure at the intensity of the attachment. It is not nearly as uncommon as it used to be for a man to be seen in a business suit or jeans pushing a stroller or sitting on the edge of the sandbox chatting with other parents (mostly mothers) as he supervises his toddler's sand play. And yet, lest we be deceived into believing that things have fundamentally changed and that the implicit obligations and rights of a "working" mother are no different from those of a "working" father, let us be reminded that mothers do not think of themselves as "helping out" when they bathe, feed, soothe, or play with their babies. What's more, it would never occur to most fathers to commend their wives for the love and devotion they give their children. A mother's responsibility for the care of the children is a given, whether she works outside the home or not. A father's responsibility is still perceived as primarily an economic one, though today affection and attachment are also considered characteristics of the "good" father. Whatever he gives in the way of actual caretaking is a bonus, an exception that proves the rule, or even an act of philanthropy, for which he expects—and usually receives—special commendation.

If some men resist conforming to this mold—and of course some do genuinely share the responsibilities with their wives—the very fact that the mold exists and continues to be prevalent confers an aura of specialness on the father who deviates, and this in itself makes his experience different from his wife's. The individual's behavior cannot be divorced from its social context, and the father who does the unexpected knows that he will not be censured when and if he decides to change his mind and assume a more peripheral parental role.[2]

Some women prefer it this way; they are secretly if not openly pleased that they, not their husbands, are incontrovertibly the primary parent. Although they lament the loss of free time and the missed opportunities for career advancement and adult forms of entertainment, they express no desire to live, work, or parent as their husbands do if that would mean that they would have to give up some of their domestic power. "He lets me be the authority in matters having to do with the baby, and this suits me because I don't like to be questioned very much. He basically thinks I'm a good mother." And they are amused or even horrified at the idea of changing places with their husbands. "I'd feel I was missing something," says one woman; "I'd be terribly jealous," says another. Elizabeth even found it disconcerting when her friend Claire temporarily assumed a relatively peripheral role in the day-today care of her daughter, interpreting it as a reflection of some unresolved psychological conflicts. And Judith, a working woman herself, could not suppress the feeling that there was something peculiar about a particular couple she knew only superficially, in which the husband and wife had reversed roles completely. Apparently in some circles it is acceptable for a woman to work outside the home as long as she continues to function as primary parent. But when a man adopts the role of homemaker he and his wife are automatically viewed with suspicion. Women as well as men often wonder whether there isn't something askew in the marriage—is he "hen-pecked"? Or is something wrong with him—is he slothful? disabled? unambitious?

Many women, however, are far more ambivalent than Elizabeth claims to be, and though they have difficulty asking their husbands for help with the baby, they feel frustrated and resentful when help is not forthcoming and their husbands fail to volunteer their services and participate on a more equal basis. "Unless I specifically ask Steve to read to Mara so that I can make the dinner without interruptions, he'll just sit there and read the newspaper and let me handle everything. It would never occur to him that I have worked all day too, and that perhaps I, as much as he, would enjoy retreating behind the paper for a few minutes. Of course I could never retreat as he does, or be so oblivious to Mara's desire for attention. It would be inconceivable to me to ignore her after being away from her most of the day, but it seems to come naturally to him!"

Although Judith envies her husband's apparent freedom, and wishes sometimes that she were the one who could screen out the world at will, she claims that this way of being does not suit her temperament, and what she really wants is for her husband to be more like her. This she often feels is a losing battle, and one she is not even convinced she has a right to wage. Her husband argues persuasively that husbands and wives are not and should not be expected to be clones of one another, and therefore she has no right to ask him to respond differently; does he ask her to be more like him? She agrees in theory, but she continues to find it hard to accept their differences when it means that she, not he, is on call twenty-four hours a day.

While some mothers are hesitant about diluting the intensity of their relationship with their child and find it difficult to relinquish control over their child's care despite their protests otherwise—"When Teddy had colic and it was Stuart's turn to rock him I usually hung out with them. . . . I felt too anxious and guilty to just read a book or take a bath"—there are many others who are certain that it is their husband's unconscious assumptions about the roles and capabilities of mothers and fathers, not theirs, that are the overriding cause of the imbalance that develops in the marriage. Moreover, they are frustrated and unwilling to tolerate what feels to them to be an anachronistic arrangement, especially one that is inherently inequitable.

Diane describes her husband as having "regressed" during the first several months of parenthood to an earlier stage in their relationship, when he behaved as if he didn't know how to shop, or cook, or clean. It was as if now that there was a baby in the house, all the chores they had shared as a married couple mysteriously fell within her domain of expertise simply because she was a mother now. This did not sit well with Diane at all. At forty, holding down a full-time administrative position in a hospital, she had no inclination to transform herself into the traditional housewife. Being the expert cook, cleaner, and homemaker had little romantic appeal. After months of intense conflict with her selectively "helpless" husband, during which time she adamantly refused to succumb to stereotypic notions of what men can do and what women can do, marital equilibrium was restored.

Since sex roles are often symbolically linked to men's and women's sexual identity—the "masculine man" does not do housework, the "feminine woman" is protected and supported by her husband—they resist bending to reason, and even pleas for justice fall on deaf ears. Consequently, many women are not as successful as Diane in challenging their husband's assumptions about domestic responsibilities (or their own assumptions about what they *should* be doing at home), and most surveys indicate that in addition to being primarily responsible for child-care arrangements women continue to shoulder most of the responsibility for cooking and cleaning even when they work outside the home full-time. What these studies do not investigate is how this imbalance affects the marital relationship. In many cases feelings of bitterness or resignation develop, and these sentiments invariably contaminate other aspects of the marital relationship, particularly when verbal means of communication are abandoned and compromise is not forthcoming. The child, being acutely attuned to the emotional tenor of his parent's relationship, may conclude that marriage and family life are the bane of existence and that intimacy between men and women is emotionally draining rather than restorative. The child is thus a casualty in the silent war between the sexes.

Sometimes the only way a woman can restore a sense of balance in the marriage is to either go on strike and stop giving or else find alternate means of replenishing herself. She may let the house go, neglect to buy her husband his favorite beer or make him his favorite dishes, or she may gradually become uninterested in sex. In short, she withholds from her husband what is in her power to withhold. Or she may do as Charlotte did when she felt she was not getting enough support from her husband, and go on spending sprees. Both strategies are indirect ways in which a woman can take back when she feels she has given too much and her husband has not given enough, but both measures ultimately lead to more disappointment and more conflict. A husband becomes sexually frustrated and angry, and instead of giving more time and tenderness to his needy wife he begins to work overtime or glues himself to the television set as soon as he comes home from work. Or anxious over his wife's mounting credit card bills and their rapidly dwindling bank account, he may economize on his wife's next birthday present.

Alternatively, a woman may decide to decrease her hours on her job, or even quit her job altogether out of exhaustion—and anger. Although this may alleviate some of the pressure she experiences while trying to do two jobs at once, it will not eliminate any lingering feelings of resentment over the fact that her husband was not willing to pitch in so that she could manage both. She has had to sacrifice the work she enjoys in order to have the pleasures of family life, whereas, from her perspective, her husband sacrifices nothing and seems to be able to have his cake and eat it too. If he misses out on the pleasures of being home with the baby (which he does), his loss is not equivalent to hers, because in most cases he does not experience it as a loss, undoubtedly preferring to continue to do just what he is doing.

When a woman decides to leave work or radically reduce her hours, this can create a whole new set of pressures on the marital relationship, particularly if she misses the outside involvement or the family depends on her income to make ends meet. Feelings of mutual resentment may develop, expressed by a wife who suddenly begrudges her husband the business trips that take him away from the family, or a husband who patronizingly scrutinizes his wife's credit card bills suspiciously.

A woman who suddenly finds herself largely isolated from her peers because of changes in her work involvement may become overly dependent upon her husband to fulfill her needs for adult contact, emotional support, and intellectual stimulation. Moreover, she may feel disappointed and angry when he fails to satisfy these needs— and being just one person, he is bound to fail. Her increased emotional and financial dependency creates tension within the marriage, tension that did not exist when their lives were more similar and their needs more complementary. Her husband may start to feel that she is cloying or critical and overdemanding; the wife may berate herself for her dependency needs and absorb the blame for the marital conflicts. (She, not her husband, is the one who is complaining; she has become the proverbial nag.) Her loss of self-esteem may further compound her experience of dependency on her husband to affirm her worth as a wife and a mother, and the cycle of dependency and anger recommences. Neither partner may realize that the wife's "personality" changes are an outgrowth of changes in her daily life, and it becomes *her* problem, rather than *theirs*.

Although Denise's decision to leave her job, one to which she had returned after a seven-month leave of absence, was motivated by many factors, it is not insignificant that she describes her husband as *completely* unwilling to help with the housework. Of course, Marty had never helped before the baby came along, but Denise naïvely assumed that as a fair-minded person and loving husband, Marty would automatically pitch in when the work began to mount and she began to feel debilitated.

Whether Marty's refusal to help reflects an unconscious dynamic between the couple, which allowed each partner to do what he or she really wanted to do but did not dare ask for explicitly, is unclear. But it is evident that his behavior wittingly or unwittingly encouraged her to make the decision she ultimately did, which was to leave work and stay home full-time.

Since Denise and her husband were unable to afford paid help (this they agreed upon), and Denise was unable to induce her husband to change his ideas or his behavior regarding housework, she was left feeling exhausted and unhappy. This was not what she had envisioned when she became a mother. The traditional arrangement between husband and wife, which she grew up with and had never really rejected, gradually became more and more attractive to her. It was a respectable way out of an otherwise untenable situation. If Denise's husband's response to parenthood had an impact on Denise's decision to stay home full-time, her decision to leave her job put pressure on him to be a "success" since he now had to earn enough money to support his family single-handedly. Making a name for himself in his field became more crucial than ever. This means overtime and less time with the family. Whether these changes in Denise and in her husband will successfully restore the balance within the marital relationship, which was disturbed when Denise and her husband became parents, or whether the changes will sow the seeds of future conflict and alienation, is impossible to know. For that we would have to explore more fully how Denise feels about her husband's lack of cooperation in the home (does it aggravate her, or secretly please her?), and how her husband feels about the new financial pressures brought about by Denise's unanticipated withdrawal from the work force (does it make him mostly anxious, or mostly proud?). It is clear, however, that the new arrangement has altered the relationship between husband and wife and that the baby was the impetus for this transformation.

It is not only the women who work full-time and who then come home to work the "second shift" who are disturbed by the rigid sex roles and role-related expectations and values that insidiously shape their relationships to their husbands. The women who cut back on their work outside the home while their husbands continue, as usual, in their careers find that they are confronted with perhaps an even more complicated set of problems. They sometimes feel that they are neither fish nor fowl, neither "homemaker" nor "working woman." This is particularly true for women who work part-time at home such as editors, designers, and various consultants, who, on account of the flexibility of their work schedule, may not only be vulnerable to intrusions but may also minimize the extent of their work commitment. Their arrangements with their husbands do not really fit the "traditional" mold, because they are committed to their identity as workers and may intend to return to full-time employment at a later date. But their role within the family is clearly not the same as their husbands' role; though there is some overlap, it is unclear just how much.

Since these women are not technically "working" full-time, they may feel obligated to do all the unpleasant domestic chores that, prior to having had the baby, they shared with their husbands more equally. Both husbands and wives often assume that since the wives are home part-time they should be the ones to take care of the home all the time. In the abstract this arrangement sounds quite reasonable to both husband and wife. But after the baby becomes a material reality and not just an object of fantasy, it is frequently the mother, not the father, who starts to question the justice of this division of labor. After all, she, not her husband, is home during the day with their baby, and she, not he, has the opportunity to experience directly how easily the baby consumes her time and attention and how little there is left over for domestic chores.

But even after having come to this realization, a woman who works part-time may feel that she can no longer claim to be her husband's equal in terms of the marketplace and may conclude therefore that she is no longer justified in asking him to take equal responsibility in the home. Through some peculiar logic, it seems that the person who is not earning the bulk of the money should "naturally" do all the unpaid domestic work by way of recompense.

This may mean that a woman has substantially less leisure time than her husband, since it is assumed that he, having worked all day, has the right to relax on evenings and on the weekends. Or it may be that they work an equal number of hours, but that a greater proportion of her work time is spent doing unskilled and tedious activities. While initially this may seem as equitable as it seems to be inevitable, after months of ninety-five-hour weeks, which include part-time work, child care, and domestic chores, many women begin to get suspicious and question whether the scales are really balanced, and then the arguments ensue. What is comparable to what? And how does one measure what is fair without clear measuring rods and without precedents?

Elizabeth loved being a mother and being able to pursue her graduate work at her own slow pace, but this did not inure her to feelings of outrage at her husband, whose unspoken privilege it was to spend the evening according to his whim. She knew that there was mopping and ironing to do after Jennifer went to bed, and also knew that she was the one designated to do it, and if not then, when? She wasn't going to graduate school for this! It all felt somehow demeaning. She would ask herself on bad days whether she wasn't selling herself short. And yet, how could she ask her husband to help when she had chosen to be home with the baby most of every day, loved it, and her earnings since the baby arrived were negligible?

The legacy of sex roles emerges as a source of conflict between husband and wife when one partner resists conforming to the other's definition of these roles. This is not uncommon today. Women often expect their husbands to be less like their fathers than they actually are; men often expect their wives to be more like their mothers, yet expect them to be modern women who can supplement the family income all the same.

And for many women and men there are moments when they are only too eager to assume the role of the prototypic mother or father. It is a familiar and comfortable pleasure (fleeting as it may be) to talk with other mothers about motherhood and babies while the men discuss money, politics, and other "worldly" concerns. It is a déjà vu experience, a childhood fantasy come true, a dance sequence witnessed hundreds of times and one they have been waiting for years to try out for themselves. Although we are "wiser" about these things than our mothers and fathers, and wary of the seduction of traditional sex roles, parenthood gives women and men the permission to play the parts that have been choreographed

through the ages (if only for a brief interlude), a reprieve
from the realities of modern times.

Competing Loyalties: Baby Talk and Adult Forms of Communication

> *There is simply no question who comes first. Billy does.
> He is two years old and Neil is thirty-eight.—Ann,
> thirty-seven, mother of a two-year-old boy*

> *According to my husband's philosophy, our relation-
> ship is the most important, because one day our daugh-
> ter will be gone and what we have as a couple will be
> vital. I agree in principle, but my feelings are less
> clear-cut. When there is not enough time or energy to
> give to the baby, and to my husband, and to me, I give
> to her and to me, and leave him out.—Deborah, thirty-
> five, mother of an eighteen-month-old girl*

> *My husband says we don't have sex enough, and I say
> we don't do enough of the things that naturally lead up
> to having sex. I worry that we don't talk to each other,
> but then he brings it all back to sex, and then I have to
> worry about that too.—Susan, forty-four, mother of a
> three-and-a-half-year-old boy*

In love and in marriage we keep accounts, compute
balances, and silently tally our credits and debits as much
as we share and compromise. If we are not aware of our
secret system of bookkeeping (and under "good-enough"
circumstances we generally are not), it is only because our
gains and our losses cancel each other out and we come to
trust that as we give of ourselves we are being replenished in one form or another.[3]
Although many of us may find this description of the
marital relationship difficult to reconcile with romantic
and religious images of union and selflessness, most of us
who have experienced imbalance or inequity, fleeting as

the feeling may have been, can vouch for the fact that
accounts are kept even among intimates. And why not?
Don't all human relationships hinge upon questions of
loyalty and betrayal? Aren't balance, reciprocity, and mutual gratification worthy goals for which to strive? As
anthropologist Jules Henry notes in his analysis of love:
"Saints in remote eastern deserts may be able to imagine a
blending of two souls in love, but other people experience
love as getting and returning (requiting)."[4]

From the moment we realize that our desires do not
always correspond with the desires of those we love and
depend upon, we are faced with the problem of having to
choose between competing interests. This is why, according to Freud, conflict and compromise are inherent to the
human condition.[5] At the very earliest stage of development the question may take the form of "me versus
mother"—"my desires versus hers"—a most difficult dilemma to resolve if neither me nor mother is unwilling to
negotiate a compromise. When a third party enters the
picture, as invariably happens sooner or later, the problem of loyalty and betrayal takes new, more complicated
forms—me and daddy versus mommy, or me and mommy
versus daddy, or me, mommy, and daddy versus everybody
else are obvious, though often unfortunate, possibilities.

In addition to the conflicting loyalties each of us experiences within the family, by the time we reach adolescence
our loyalty to friends and to a particular peer group with
which we identify represents a challenge to the authority
and influence of our parents; we waver back and forth
between home base and the outside world even as we
explicitly reject one for the other.[6] Marriage is one more
complicating factor, and loyalty to a spouse competes
with loyalty to parents and friends ("those wedding bells
have broken up that old gang of mine").

But just as marriage represents a turning point in a
person's relationship to his or her family of origin, loosening the bonds between parents and their adult children as
new alliances are formed and old allegiances yield pri-

macy to the new, so too the birth of a baby destabilizes the marital relationship. Although the relationship between husband and wife may continue to be the focal point of the family (and most family therapists and theoreticians would argue that it is critical that it does not become submerged in parenting), the marital relationship is no longer exclusive.

The baby is an additional source of energy, love, anxiety, and frustration and requires a goodly portion of the time, energy, and love that husband and wife have previously shared among themselves. Precisely because a baby is so helpless, so vulnerable, and so dependent upon its parents for its very survival, it is simultaneously an object of their identification and a fearsome rival for their attention and affection. Love and duty conspire to silence a jealous parent's protest, and feelings of competition, deprivation, and neglect are often forced to fester beneath the surface. But then there are the explosions about who has more time, who has more freedom, who is being left out, and finally, who is spoiling everything by being so ungenerous and so witholding?

Competing loyalties are most painful and most difficult to resolve when the attachments on either side are intense and the stakes are high for preserving both relationships. This is precisely the predicament a new mother finds herself in when her baby competes with her husband for her care and attention. Evenings, dinnertime, weekends, and vacations are situations particularly conducive to conflicts of this nature, because these are times when the adults are most likely to expect and want the adult forms of intimacy they were accustomed to getting before the baby arrived. Making love, talking, "going out," or just spending a quiet evening at home listening to music are activities that can no longer be taken for granted with a baby or small child in the house, yet these are nourishing to women and men and sustain the intimacy between a husband and wife.

Family therapists speak of the problems that ensue when

the marital relationship is subsumed in the relationships between parents and their children, and they emphasize the importance of preserving intergenerational boundaries by which the adults and their relationship are clearly separated from the children. (We are not talking about an authoritarian model of the family, but simply one in which there is respect for differences, and parents do not surrender their personhood at the door.) Salvador Minuchin, a psychiatrist who is known for his "structural" approach to family therapy, emphasizes the importance of maintaining clear and distinct roles for parents and children, noting that "a boundary must be drawn which allows the child access to both parents while excluding him from spouse functions."[7] This boundary protects the children from being pulled into the middle of their parents' quarrels, while at the same time it grants parents the permission to continue to function as husband and wife.

What may be self-evident from a theoretical point of view (who would disagree that the marriage must not be neglected?) is, practically speaking, a very complicated affair. Where loyalty to one's marriage leaves off and selfishness and immaturity begin is a question many mothers of good conscience ask themselves. Moreover, once it has been decided that a baby or young child has gotten a fair share of attention, interest, and love, and that it is time to attend to other concerns, namely the needs of the woman and man who are serving as its parents, the protests, temper tantrums, and debates that ensue are themselves time-consuming and depleting.

The toddler whose desires have been postponed so that its parents can continue their discussion about the crisis in the Middle East or the latest Supreme Court decision escalates the crisis in the family as he takes this opportunity to engage in a battle of the wills. The three-year-old argues each case so exhaustively and responds so indignantly when a judgment is not in her favor that at least in the short run setting appropriate limits may take more time and energy away from the marital relationship than not attempting to set limits at all. In either case, the focus remains on the child and the parent-child relationship, and the spouse and the marital relationship are relegated to the periphery.

The external barriers to intimacy between husband and wife are obvious to everyone—parents are exhausted, children are demanding, there's no time to talk, it is not the right moment for sex; and when people feel deprived and depleted, tempers flare. But the seldom-articulated internal conflicts of loyalty are as much an ingredient in the atmosphere between husband and wife as anything else.

Gina, for example, feels torn between her husband's desire to talk to her when he comes home from work, her desire to get dinner on the table, and her daughter's desire, which she expresses loudly and clearly, for undivided attention. Gina would like to hear about her husband's day; moreover, she would like to talk with him about hers—but she is acutely aware that her three-year-old daughter hasn't seen her since early in the morning and needs the intimacy, the focused contact more than anyone. Since she must frustrate her husband (and herself for that matter) to satisfy her daughter, whose needs are, after all, more pressing, and with whom she is intensely identified she feels tied in a knot. When and if she explodes, her husband (who, after all, is only asking for what he always asked for and what they both want) is the most likely target. When and if he explodes ("Why is she so preoccupied all the time with the baby? Why is she so uninterested in what concerns me?"), she is likely to feel unjustly accused of crimes she has indeed committed, but under extenuating circumstances. She may oscillate between feeling twinges of guilt over her inattentiveness to her husband (she must admit she does not listen as carefully as she should, did, and wants to) and feeling enraged at her husband's insensitivity to her dilemma.

When a mother feels that by giving to the baby she is unintentionally betraying her spouse, or vice versa, she may become so angry at having been placed in such an impossible situation that she resolves the problem of conflicting loyalties by disavowing her loyalty to one or the other. For example, Roseanne and her husband had fundamental disagreements about their daughter's eating habits and preferences. Roseanne believed that their daughter should eat when she was hungry and that she should not be pressured to eat what she did not wish to. Her husband thought otherwise, and mealtimes became a battle of wills as he, despite her pleas, urged their daughter to have just one more bite. It was not simply a matter of nourishment, but a matter of principle. This situation presented a conflict of loyalties for Roseanne as she agonized over whether or not she should intervene in order to rescue her daughter (herself as a child) from her husband's intrusiveness at the risk of incurring his wrath and wounding his pride.

The conflict between Roseanne and her husband began as a disagreement about the best way to approach feeding, but developed into a battleground upon which Roseanne felt forced to choose between her daughter's welfare and her husband's need to father in the way he knew how. Unable to be both a loyal wife *and* a protective mother, and feeling that her daughter was at a disadvantage in her struggle with her father to get her to eat what he thought she needed, Roseanne secretly joined forces with her daughter and began to lie to her husband when he asked her about their daughter's food consumption during the day. Although she managed to preserve a semblance of marital unity, her duplicitous behavior represented a betrayal of her loyalty to her husband, and this reinforced a growing sense of alienation from him and their relationship.

Most schisms that develop within the marital relationship are more subtle, as when a husband settles into a peripheral role in relation to his wife and child, and both partners resign themselves, if only temporarily, to the loss of the romantic. But if this gradual resignation and emotional withdrawal are less tumultuous than the bitter arguments and childish tantrums other couples such as Roseanne and her husband engage in, the loss of intimacy may be as far-reaching, and perhaps more insidious.

Fleeting feelings of deprivation and resentment between a husband and wife are common, but often they are balanced by a basic sense of sharing and trust ("every night we look at each other and marvel at how he's the best baby in the world"). Nevertheless, even when parenting is more a source of mutual joy than antagonism, many women acknowledge that their relationship with their husband has taken a back seat and that both of them have suffered on that account.

Some Properties of Triangles

> *His love for that baby is so intense that sometimes I feel that I'm a baby-machine and that is why he married me.—Nancy, twenty-nine, mother of a four-month-old girl*

> *When I was nursing all the time, my husband felt jealous because I had nothing to give anybody else. . . . Now he tells me Jesse and I enact the oedipal crisis every day—he's smitten and I adore him.—Cheryl, thirty-nine, mother of a two-and-a-half-year-old boy*

> *My husband can't not be jealous of the relationship I have with Sarah. . . . She clearly prefers me.—Deborah, thirty-five, mother of an eighteen-month-old girl*

From *Oedipus Rex* to *Anna Karenina* to *Gone with the Wind*, triangular relationships have featured prominently in love stories.[8] Perhaps this is because the triangle has the power to trigger deep-seated and unresolved feelings of jealousy and competitiveness, deprivation and triumph. In a triangle, alliances form and shift, loyalties are affirmed and betrayed, and communication between any two points is reflected through the eyes of a third party.

Hence, there are multiple layers of meaning. An attack on one person may be experienced as an attack on his or her "ally"; whether it is meant as such or not, intimacy between two threatens the third with exclusion. With the triangle, the stage is set for us to act out dramas that originated in our own childhood relationships with mothers, fathers, and siblings.

Before the baby is born conflicts between a wife and a husband are more likely simply to be conflicts between the two of them. Of course, it could be argued that each partner brings to the marriage a large cast of real and imaginary characters from the past, and that each character volunteers an opinion about all aspects of the marital relationship, transforming a dialogue between spouses into an open forum.[9] But this is mixing fact and fantasy, and whatever archaic characters we surreptitiously introduce into our marriages there are always only two directors, and they are ultimately responsible for the action. When a husband sends a message to his wife, it may be tender or angry, distancing or engaging, insensitive or finely tuned; he may express it directly in words or indirectly through his actions or omissions; but the message is meant for her and has significance for their relationship alone. (Unless there is another triangular relationship involved—a mother, a lover, a sibling—in which a third party is directly affected by the marital relationship.)

When a baby is born, this changes. Messages get crossed, relationships blend into one another, feelings are unintentionally hurt, power struggles arise, and a cycle of hurt and reprisal begins. Women may find themselves jealous of the tender, loving attention their husbands shower upon their baby— attention they themselves hunger for at times and do not now receive.

Nancy, for example, had pleaded with her husband for a year to buy a humidifier, and then an air conditioner, for their home, but it was not until the baby came along that he relented and agreed to make the necessary purchases. Whereas her husband could dismiss her discomfort, he could not or chose not to ignore their baby's. From an objective point of view Nancy's suffering was not tremendous, and moreover, she could have gone out and purchased the appliances herself if the issue had been simply her physical discomfort—but it wasn't. The conflict between her and her husband was about giving and taking within their relationship, as well as about the value of self-denial versus self-indulgence, hers and his. It assumed yet greater symbolic significance when Nancy's husband responded to their daughter more indulgently than he had responded to her. In the context of the threesome she felt like the proverbial stepdaughter, the family member who was "relatively deprived."[10]

More commonly, however, it is the husbands who feel excluded and peripheral as their wives become absorbed in the baby and are too preoccupied to participate wholeheartedly in what concerns their husbands—sex, food, literature, and politics, in his office or in the world, to name a few possibilities. For many women, sex, the household chores, and the world outside are clearly not their priorities, and though husbands may be able to acknowledge that comforting or playing with a baby is a more immediately pressing concern than what is on their minds or what is being experienced in their bodies, they feel that their wives have become selectively callous. If they do not explode, husbands may retaliate in more subtle ways, and months later their wives may complain that they are insensitive, or may accuse them of being interested only in sex. This may be an accurate appraisal of their husbands' behavior, but it is only one link in the intricate chain of interpersonal events.

Laura reports that as soon as she found out she was pregnant her husband began to worry whether there would be room for him in the family. Ironically, the tables turned once the baby came, and her husband's fears inspired him to devote himself so fully to his role as father that Laura began to feel left out. Not only did he not allow himself to dangle unconnected at the edge of the family, but from

her vantage point, he allowed the baby and his relationship to the baby to put a wedge between him and her.
"Fred refuses to spend time away from Tom, he puts a lot
of his energy into being a father, and I feel it is a way of
avoiding our relationship."

Being second fiddle is rarely a comfortable position, and
when a husband or wife feels as if he or she is in the
process of being relegated to that position in the family,
eating leftovers in the kitchen while the others are feast-
ing in the dining room, the response may be either to
withdraw even more into the shadows and seek solace
elsewhere, or to fight to maintain a foothold wherever
possible. When the coming of a baby means being second
in the eyes of the baby as well as second in the eyes of a
spouse, the sense of loss is compounded and the battle to
regain love and power may be fought on two fronts.

When one partner feels left out in the cold, hurt and
angry feelings contaminate the relationship between husband and wife, as well as the relationships each parent
has with the child, in what can become a vicious cycle. A
husband or wife who feels neglected and angry at the loss
of marital intimacy may displace these feelings onto the
baby, irrational as this may be—"If it weren't for him [the
baby]. . . . He's already spoiled." Alternately, frustration
with the baby may be displaced onto a spouse: "If only he
[my husband] had been gentler, more patient, less indulgent the baby would be calmer, more independent, less
demanding." In the first case the baby is placed in the
middle of the martial relationship; instead of one spouse
lodging complaints against the other for his or her failure
to satisfy, the baby is blamed for their problems. In the
second case the husband is placed between the mother
and the baby, and he becomes the target of her frustration.
The scapegoat, he allows her to retain an image of herself
as a perfectly loving mother of a perfectly lovable child—
she is not angry at her child but at its father. In either
instance the boundaries between relationships have be-

come blurred and communication within the marriage has broken down.

Of course, marital conflicts rooted in feelings of deprivation and frustration exist prior to and independently of babies and children. It would be naïve and dishonest to suggest otherwise. In his analysis of family problems, Nathan Ackerman notes that "marital partners who are caught in conflicts that they cannot resolve often maintain a defensive distance by putting other family members between them."[11] The birth of a baby may intensify these feelings by cutting off access to the customary channels of satisfaction within and outside of the marriage. Moreover, by introducing a third party into the family the troubled couple may find it easier to avoid confronting their feelings about each other head-on. Inadvertently, the baby becomes a buffer, a scapegoat, or simply a diversion from the problems within the marriage.[12]

Many new parents are aware that they should avoid arguing in front of their child, particularly about things that concern him. Not only might it be upsetting for a child to see his parents angry at each other, but also it may encourage his natural propensity to try to split the marital pair and seduce mother or father into an unholy alliance. In the long run, this spells disaster.

According to Freud, the desire on the part of the child to do away with one parent or the other who is a rival in love is "all too human" (to borrow from Neitzsche), and the basis of the oedpial conflict. As psychoanalysts have discovered, however, the so-called oedipal victory, in which a boy or girl succeeds in his or her quest for his parent's exclusive love and symbolically supplants his parent as a primary love object, is really no victory at all. Caught in the middle of an unsatisfying marital relationship, the child will have to pay a very high price for his "favored" position. He feels guilty at having usurped one parent's position, but also feels guilty when he tries to extricate himself from his role as surrogate spouse, because in doing so it feels as if he is betraying the parent who depends upon him to fulfill this function.[13] But when the bond between a husband and wife is frayed by repeated arguments about sex, love, time, and space, the child offers a parent not only an alternative source of gratification, but also functions as a lovable and loving ally when the marital partner appears neither lovable, loving, nor or an ally. When this happens, the "united front" is abandoned, if only temporarily, and the superpowers compete for control of the developing child.

Although sometimes struggles for control over the child's life are just that—struggles for control, with the content being largely irrelevant—many times there are real, substantive conflicts between a wife and husband about what constitutes "good parenting." These ideological differences divide wives and husbands and create the conditions in which child-parent alliances encroach upon the marital relationship. Ideas about "how to parent" and "what a good child should and should not do" are rarely motivated purely by reason and therefore do not bend to reason. They generally express a spouse's individual personality characteristics, predating the baby and the marriage. As such, these ideas are highly resistant to change and may represent an unending source of marital conflict.

It is not uncommon for the personalities of husbands and wives to complement rather than to mirror each other. Jack Sprat and his wife are paradigmatic of the maxim "opposites attract." Personality differences between husbands and wives often create a balance within the marriage, even when they foment conflict, because they allow each partner to express vicariously what he or she finds difficult or impossible to express directly. Some obvious examples are the socially awkward man who enjoys his wife's sociability and garrulousness but who also finds these qualities embarrassing and even contemptible; or the emotionally intense woman who admires her husband's cool-headed reserve but who nevertheless challenges him to "feel" as fully as she does. But when one person's personality encroaches upon the other's freedom to be different and to shape his life as he sees fit, then the attraction wanes, and a power struggle is likely to ensue.

Parenting is a special case in which an attitude of tolerance toward a spouse's differences is difficult to maintain. Parents often experience their child as an extension of the self, and yet unlike the self, the child is rightfully subject to the influence of both parents. When either a husband or wife feels that the other is jeopardizing their child's psychological or physical well-being, the impulse to intervene can be irresistible.

In the context of parenting, differences between a wife and a husband are magnified as each approaches the impressionable child in his or her own particular way. One partner may, for example, implore the other to be more indulgent, the other in turn may rebuke the first for being insufficiently demanding. One pleads for more leniency, whereas his partner insists that their child needs limits and structure, not empathy. A husband wishes his wife were more flexible, less concerned with being the virtuous mother, and she in turn wishes he were less carefree and more thoughtful. These conflicts about how best to care for a child are infused with a passion and intensity that belie their surface content because they express more fundamental conflicts about meaning, value, and how best to live one's life. Indoctrinated into believing that they should present a united front to their child, husbands and wives may feel that they are forced into a battle of wills in which one parent's personality preferences must defer to the other's. The prospect of becoming homogenized parents can represent a "clear and present danger," however, when a husband and wife have distinctly different personalities, and compromise feels too much like a betrayal of the baby and through identification a betrayal of the self.

Judith, for example, acknowledged that her husband

has always been perfectionistic with himself, with her, and with his work. Although she admits that his demanding and critical attitude has disturbed her since the beginning of their relationship, she claims to have been able to distance herself emotionally, accepting more or less that this is a part of her husband's character, well intended if misguided, and unlikely ever to change. Once the baby was implicated, however, such objective analysis of her husband's psychology felt irrelevant and trivial. Judith believed that her husband's expectations for their daughter's cleanliness, obedience, and independence were absurdly unrealistic and even at times a design for failure, and she felt obligated to protect her daughter from what she saw as her husband's overdemanding aspect. But to her husband, Judith's interventions on behalf of their daughter were perceived as a challenge, and he often accused her of "spoiling" their child and undermining his authority as a parent. Provoked to prove that he as well as his wife had the right to relate to their daughter in whatever way he felt fit without being "reprimanded" by his wife, Judith's husband dug his heels in deeper and became more rather than less perfectionistic.

The alliance that developed between mother and daughter added a new dimension to the personality conflicts in Judith's and Steve's marriage. Whereas in the context of a twosome there was a sense of balance, the baby created an imbalance of power, and both husband and wife struggled to exert an influence on her.

Because mothers and fathers identify with their children and often have difficulty separating their children's feelings from their own, a wife may experience her husband's relationship to their child as a measure of his feelings about her, and a husband may experience his wife's relationship to their child as a measure of her feelings about him. This tendency to feel vicariously through the process of identification with the child has positive as well as negative implications, depending upon how a wife or husband perceives the partner's relationship with their child. When a husband is loving and sympathetic to the baby and extols her virtues to friends and family, a wife may feel that she has been given to herself, that his love for the baby indirectly confirms his love for her. When a husband see his wife mothering their child as he would like to have been mothered himself, he may regret that he wasn't loved as fully as his own baby now is, but he may also partake of his baby's pleasure, and feel that he, too, is being well cared for by his wife.

When asked whether she thought her husband ever felt jealous of the love and attention she gives their baby, Elizabeth replied, "Paul feels that his parents didn't give him enough attention, and it comforts him when he sees me give so much to Jenny." Judith says that sometimes it brings tears to her eyes when she sees her husband and daughter cuddling together on the couch reading. "My father and I never touched in such an innocent and tender way, and when my daughter and husband do I feel loved and soothed myself." In these instances parenting can nourish the marital relationship by allowing spouses to express and absorb love without the encumbrances of adult mediations.

On the other hand, when a husband appears bored with the baby and baby talk, irritated with his fussiness, or insensitive to his feelings, his wife may experience his responses to the baby as personal affronts, signs that his love and respect for her are waning. His nonchalance about the baby's latest accomplishment may translate into indifference to her; his irritation or impatience may feel like an implicit criticism of the baby and indirectly as an attack on *her* character. His failure to consider the baby's needs and preferences when planning vacations or weekend activities may be felt as a message to her that her needs are bothersome and inconsequential.

Elizabeth finds herself frequently irritated at her hus-

band's behavior, which she describes as careless about
their daughter's safety—he forgets to put his razor safely
out of her reach each morning and may not notice that
she has slipped out of the apartment and has run down
the hallway when he opened the door to get the morning
paper. There have been no serious mishaps, but his carelessness, which she attributes to characteristic preoccupation with more esoteric matters than day-to-day existence,
affects her now more than ever. While Elizabeth is genuinely anxious about her daughter's welfare and irritated at
her husband Paul's occasional inattentiveness as a father,
she also appears to be troubled by the thought that Paul's
distraction has a deeper significance for the relationship
between the two of them. What does it mean in terms of
their marriage that he continues to forget to take care
despite her repeated reminders?

Since parents do sometimes express their feelings for
one another through their manner of relating to their
child, suspicions that there is an implicit as well as an
explicit message are not always unfounded. Messages sent
by way of the child are often unconscious; and their connection to the marital relationship may be ambiguous. But
the dangers of overinterpretation are perhaps as great the
dangers of underinterpretation. Reading hidden motives
into a spouse's every word and action results in as much
distortion as naïvely taking everything he says at its face
value. Even Freud admitted that "sometimes a cigar is just
a cigar," though he could not devise a simple rule by
which to know when it is and when it isn't.

It is in the nature of triangles that alliances shift, and so
husbands and wives not only feel jealous of the love and
attention the baby receives in their stead but also may feel
jealous of the baby's love and attention, which is frequently distributed unevenly between the marital couple.
Then husband and wife not only compete with the baby
but also with each other, and in effect become rivals in
love.

Deborah, for example, is aware that the baby's preference for her has had a "devastating" effect on her husband, even though she reassures him that he is indeed a good father. Her husband was not prepared for being ignored or rejected again and again when he returned home from work with open arms, searching for some evidence that his daily labors were appreciated. Until their daughter is able to include him in a threesome, there is little in the way of compensation for the loss of his wife's attention.

Nobody likes to be rejected, particularly by someone he loves, and though a baby's responses are often as fleeting as they are irrational, this is not always a comfort to the parent who has fallen out of favor. Most parents are able to admit to having preferences for a particular stage in their child's development—some find infants and toddlers the most captivating, while others only come alive when their children begin to speak in sentences or can play ball. Nevertheless, they find it difficult to accept the fact that their babies also have preferences, and that these are often transitory and should not, moreover, always be taken personally. Yes, the baby is a separate human being, too, who does not always respond as we would like him to.

At least during the first several months of the baby's life mothers are generally favored by their babies over fathers, which reflects their greater involvement and the strength of their initial bond. Consequently, mothers are probably less likely, at this stage, to suffer from feelings of exclusion. This has its rewards as well as its disadvantages for both parents. It is gratifying to be the one who can most readily comfort a baby in distress, but it can be frustrating and a source of marital conflict when the baby's preference for its mother is used as an excuse by the father to bow out of child-care responsibilities, leaving the mother feeling entrapped by her baby's too-exclusive attachment. When a husband reports, "he wants you," it may be an accurate description of his son's conscious desire, but the evolution of this desire and its meaning in the context of a particular family are far from self-evident. Family systems theory alerts us to the fact that the child often expresses one or another of his parent's unconscious needs or feelings. Does the child's expressed preference gratify or frustrate the mother? Relieve or wound the father? Does the father somehow encourage the child to gratify or frustrate its mother in this manner? Does the mother somehow encourage the child to relieve or wound its father in this manner? And, most significantly, is the couple drawn closer together by their child's communication, or pushed farther apart? No point on the triangle can be understood without reference to the entire figure.

Judith found herself exhausted and frustrated at being continually on call for her toddler, who protested vehemently whenever Judith suggested that her father read, bathe, or otherwise take charge of her care. (He rarely thought to volunteer his services himself.) She felt envious of her husband's relative freedom to read, relax, or converse with friends unencumbered by the baby and angry that he seemed to be so insensitive to her desire for the same freedom. Although Judith tended to vent her frustration at her husband and not at her daughter, she honestly found it difficult to know for sure who was the appropriate target of her frustration, her husband, her daughter, or herself—why, after all, couldn't she just accept the "fact" that fathers, or at least this father, are simply not as involved? Was her frustration with her daughter's "unreasonable" demands for only mommy spilling over and coloring her feelings about her husband, or was her resentment of his relative disengagement spilling over and coloring her feelings about doing what she ordinarily liked to do with her daughter? Judith's daughter's insistence on mommy may have been simply a passing phase in her development, but Judith was not convinced of this. She suspected that it had something to do with her relationship with Steve and the messages they were sending each other via their daughter. In any case, for several months the interaction among the three became a ritualized part of their lives, and its meaning and function remained elusive.

Triangular relationships are difficult to untangle, and the marital relationship cannot be completely insulated from the relationship each parent has with his or her child. Judith and her husband, Steve, might well ask themselves whether Steve's peripheral role developed in response to Judith's proprietary relationship to their daughter, or whether his withdrawal encouraged her to cultivate such an alliance. Often it is an interaction effect, as preexisting tendencies within each personality complement each other.

In this case, for example, Judith's husband seems to have withdrawn in reaction to Judith's willing absorption in her daughter during the early months. Perhaps he felt this was preferable to competing with the baby for her attention or with Judith for parental authority. And perhaps, moreover, it was consonant with his desire to continue to pursue his extra-familial interests unimpeded. But Steve's retreat only frustrated his wife and alienated his child and reinforced Judith's tendency to overidentify with her daughter. This in turn created an alliance between mother and daughter that excluded father and gave him reason to feel left out and ungiven-to.

As psychological development proceeds, mothers also find themselves being shunted to the periphery of their child's emotional world. This is normal, and if it feels like a rejection, mothers can reassure themselves that it reflects their child's healthy effort to become a separate and unique individual. But just as wives sometimes collude with a child in excluding a husband with whom they themselves are angry, so too husbands sometimes consciously or unconsciously collude with a child in excluding a wife, in revenge perhaps for an earlier slight. Whereas a child's anger and rejection can hurt, the injury is compounded when a spouse has cast himself in the role of the good parent, the confidant.

Susan acknowledged that she felt a twinge of envy and pain when her three-year-old son proclaimed his love for his father repeatedly without mention of his love for her, but she also felt furious and manipulated when it became evident that her son was responding to her husband's more lenient (she would say overly indulgent) approach to parenting. The "rejection" was no longer solely an issue between her and her son, but also an issue between her and her husband, a competition about who was to be the good guy in the family and who was to get all the love.

Though it may be more common for a mother's identification with her child to result in an alliance between mother and child, which in turn creates a schism within the marital relationship, a father's identification with his child may also divide the couple when he feels that he, not his wife, is better attuned to their child's needs and assumes the role of child advocate. Roseanne, for example, described her husband as very protective of their daughter, and he became highly indignant when Roseanne proposed that they try letting her cry herself to sleep after they had suffered through eight or more months of sleepless nights. Her husband responded to her suggestion as if it were a personal attack. He accused her of being selfish and characterized her suggestion as barbaric, evidence that Roseanne didn't really care about their child. While her husband perceived her desire for undisturbed sleep as a sign of weakness, a betrayal of their daughter, and hence a betrayal of him, Roseanne perceived it as a sign of strength, an affirmation of her identity as an individual and a wife as well as a mother. Roseanne believed that the pattern that had evolved over the course of nine months was not only fostering a pattern of dependency between her and her daughter, which would be difficult to break later on, but also interfering with her ability to function as a wife. "I wanted some time with him alone in the evenings, but it got to the point where I felt 'if he doesn't want to spend time with me, why should I want to spend time with him?'"

Although in this scenario husband and wife have reversed what may be the more typical male-female roles—stereotypically, it is the husband who protests that his wife has neglected sex and other forms of marital intimacy by being an overly solicitous mother and the wife who cringes when her husband demands that their child take a back seat and learn to tolerate frustration—the underlying process remains the same. The child, who is not simply the child, but also the child within the wife and the child within the husband, has become the vehicle through which conflict is expressed. Roseanne is mothering not only the real child, but symbolically mothering herself as a child, while the child in her husband cries out for attention; Roseanne's husband is fathering not only the real child, but also symbolically fathering himself as a child, while the child in Roseanne cries out for attention. Each of the real and imaginary children needs something different from its parents, and each parent responds to the child *he* sees and hears at the risk of misreading or neglecting the others. When a husband and a wife feed one child at the expense of another, feelings are bound to get hurt despite the best of intentions.

Symbolic Interaction

> *I've been on a spending binge around the holidays because I feel I don't get enough, and it has become a real battle. Being able to spend money is a sign of security for me because as a child we never had any. I want to buy Teddy a million things, but my husband doesn't think we have the money and feels that I'm spoiling Teddy. He gets angry and I end up feeling*

deprived.—Charlotte, thirty-three, mother of a three-year-old boy

My husband has been more willing to turn himself into a pretzel so as not to disturb Brendan. So when I set normal limits, and for example refuse to make three different meals for dinner when Brendan doesn't like what I've served, my husband reacts as if I were a mean mother. Now it is clear to me that it is his mother he is seeing, but at the time this happened I went into a rage and even hit him.—Susan, forty-four, mother of a three-and-a-half-year-old boy

Who writes the scripts? What are the plots about? And where are they performed?
Language informs us that the scriptwriter is called I. Psychoanalysis has taught us that the scenarios were written years ago by a naïve and childlike I struggling to survive . . ."—Joyce McDougall, Theaters of the Mind, *1985*

Because we are capable of creating symbols, of transposing feelings from one relationship to another, and of infusing meaning into seemingly trivial aspects of experience, a battle over a Christmas present, an uneaten plate of chicken, or some such minor details of family life cannot be taken at face value. In *The Interpretation of Dreams*, Freud distinguishes between manifest and latent content, suggesting that the surface meaning of a dream is merely a subterfuge, a screen beneath which lies its real meaning. This distinction between the surface and the depth, the conscious and the unconscious, the real and the symbolic applies not only to dream life, of course, but has relevance for the interpretation of any experience in which the feelings evoked are out of proportion or otherwise unexplainable by the bare "facts."

During the first years of parenting, husbands and wives often become embroiled in fierce arguments revolving around what appear to be relatively inconsequential issues. Diane (a highly educated and ordinarily unflappable woman) described how she and husband argued ferociously over how to measure the temperature in their baby's bath water—whether to use the elbow or a more sophisticated instrument! An "objective" observer might wonder how intelligent and otherwise mature individuals can behave so foolishly and irrationally, but as soon as it is recognized that these interactions are *symbolic*, the problem becomes one of decoding the symbols; labeling these parents as childish or neurotic is not helpful.

There are no a priori guidelines that might inform us as to what will trigger a major conflict between a particular husband and a particular wife, because it is not the situation but the personal meaning a situation has been imbued with. If Rebecca and her easy-going husband nearly come to blows (and they did) when they have to decide whether to risk awakening their son from his nap in the car when the family has arrived at a shopping mall or to allow him to continue to sleep undisturbed while one parents stays behind, this is because each attaches some hidden significance to whether the child is allowed to sleep or not. To Rebecca her husband's desire to awaken their sleeping baby is evidence of his tendency to be irresponsible, flighty, and impractical, a tendency that irritates her as a parent and as a person. But perhaps to her husband Rebecca's reluctance to get on with the shopping, baby in tow, is evidence of her rigidity, her constriction, and her generally overcautious manner. They are married, so it is likely that Rebecca finds Daniel's impulsive character attractive as well as enraging, and Daniel finds Rebecca's orderliness reassuring as well as confining. Their private tug of war between passion and reason is being enacted on the stage of parenthood. But without speculating further about the reasons for Rebecca and Daniel's argument in the parking lot, we need only point out that their dispute is not what it appears to be at first glance and that another couple might have no problem whatsoever agreeing on one course of action rather than another.

The process of interpreting social interactions is a complicated one, and there are multiple layers of meaning to be discovered. Each interaction has significance for the wife in terms of her personal history, significance for the husband in terms of his personal history, and meaning in terms of the relationship between husband and wife. Consider the following scenario:

Susan, her husband Bruce, and their son Brendan, two-and-a-half years old at the time, were sitting over breakfast before going their separate ways for the day. These early-morning breakfasts were generally rushed and somewhat disorganized, but on most mornings everyone was relatively good-natured and enjoyed the few minutes of togetherness before beginning the activities of the day. However, on this particular morning Brendan protested vigorously when his bowl of cereal was placed in front of him with the milk already poured, as was customary. *He* wanted to put the cereal in the bowl himself this morning. This request was something new, though it was certainly consistent with other demands he was making to do everything himself and in his own way. But that morning time was short; the cereal was poured and already soaking up the milk, making it impossible to simply reverse tracks, and Susan felt that Brendan would just have to live with the frustration of having had his cereal poured for him and have to find some other means of asserting his "autonomy" until breakfast the following morning. Reasonable, but as his whimper escalated into an angry wail, Bruce, Susan's husband, took issue with her (after she had just explained her position to their screaming child). "Why not give him another bowl of cereal and let him pour it himself?" he asked with an edge of resentment in his voice. "What does it cost, twenty-five cents? Why do you have to get into a power struggle over it?" His argument continued. "He has just begun nursery and has enough to deal with." Almost instantly, Susan's anger and frustration with her son was transferred onto her husband, whom she felt was impugning her motives and casting her in the role of the "heavy." His tone of voice, his allusion to a power struggle, and his depiction of Brendan as a victim of an unsympathetic mother led her to believe that the cereal was not the only issue that morning. It was not her only issue, either. She began to defend herself, arguing with her husband that he couldn't tolerate seeing Brendan upset, whatever the circumstances, and that he would do anything to placate him, all the time questioning whether she was indeed being unsympathetic and inflexible. By the end of breakfast, Brendan's cereal was untouched, and his wail had died down into a whimper as he watched his parents argue with each other. The marital dispute was unresolved as Susan and Bruce parted for the day, each fuming inside.

This incident over cereal is paradigmatic of the conflicts that occurred between Susan and her husband during the third year of their son's life. From Susan's perspective, and this is all we have to go on, her husband had problems setting limits on their son because as a child he experienced his parents as inflexible and coolly indifferent to his needs and desires. Susan also experienced her mother as emotionally distant and withholding, and both she and her husband were conscious that they did not want to repeat this pattern with their child. In this emotional context, being restrictive and setting limits on Brendan was a particularly arduous task for them both.

Susan often felt that her husband's identification with their son was so intense that his own experience growing up with his mother and father distorted his perceptions of what was happening to Brendan. Susan admitted that she too had problems keeping separate the memory of her feelings of deprivation as a child from the reality of her son's experience. Nevertheless, she was certain that she did not want to "turn herself into a pretzel" and their son into a "little prince" in order to compensate for her past. For Bruce, the line between being empathic and being indulgent was more ambiguous.

Regardless of who was correct about how to handle the cereal incident (if indeed such a judgment could be made), the intensity of Susan's response to her husband and his response to her indicates that the interaction was imbued with symbolism for both of them and cannot be interpreted solely in terms of a disagreement about cereal or even a disagreement about a child's need for autonomy. In the context of the triangular relationship that had developed between Susan, Bruce, and Brendan, Susan's refusal to get Brendan a fresh bowl of cereal that morning represented to Bruce an insensitivity that was magnified and became monstrous by its surface similarity to his own mother's. At least according to Susan, she stood in for his "bad mommy" and received the residue of antipathy he had felt toward her as a child. Susan's rage, which in the context of another argument over a dinner menu led to her striking out physically, was also evidence that the husband-wife interaction was symbolic to her. Bruce's characterization of Susan as the "bad, withholding mommy" resonated with her own conflicts about her own too-distant mother, whose style of mothering she adamantly did not want to replicate.

Charlotte's "battle" with her husband Stuart over holiday shopping is another example of a symbolic interaction in which the present is colored by the past (Charlotte's relationship with her own mother detailed in Chapter 2 seems particularly relevant), and the child becomes a vehicle through which husband and wife express their conflicts with each other. Charlotte acknowledged that as a mother she tended to stretch herself beyond her limits, and at times was left feeling emotionally depleted and needy. Because she has difficulty asking her husband directly for more of that intangible something that might make her feel less drained, she overate and overspent, symbolically replenishing herself.

But in the context of the family triangle, communication between her and her husband became yet more oblique when through the process of identification she transferred her desire to be taken care of by her husband onto her son. It was no longer solely *Charlotte* who wanted more in the way of tenderness, emotional support, and financial security, but their son, who she felt, was or was not getting enough in the way of Christmas presents from his father. Her husband's thrift at Christmastime felt tight-fisted, and his insistence that she was spoiling their son by wanting to shower him with presents felt unduly critical. The ensuing battle, ostensibly over their son's Christmas presents and about *his* needs for toys, and books, and celebration, was an extension of an ongoing conflict between Charlotte and her husband about giving and receiving, generosity and withholding, and the balance within their relationship.

Nancy's daughter is only four months old, and she and her husband, Robert, have had no major disagreements about child care as yet and are still basking in the joy of having produced a happy and easygoing baby. Yet, projecting into the future, Nancy anticipates that her husband's overanxious and overprotective attitude will present a problem for her, since she is committed to raising their daughter in the atmosphere of freedom and autonomy she remembers from her own childhood.

The issue of autonomy and freedom figured in their marriage well before the baby was born, and Nancy frequently rebelled against what she perceived to be her husband's tendency to be overly possessive of her and her time. He would protest when she frequently came home late in the evening after going out with friends after work, and she would refuse to submit to his attempts to control her comings and goings, escalating matters by not calling to tell him where she was.

When Nancy became a mother these conflicts seemed to resolve themselves. She no longer wanted to socialize after work but was anxious to come home and spend her evenings with her daughter and husband. Moreover, as her husband's partner in parenting she found herself less critical and more appreciative of his anxious care. "I've learned to be more sympathetic seeing how much he loves her . . . I can see his insecurities whereas before I was more in my own world." Actually, the struggle between Nancy and her husband has not magically resolved itself, and from Nancy's description, the pattern of interaction that developed in their marital relationship has gradually been transferred onto their relationship to their baby. In the context of the triangle, Nancy's husband continues to be the more anxious and more protective of the two (he was fearful of letting their daughter ride in a car, car seat and all, so Nancy just took off without consulting him), and Nancy continues to be his counterweight—"I don't have the pressure because he takes it all and I have to lighten up."

Nancy attributes her husband's anxiety about parenting to the fact that he was an adopted child. "Our daughter is his only blood relative, so it is very important to him that the baby looks like him and very important to him that he be a good father." For him this translates into financial pressure, and according to Nancy, he is intent upon having one hundred thousand dollars in the bank by the end of the year for their four-month-old daughter's college education. His parents apparently left him with the responsibility of repaying student loans, and he does not want *his* child to have to worry about money when she graduates from college, as he did.

Whether in his mind the financial burden he shouldered as a young man was symbolic of the fact that his parents did not love him well enough (perhaps because he was adopted), or whether money is just one of many ways in which he has learned to secure his love and attachment, the baby's present and future material needs have become the focus of his anxiety. From Nancy's perspective, the pressure her husband experiences and tries to impose on her is largely his own creation. Insofar as the baby represents himself, and her material comfort represents Robert's capacity to love and protect that baby (self), the arguments that arise between the marital pair over whether the baby should have more furniture, more clothes, more toys, and more living space, which lead into arguments about whether they need to earn more money and how much more, are not to be taken literally. They are laden with symbolic significance. Realistically speaking, money is *an* issue, but it is not *the* essential issue for this couple. At the heart of their arguments are disagreements about how to live, how to love, and how to be the best possible parents to the new baby as well as to the babies that continue to live inside each of them. Nancy and Robert do not always agree on the meaning of the symbols they use. Robert equates material security with love, and so to him his anxiety about money or college tuition or car safety is proof of his maturity, a manifestation of his devotion to his family. Nancy, on the other hand, insists that to love means to relax and let go, and finds her husband's cautiousness and anxiety unnecessarily confining. Whereas she resists being cast in the shadow of his darker vision, he struggles to curb her naïve "childishness." Their early marital conflicts about freedom and commitment in which the "free spirit" played opposite the "pragmatist" are infiltrating the triangular relationship between parents and child as each of them attempts to instruct the child in his or her own language.

Conclusion

> *Much will be gained if we succeed in transforming your hysterical misery into common unhappiness.*
> —*Sigmund Freud*, Studies on Hysteria, 1909

In the Golden Age (which never was, or "is always of the past"), men and women lived together in perfect harmony, and love was quite enough.[14] But since that time (which never was), intimacy has breed conflict, and in the context of the marital relationship, experiences of tenderness, sexual passion, and communion intermingle with those of anger, jealousy, and alienation. "Happily ever after" is not the end, but the beginning of the romance.

But if the "real world" is not the world according to fairy tales, and struggle and compromise are inherent in human relationships, as Freud would have it, this does not mean that much of our "misery" or many of our conflicts are not of our own creation and hence would evaporate if we would only expose them to the light of present-day reality. Relics of former times outlive their usefulness but are superimposed upon present-day relationships. Real conflicts between husbands and wives are infused with symbolic significance, and battles with ghosts who will not die can never be won.

As men and women become parents in a world in which sex roles are ambiguous and the rights and responsibilities of men, women, and children are no longer clearly defined, the potential for controversy and conflict between husbands and wives is greater than ever. On a projective test with little structure and no clearly discernible right or wrong answers, the individual is forced to create his own meaning out of an infinite number of possibilities (an inkblot, for example, can look like a many different things, depending upon who is looking at it and from what angle). The lack of structure leaves room for creative expression, but it may also be disconcerting when internal conflicts originating in childhood are superimposed upon external reality.[15]

Similarly, now that the traditional model of the family, in which the man is sole breadwinner and the woman is housewife, can no longer be counted on to organize and structure our family life for us, husbands and wives have to create and shape their own realities, their own family relationships. Family relationships are built on needs, memories of what was, and fantasies of what can be. But these needs, memories, and fantasies may color parents' perceptions of one another and their child unrealistically, particularly when husbands and wives and babies stand in for fathers and mothers and other babies. The real conflicts that emerge as husbands and wives attempt to build a family together become mixed up with symbolic ones, and real solutions are sacrificed for the sake of completing the drama as written.

If there is a conclusion to be drawn from this analysis of parenting and marriage, it is that in most interactions between husband and wife or parent and child there are multiple levels of meaning, and the manifest content often obscures rather than illuminates its deeper significance. We live symbolically and are adept at creating smoke screens that camouflage our feelings from ourselves and each other, and blur the distinction between past and present realities. The child is but one means of obfuscation. Symbols must be translated into a common language, diversionary tactics must be identified as such; we all engage in them, but at least we should be aware of doing so. Indirect forms of communication can be elusive and should be confronted. Only then can husband and wife get on with the job of being just that, husband and wife to each other, and mother and father to their child.

8

Beyond the Nuclear Family: How Your Baby Fits into the "Family System"

The Family as a "System"

> *A family has body, mind, and spirit. It has a heart; it throbs with the pulse of life. Like the individual, it has both depth and surface expression, an inner face and an outer face. . . . Often, things that are consciously felt but that the members tacitly conspire not to talk about are of the essence in family interaction.—Nathan Ackerman,* Treating the Troubled Family, *1966*

The way in which family members interact with one another is never random; there is always some pattern, and, even in the most chaotic families, a "method to the madness." Everyone plays a role, however minor, and every role has a function: the Prodigal Son who recklessly spends his parent's hard-earned money; the Devoted Daughter who sacrifices herself to care for her ailing father; the Black Sheep who gets pregnant at age seventeen; the Shining Star who is slotted to be the first woman President; the Tough Disciplinarian whose perfectionistic standards inspire rage as well as awe; the Understanding Parent who is perfectly blameless and who nobody can ever be angry with. These are just a few obvious possibilities. The roles come in pairs, and each family member depends upon a counterpart to play his or her individual part. Thus, when one member of the family drops out or introduces variations into the script, the entire scene is thrown off its customary course and the action comes to a screeching halt.

As adults, we often find ourselves behaving one way when we are among family and another when we are not, and despite our intentions to break out of the mold, the pull to be what we always were feels at times irresistible. But it is not simply the past that mysteriously insinuates itself into our present-day lives and distorts our perceptions of who we are and how we are to relate. Rather, within a family there are at any moment implicit rules that regulate the behavior and experience of each member, and as loyal soldiers we respond to them accordingly. Outsiders are not privy to these informal, but often inviolable codes; there is no written record, and communication is frequently indirect, with messages being sent and picked up subliminally. This is what we mean when we say that the family is a "system."

Psychiatrist and family therapist Boszormenyi-Nagy summarizes the systems approach to understanding a person's experience in his family in the following manner: "This concept conceives of the individual as a disparate biological and psychological entity whose reactions are nonetheless determined both by his own psychology and by the rules of the entire family unit's existence."[1] In other words, in order to understand an individual's experience and behavior it is necessary to understand its relationship to the family culture in which he was raised. The individual's needs and conflicts (conscious and unconscious) are expressed (or not expressed) according to the needs of the family as a unit, and the behavior of the individual assumes interpersonal as well as personal significance. Other well-known family systems theorists are Salvador Minuchin, M.D., and Nathan Ackerman, M.D.

While each theorist has a somewhat different emphasis, all would agree that the birth of a baby has an impact not only on its parents and their individual psychologies, but also on the entire system of relationships within each new parent's family. Changes in the emotional tenor between a husband and wife, a daughter and mother, a sister and sister-in-law precipitate changes in all the other family pairs, as alliances shift and similarities and differences crystallize along new dimensions.

When one member of a family experiences a psychological change, or when a new member is added to the existing family structure, the system is destabilized. Almost invariably this leads to conflict. But conflict within a family is *not* in itself a negative. In the "healthy" family, conflict leads to new accommodations, and family cohesiveness is not sacrificed in the process of individual growth. Under such circumstances, the birth of a baby is an opportunity for renewal, a chance for everyone to try out new roles and break free of stale patterns of relating to one another that have become habitual over the years.

Under less than optimal conditions, however, the "system," or one element of the system, violently resists change, because change is experienced as a threat to self-esteem and identity. As differences among family members emerge they are denied or else magnified; scapegoats are created, heroes are made, skeletons are pushed into the closet and others are pulled out, and the family splits into factions. Consider the following imaginary, but not unrealistic, sequence of responses to the birth of a baby:

A new grandmother feels neglected by her daughter, who as a new mother herself has less time to spend with her own mother and less patience for her mother's idiosyncracies. The grandmother does not feel comfortable telling her daughter how she feels (she scarcely understands why she has been so irritable herself), but instead becomes critical of her daughter's husband, who, after all, is indirectly responsible for her loss, having first usurped her role as her daughter's confidant and then having had the audacity to father a baby without including her in the decision-making! The new grandmother begins to find fault with her son-in-law's job and his relationship to the baby, and insinuates to her daughter that he is not as attentive to her needs as he should be. The grandmother does not attempt to compensate for her daughter's own inattentiveness by offering to help with the new baby, or by trying to establish a relationship with it; instead, she becomes depressed and anxious about her physical health and makes sure that her daughter is aware that she is not doing very well. (Indirectly, she sends her daughter the message, "Your husband does not deserve you. You should take care of me. I need you.")

Meanwhile, an older sister feels abandoned by her "baby sister," who has managed to distance herself from their parents and their parents' problems by having become a mother. She feels that she has been left to shoulder the burden of caring for their aging mother and father single-handedly, and she resists, having always been told, moreover, that she was the more rebellious, less responsible of the two sisters. The older sister responds to the birth by simply refusing to acknowledge that anything has changed. She continues to invite her sister to social functions that she cannot possibly attend under her present circumstances and takes umbrage when her sister repeatedly declines her invitations. She conscientiously informs the new mother of their parents' arguments and their mother's ailments, claiming that she does not want her sister to feel excluded. (Indirectly, she sends her sister the message, "You cannot disengage and you should feel guilty if you do.")

And finally, the father of the new mother, who is also the husband of the new grandmother, feels additional pressure from his wife to respond to her emotional needs now that their "favorite" daughter has "left the nest." Having maintained a peripheral position in the family for many years while the children were growing up and occupying their mother's attention, he resists the pressure to become more involved in his wife's concerns and feels angry that their daughter is less available to play her customary role. Is she in fact the devoted and unselfish daughter he always pictured her to be? Suddenly, the grandfather finds himself disaffected with his son-in-law (with whom he always felt competitive anyway), and sides with his wife against him when sides are taken in any controversy. He suspects that his son-in-law may feel, as he does, overburdened by domestic responsibilities now that he is a new father, but rather than defending him against his wife's criticisms, he allows him to be used as a kind of scapegoat. By allying himself with his wife against his son-in-law, the grandfather successfully deflects his wife's attention away from their own marital problems—it is the other man in the family who is guilty of negligence, not he. (Indirectly, he sends his wife the message that he is an innocent bystander and that she should continue to look elsewhere for emotional nourishment.)

This family is imaginary, but the behavior of its members serves to illustrate the principle underlying family systems theory. Every event within a family sets off a chain of reactions as each member responds to every other member's response, and a new equilibrium is established. One might well anticipate that unless this family stops in its tracks and make an honest appraisal of what they are feeling and doing, the baby, the newest and potentially most vulnerable family member, will surely suffer. What distorted images of itself will the baby absorb and reflect back into the "system"? And how will he or she fit in? This example is one end of a continuum. As we shall see, in most families, the changes that occur when a baby is born generate feelings of renewal and generosity along with feelings of resistance, and the baby embodies both new hopes for intimacy and new fears of diminishment, aging, and loss.

The Plot Thickens

My mother's initial response to my pregnancy was as if a horse had kicked her in the stomach. But now she loves the baby and knits clothes for her all the time. Although my mother wasn't a single mother like me, she raised us pretty much on her own, what with my father being away months at a time in the merchant marine. . . . I'm thinking of moving back home to Australia because both my parents are very eager to help take care of Vicki, and here she has to be in day care more hours than I like.—Celia, forty-two, single mother of a two-and-a-half-year-old girl

Everybody in my family is a doctor except me—my mother, my father, and my brother—and having a baby has given me something in common with the rest of the family. My father, for example, seems to be more interested in having a relationship now that there is a grandson. However, I do not share my brother's lifestyle or the values that go along with it, and I assume that his children will eventually absorb his values. When this happens, it will be a source of added tension. —Julie, thirty-two, mother of a ten-month-old boy

Conflict between the minds of family members and conflict within the mind of any one member stand in reciprocal relation to one another. The two levels constitute a circular feedback system. Interpersonal conflict affects intrapsychic conflict and vice versa.—Nathan Ackerman, M.D., Treating the Troubled Family, 1966

Judith reports the following *true* story: ecstatic, after having just heard from her doctor that she was indeed pregnant, she telephoned her mother-in-law, Miriam, to tell her the news. "That's wonderful," her mother-in-law replied, "but of course you know that now your career is kaput!" Momentarily too happy to brood over this comment, Judith waited for another opportunity to make her rebuttal, and sure enough, another one arose. Four months later, Miriam heaved a sigh of disappointment when she was informed, this time by her son, that her new grandchild was to be a girl, and Judith exploded. "You just don't like women do you?" she fumed, and then, for the first time, it was open warfare between the two. Old wounds that had never fully healed were opened up (some predated their particular relationship but were exposed all the same), accusations were made, and then everything was sealed over once again . . . pending another crisis.[2]

Among intimates, we often allow ourselves the liberty to express, if only indirectly, our deepest conflicts, and, as Nathan Ackerman suggests, by the time we are adults our family relationships reflect our internal world as much as our internal world reflects our family relationships. The birth of a baby provides each family member with the opportunity to express, through the mediation of the baby, feelings that are otherwise off-limits—feelings of tenderness, pride, generosity, competitiveness, resentment, or hurt. While the baby itself may elicit these feelings in a new grandparent, aunt, or cousin, the baby also serves as a convenient vehicle for indirect communication between new parents and their extended family.

Miriam's response to her daughter-in-law's pregnancy is a case in point. It is laden with ambiguous meanings and intentions, and no single interpretation of its meaning, however accurate, would be sufficient *unto itself*; her response has at least as much to do with herself and her life as it has to do with her daughter-in-law's. Judith and her unborn baby girl were being enlisted as players in Miriam's personal drama as she struggled to make sense out of *her* life.

Judith informs us that Miriam had always voiced regrets at having never made a career for herself, attributing her failure in this regard (and she seemed to experience it as a failure) to her responsibilities as a devoted daughter, wife, and mother. It is against this backdrop of disappointment and missed opportunity that Miriam hears Judith's good news. Is it conceivable that her daughter-in-law could have a career *and* a baby, when she had to sacrifice one for the other? Miriam's gloomy expectations reflect not only her understanding of the ways of the world, based, as it were, on her own experience, but also her fears and wishes for her daughter-in-law who, by virtue of the fact that she married her son, has always figured as a competitor of sorts.

Judith, on the other hand, is not without her own psychic baggage, and her mother-in-law fits neatly into *her* life drama, in which an older female figure threatens to undermine her self-confidence and indirectly sabotage her success. Miriam can easily be cast in the role of the mother who does not like herself and who cannot but envy her daughter her happiness. These imaginary figures recite their lines from memory, hypnotized and hypnotizing, and color Judith's response to Miriam's competitiveness. She admits, post hoc, that she blew it all out of proportion and believes that under ordinary circumstances she would simply shrug off Miriam's deflating remarks as "typically Miriam." But as a mother-to-be Judith felt more fragile than usual, and in that state Miriam appeared truly monstrous.

The baby girl whose impending arrival triggered such a commotion between Judith and her mother-in-law is not really at the center of their controversy. Nor are the very real problems Judith will face as she tries to juggle motherhood and career at the crux of the conflict. The conflict between Judith and her mother-in-law is about self-esteem and about being different from one another—in age, in life experience, and in their dreams for the future; and at issue when they argue about careers and the advantages and disadvantages of girl babies versus boy babies is whether these differences complement each other or pose a threat to their respective identities.

As Nathan Ackerman points out, conflict in itself is not a positive or a negative aspect of family life. "Conflict can be catalytic or paralytic; it can integrate or disintegrate human experience. It may enhance human growth and adaptation or it may induce its arrest or distortion or both."[3] The changes that motherhood brought to Celia's relationship with her mother are illustrative. Celia's pregnancy brought long-standing conflicts between her and her mother to the surface, and as tension mounted, it became evident to both that they must either sever all relations or learn to live with each other's differences. Because they chose the latter course of action, the conflict was ultimately a catalyst for positive change.

It had been years since Celia and her mother had more than superficial contact with one another. Celia's move from Australia, where she was born and raised and where her parents have continued to live, was only a concrete manifestation of the emotional gulf that separated her from her home and family. In fact, physical distance and the expense of airline tickets provided Celia and her family with a convenient cover, enabling them to avoid acknowledging that the barriers to intimacy were first and foremost psychological. Celia's pregnancy was a jolt to the system, and feelings—hers and her mother's—spewed forth when they might otherwise have remained bottled up.

Though Celia's mother was initially shocked and horrified when her unmarried daughter told her that she was expecting a baby—there were angry words, tears, accusations from both directions—after the initial upheaval, the baby and the events surrounding the birth brought Celia and her mother closer together. Apparently, after diving into the arena head first, Celia's mother took a step back, reconsidered her prejudices, reviewed her options, weighed her potential losses against her potential gains, and proceeded to take two steps forward, this time with the hope of reconciliation. She offered to come to America and help Celia with her new grandchild (the only one she has), and though she was wary at first, Celia accepted her mother's offer and has been grateful ever since. Three years and several intercontinental visits later, Celia is seriously considering returning to Australia. Her mother adores her granddaughter, is eager to care for her, and Celia is happy for the help. Her needs and her mother's complement each other, and now that their past differences have been aired, not simply glossed over and denied, they can be put to rest.

Uniting the Family: Birth and Rebirth

Hope springs eternal in the human breast:
Man never is, but always to be blest.
—Alexander Pope, An Essay on Man, *1733*

I definitely feel closer to my mother, and she feels better about me too. She was probably angry when I didn't rush to have children after waiting until I was thirty-two to get married, and Michael has become a project of sorts for her.—Rebecca, thirty-seven, mother of a one-year-old baby boy

Having a baby strengthened my bonds with my siblings. Before the baby I was the aunt with no children. Now my older sister talks with me about taking custody of her children if something ever happens to her and her husband—she never would have considered this before I became a mother.—Charlotte, thirty-three, mother of a two-and-a-half-year-old boy

With new beginnings come new hopes and dreams for a better future. When one member of the family has a baby, it is not only the beginning of one new life, but also the beginning of new stages of life for all involved. With birth comes the implicit promise of regeneration and rebirth, practically and symbolically. A new generation is born and the older generation is forced to move forward. With the birth of the baby a woman becomes a mother, a man becomes a father, their parents become grandmothers and grandfathers, their siblings become uncles and aunts, and their nieces and nephews become cousins. The baby is the gift of the future—a future we alternately embrace and protest against as we cling fearfully to the past.

Many women find that having a baby is not only the fulfillment of their dreams but also the fulfillment of their mother's dreams for them. Their mothers want to be grandmothers, enjoy fauning over their grandchildren, and relish the chance to open up channels of communication with their daughters that may have gotten clogged over the years. Through the mediation of the baby, intimacy is once again possible.

Elizabeth, for example, finds that suddenly her mother has become very interested in helping her. Before the baby, she never asked her mother for anything, and, at least in concrete terms, little was forthcoming. To be sure, their relations were friendly, but they were somewhat strained, each woman harboring some suspicion that the other was critical of her. Apparently, feelings of competition between this mother and daughter, which had reached a peak during Elizabeth's adolescence, had not entirely dissipated.

Now, however, the two women meet on common ground, and neither challenges the other's ability to mother a small child. (Adolescence may be a less comfortable time for them, and there may be a resurgence of conflict.) Their differences are no longer salient as they engage in the cooperative enterprise of mothering the new baby. This is a relief to both Elizabeth and her mother—finally they can let down their guards and be tender with one another. When Elizabeth asks something of her mother now, she asks not only for herself but also for Jennifer, and when her mother responds by giving she does not give directly to Elizabeth (with whom she still feels competitive), but gives to her indirectly by giving to her daughter. This indirection feels more comfortable to both.

Not only has Elizabeth's mother agreed to baby-sit one afternoon each week, but she continually thinks up things to do for Jennifer, the kinds of things she used to do for Elizabeth when she was a young girl, before adolescent rebelliousness and sexuality created a strain in their relationship. She makes Jennifer dolls out of *her* old clothes and eventually plans to build a doll house and doll furniture out of papier-mâché and clay when Jennifer is old enough to participate in the project. She is at her best.

Elizabeth's mother has found a creative way to give of herself, which by its distinctiveness ensures that she will not be forgotten, and in giving she is simultaneously expressing her special talents and replenishing herself and her self-esteem.

Because the focus is almost exclusively on baby Jennifer—what she is doing or saying or wearing—Elizabeth enjoys just sitting and chatting with her mother, and there have been times when she has ended up spending the afternoon at home visiting her mother rather than availing herself of her mother's baby-sitting services. This cannot but flatter her mother. Jennifer is a mutual object of interest and affection, and both Elizabeth and her mother are relaxed in their complementary relationship to her. Neither feels left out, each has her own very different function, and all three feel loved and loving.

By making a mother into a grandmother, a woman gives her mother or mother-in-law the opportunity to relive the past at a comfortable distance, and at the same time to fill up the empty spaces in her present-day life. Moreover, a grandmother can love and be loved without all the complicated and conflicting emotions she had when she was mothering her own children. According to Rebecca, her relationship with her mother was always burdened by guilt, and up until she became a mother herself she felt that her mother was vaguely disappointed with her, although she is not able to pinpoint the specific reasons why.

As you may recall from Chapter 2, Rebecca experienced her mother as overly involved in her life and at the same time perfectionistic—Rebecca was all-important yet never quite right. Rebecca was an only child, and although her mother had interests outside her family, her daughter embodied her hopes and dreams for herself. Rebecca had always remained a loyal daughter to her mother and adopted many of her mother's characteristics—her willfulness and her unbounded energy—yet she kept her distance from her lest she be trampled under by the force of her mother's opinions and desires. Intent at keeping herself safely at arm's length, Rebecca could not allow herself to consciously appreciate her mother's good qualities, and their relationship suffered on that account.

Rebecca's pregnancy set in motion a process through which she and her mother could shed their feelings of mutual distrust and meet each other on new terms. Her aging mother had retired from teaching twenty years earlier, and though she became actively involved in volunteer organizations, Rebecca has no doubt that she had longed for a grandchild for many years. "She's not fulfilled as a person. . . . My mother is very intelligent, organized, and creative, and she doesn't have enough outlets." By having a baby when she wanted to (at age thirty-six, after having established herself in a career) and in the manner she wanted to (with midwives), Rebecca was able to discharge her obligation to her mother, to give her something she wanted and repay her emotional debts—but without sacrificing her sense of her own integrity.[4]

While Rebecca had always been one of her mother's "outlets," she had served in this capacity reluctantly, and consequently she and her mother were engaged in a perpetual tug of war. Now Rebecca's son, Michael, is "a project" —"She baby-sits and she's been really great with him. . . . She thinks of all sorts of different things to do." But, from Rebecca's perspective, there is a big difference. As a grandmother who lives more than an hour's subway ride away, there are limits to her mother's involvement, and this makes it not only tolerable but most appreciated. Moreover, in contrast to her husband's mother, who is a socialite and, according to Rebecca, an inattentive grandmother, Rebecca finds her mother's interest in her grandson gratifying rather than intrusive. "My mother-in-law never engulfed her children; she gives kids space, but then there is the flip side. . . . Michael doesn't even recognize her, and he definitely knows who my mother is." As in the case of Elizabeth and her mother, Rebecca has found her baby to be a vehicle through which she and her mother are able to express their needs and affection for one another at a comfortable distance.

Because a grandmother is generally not primarily responsible for her grandchild's physical or psychological well-being (nobody will raise his eyebrows if she continues to work full-time or prefers to play cards one weekend rather than baby-sit), she may feel less burdened and more generous toward her children and their children than she did when she was a mother herself. She need not be the one to set limits, engage in power struggles, or feel personally responsible when her grandchild misbehaves and embarrasses the family in public. Moreover, since she is not the mother now but the grandmother, what she gives is "extra," and therefore, less likely to be taken for granted. This makes being a "good grandmother" an appealing and emotionally untaxing enterprise.

Because a new mother is hungry for information, support, and empathy, she may feel more receptive to her mother's or mother-in-law's desires for contact and more willing to be guided by their experience. Moreover, having had a baby herself, a woman has concrete and incontrovertible evidence that she is no longer a dependent child in relation to her mother—she has her own family and her own life, and if there were any doubts, the baby is proof that indeed she is a separate individual. Ironically, having thus asserted her independence from her mother, a woman may no longer feel obligated to prove it by keeping her at a distance and resisting her influence.

Of course, there are cases in which grandmothers and mothers continue their age-old battles, and when the one reaches out the other one recoils from her touch in a carefully choreographed dance of cross purposes. Roseanne, for example, acknowledges that her characteristically cool and distant mother relates to her more intimately since the birth of her baby, and that she remains wary, finding her mother's overtures distinctly distasteful. "She's hanging on me, wanting to share . . . waiting for this wonderful, understanding, happy, sharing relationship to sort of just appear, and I feel like saying, 'Don't push it.' " Roseanne admits that she is unable to put the past behind her or make believe that now everything is "peaches and cream" despite her mother's wishes to do just that, and in a kind of reversal of their past relationship, Roseanne observes that now she is the one who is standoffish, always pushing her mother away. Although they have switched roles, the pattern remains very much the same. This is birth without rebirth.

Relationships with siblings, the new mother's and the new father's, are also often resuscitated once a woman has had a baby. And, just as a sibling can function as a loyal ally, an intimate confidant, or a fierce competitor in childhood, so too in parenthood can siblings be divided against each other and united together. The arrival of the new baby often highlights preexisting conflicts within sibling relationships, but it also provides an opportunity to make amends and resolve these conflicts indirectly.

Throughout her life Deborah's relationship with her older sister, Valerie, was competitive. According to Deborah, Valerie had been cast in the role of the family brain, while Deborah played the part of the charming but rambunctious younger sister, which evolved over time into the role of perennial adolescent. Their early adult lives only served to reinforce the polarized images the two sisters had formed of themselves and of each other as youngsters. Valerie married, had children, and established herself in a respectable career years before Deborah contemplated "settling down." But even after Deborah did marry (outside her family's religion) and did establish herself as a serious professional (if not a very well-paid one), she always felt intellectually cowed by her sister and childish in relation to her family. She lived the family myth, and the collective family mind mirrored back to her this image of herself.

When Deborah became a mother, she and other members of her family began to see past the age-old cobwebs of their family mythology. "Before I had a reputation of being a teenager [even though it had been years since she was chronologically a teenager]. . . . But now my family sees me as more mature." Deborah's choice to become a mother was a choice to be less frivolous, less "self-indulgent," and by making that choice, she began to take herself more seriously. Not only did her perception of herself as an individual change, but her perception of herself in relation to her family underwent a metamorphosis. Deborah no longer allowed herself to be consistently typecast in her old familiar role as the captivating but outrageous baby of the family, and without her collusion, her family was forced to revise its scripts to include a somewhat different Deborah.

Deborah particularly notices a different quality in her relationship with her sister, who also has children. Knowing that she has now proven herself to be a responsible mother, Deborah feels less competitive with Valerie, and apparently this has affected Valerie's feelings for Deborah. Sensing that her sister is loosening her defenses, Valerie has reciprocated and let down her guard. And who can say which is the initiator and which the respondent, as trust builds upon trust? If Valerie has been less critical, less patronizing, and more supportive of Deborah since she has become a mother (and thus has joined her club), Deborah has been less combative and less anxious about projecting an image of herself as alternately mature and rebellious, "just as capable" but nevertheless unconventional. Feeling confident enough to admit to having vulnerabilities, Deborah can finally enjoy the maternal feelings she elicits in Valerie as they confide in one another their fears and dreams of the future.

As designated Brain and designated Charmer, Valerie and Deborah could not possibly feel tenderness or affection for one another; they were caught in their family system. The differences in their personalities were so magnified that it became impossible for them to imagine acknowledging the other's value without devaluing themselves. As mothers they share similar roles and similar experiences, and each is discovering that her sister is not the threat she thought she was. Mirroring each other's moves, each sister finds the courage to emerge from behind her family mask.

As men and women become parents they share with their brothers and sisters (who may also be parents) not only the past but also the present and the future. Their relationships to one another are set in a new context, infused with new blood, so to speak, as the family web becomes more intricate. Personality and occupational, political, or geographical differences that have alienated brothers and sisters may be surmounted as the metamorphosis of siblings and their children into aunts, uncles, and cousins is completed.

Diane observes that her single, childless sister "glories" in her chance to be an aunt, and though they live far from each other and see each other no more frequently than before, Diane feels a heightened sense of connection. The baby's existence has created another layer to their relationship, and the emotional bond uniting them as sisters has been strengthened.

For Judith, a woman who has no siblings of her own, being pregnant and having a baby represented a turning point in her relationship to her husband's brother and his wife. Before becoming a mother she felt that she had little in common with her sister-in-law, Colleen, who had stopped working outside the home after having her first child. Judith admits, somewhat guiltily, that prior to becoming a mother herself she was not all that curious about Colleen and her life, and consequently her impressions of her and her children (who were, after all, Judith's nieces) were rather vague and insubstantial. Judith imagines, moreover, that Colleen's understanding of her inner workings was similarly diffuse.

Until the advent of the baby, relations within Judith's extended family were cordial but superficial; holiday gatherings, birthday parties, and picnics in the park were not enough to break down the invisible barriers that separated family from nonfamily, and Judith continued, even after many years, to feel outside the emotional center—a welcome visitor to the family but not fully a member.

This changed markedly when Judith became pregnant. Judith had no blood relations, and her friends were mostly childless; Colleen was pleased to assume the role of confidant and mentor in matters pertaining to pregnancy, childbirth, and infancy. Whereas previously neither woman felt needed or valued by the other (being such different women and leading such different lives), as mothers they gratified each other's needs and shared in each other's excitement. When Colleen became Aunt Colleen, Judith's relationship to Colleen's children suddenly became more meaningful. She too became a *real* aunt. Technically nothing had changed, but experientially it had: Colleen, her husband, and their children were now related to Judith in more than just name.

Splitting the Family: His Family versus Hers, the Older versus the Younger Generation, and the Resuscitation of Sibling Rivalry

His Family versus Hers

> *Marriage often provokes confrontations between the two original family loyalty systems, in addition to its demands on both spouses to balance their marital loyalty against their loyalties to their families of origin.*—Ivan Boszormenyi-Nagy, M.D., and Geraldine M. Spark, M.S.W., Invisible Loyalties, *1973*

> *A mother-in-law who moves inside and takes sides soon finds herself outside.*—An aphorism quoted in N.W. Ackerman, Treating the Troubled Family, *1966*

Grandmothers, grandfathers, uncles, and aunts often figure significantly in the conflicts that arise between husbands and wives over the proper care and management of their baby. Not that these intruders are *actually* present when differences surface; they may never even voice an opinion on the topic under debate, and their names may not come up at all in the course of a discussion. Nevertheless, their presence is felt.

Rebecca, for example, is well aware that differences between her approach and her husband's approach to disciplining their son, Michael, mirror differences between her family and his. According to Rebecca, Daniel's mother erred on the side of carelessness and underinvolvement, and as a parent Daniel tends not to worry and is very flexible; Rebecca's mother, on the other hand, erred on the side of intrusiveness and overinvolvement, and as a parent Rebecca tends to be cautious and very structured. While neither her parents nor Daniel's parents have ever interfered with their decisions regarding Michael, or openly sided with one of them or the other when a disagreement arose, Rebecca is, nevertheless, certain where the lin ᴇs of battle would be drawn were it ever to come to open warfare.

Although Rebecca is reluctant to admit that as a mother she bears more than the slightest resemblance to her overcontrolling mother, she cannot help but feel irritated with her husband and his family when his freer, less regimented (chaotic?) style of parenting clashes with her own needs for predictability and control. She struggles to find a middle ground. Whether Michael eats his crackers in his high chair or on the living room couch has as much to do with the issue of whose family customs shall prevail— which is the better way to live—as it has to do with how much mess is expectable and tolerable with a toddler.

There is not a husband or a wife who enters into marriage and parenthood without experience in family life, and every family has its own traditions. Loyalty to the traditions of one family may constitute a betrayal of the traditions of another, and there is nothing like invoking family tradition to turn a dispute between a husband and a wife into a full-scale family drama. Nancy contrasts her parents with her husband, Robert's, adoptive parents, and not surprisingly finds that as a mother she feels a greater affinity for her family than for her husband's. She observes, moreover, that when she and Robert disagree about something having to do with Marissa, their four-month-old daughter, their respective positions directly reflect their varying upbringings.

Even before the birth of the baby the differences between the two future grandmothers were obvious when Robert's mother confided in Nancy and her mother that all she ever wanted in life was to be a mother. At the time, Nancy and her mother exchanged glances of wonderment at what was "just a completely different way of thinking." In broad terms, Nancy perceives herself and her mother as easygoing yet responsible, attached but never clingy, and perceives her mother-in-law as anxious to please yet potentially intrusive, loving but overly protective. She observes similar tendencies in her husband. His almost desperate need to be the "perfect father," which means ensuring that his daughter has the "perfect" room in the "perfect" house, with her college tuition securely squirreled away well before she is ready to enter nursery school, echoes his mother's almost desperate need to have a child. Nancy clashes with Robert as Nancy's mother would have clashed with Robert's mother were they to venture beyond superficial pleasantries.

While Nancy's parents are very attached to their granddaughter, their visits to the family are not noticeably more frequent than before the baby was born. Both of Nancy's parents work, and although they are clearly pleased at being grandparents, the new baby has not become the primary focus of their lives. This is not the case with Robert's parents, particularly his mother, and Nancy worries lest her own mother feel crowded out. (Since Nancy clearly identifies with her mother, her fears for her mother may also reflect her fears that her mother-in-law may crowd her out as well.) Contact with Robert's parents has increased dramatically since the baby was born—they call and ask if they can drop over whenever they are in the neighborhood. And though her in-laws make a point not to interfere—"They are exceptionally concerned with not wanting to step on my toes"—and generally stay to visit only a few minutes, Nancy anticipates that in the future they may become meddlesome. Already her mother-in-law has "reorganized" her entire kitchen.

Unwittingly, the legacies of both sets of parents have infiltrated the marital discourse as Nancy and Robert argue over whether Marissa should take a car ride (Robert is against it for fear of an accident; Nancy dismisses his anxiety and goes full-speed ahead), or whether they need to earn more money to guarantee a secure future (Robert says yes; Nancy is less sure and less worried). Nancy and Robert see the world from different perspectives, and their parents, who are their respective secret allies, affirm that their own construction of reality is the correct one.

Some relatives conscientiously avoid being seduced into taking sides in a marital dispute, while others insinuate themselves into every argument, vehemently voicing their opinions about everything from the baby's diet to the mother's work schedule and the couple's finances. But even the most reticent and disengaged of families cannot help but wield influence on the next generation. The family is the original home base and represents a potential source of allies, in spirit if not in words or deeds. The new mother or father can always think, even if it is not voiced, "They would have done it my way."

The family is always on reserve, ready to be called up when a husband or a wife senses that a marital battle cannot be waged single-handedly. Who can resist the temptation to offer oral support to a son, a nephew, or a favorite daughter-in-law? And in times of crisis even the most fair-minded person may find it difficult not to try and curry favor with a brother, sister-in-law, mother, or uncle when a spouse is so unwilling to listen to reason.

Unfortunately, what begins as an argument between a

husband and wife may rapidly escalate into a full-fledged war when other members of the extended family become involved. Alliances (real and imaginary) are invoked to bolster one spouse's position or another's, and a victory for either side bodes poorly for the marriage.

Denise's decision to leave her part-time job in order to stay home full-time with her one-year-old daughter was an extremely difficult one for her and her husband, Marty, to make, but, as we will see, it was further complicated by the fact that Marty's mother and aunt on the one hand and Denise's mother on the other became implicated in a decision-making process that polarized the family for several months.

Before their daughter, Madeline, was born it seemed crystal-clear to both Denise and Marty that a part-time work schedule would be ideal for Denise. Denise had just begun a new stage in her career before becoming pregnant and was as reluctant to sever all ties with her company as she was eager to become a mother. Being a valued employee, Denise succeeded in convincing her boss to let her return to work three days a week after a seven-month child-care leave, and this is in fact what she did. The arrangement was reassuring to Marty, who was already thinking ahead to the future when there might easily be two additional mouths to feed, bodies to clothe, and educations to pay for. He felt more comfortable knowing that the entire financial burden would not fall on his shoulders.

So when the time came for Denise to return to her job they enlisted Marty's single aunt, Betty, to take care of Madeline during the three days when Denise was at work. Aunt Betty, who lived close by and had never had children of her own, was all too willing to spend her days at her nephew's house caring for her great-niece. She loved doing so, and from Denise's point of view Aunt Betty was quite happy to "take over" the care and management of the family as well.

Although not as evident to her husband, it quickly

became evident to Denise that this "ideal" arrangement was not so ideal after all. There were a number of draw-backs, and none seemed to be surmountable. For one thing, Denise felt that she was missing something impor-tant by being away from Madeline three days a week and began to worry that Madeline might suffer on this account in the long run. Madeline was growing increasingly at-tached to Aunt Betty, but Denise began to wonder whether her daughter's attachment to herself was really secure.

In addition to these internal quandaries, troubling as they were, there were also interpersonal and practical problems that began to gnaw at Denise. Denise found herself feeling perennially exhausted, and felt even more depleted than during those first months after the birth of her daughter when she was still home with her full-time. Denise observed, moreover, that she was coming home to just as much housework as before she had returned to work, (Aunt Betty was of little help in this regard), but now she had only two days instead of five in which to accomplish what she had to do. Marty was putting in long hours on his job and was unwavering in his resistance to participate in the cleaning, shopping, and basic manage-ment of the house, and psychologically worn down De-nise began to doubt whether he was even capable of doing what had to be done if he had been so inclined. Effectively, she resigned herself to having a very "tradi-tional" husband.

Perhaps what was most disturbing to Denise, however, was the sense that she was being edged out of her rightful role as mistress of the house by Aunt Betty, who had her own very definite ideas about Madeline—what she should eat, what toys she should play with, and when and how she should be put to bed.

And so, first in private, and then in consultation with her friends and her mother, Denise began to consider making a change. Her friends neither supported nor dis-couraged her impulse to quit her job and oust Aunt Betty from her home, but they did urge her to consider her own needs as well as the needs and desires of her family. Her mother's response was more straightforward. To her mind, the solution was obvious: Denise should simply stop working altogether. Denise's mother had stayed home full-time with her children until her youngest was well into school, and though she dabbled in volunteer work at one point and taught nursery school part-time at another, she had never developed any serious commitments outside of her family. Why then should Denise? *She* had found motherhood completely absorbing and did not understand why her daughter would want to divide her attention between a career and her family if she didn't absolutely have to.

Needless to say, Denise's mother's suggestion did not allay Denise's anxiety or resolve her conflicts, and her mother's eagerness for her to follow in her footsteps only fueled her ambivalence about doing just that. From Denise's perspective, her mother was overly dependent on her family and far too insulated from the outside world. Although an efficient mother, she had failed to fulfill her intellectual potential and was paying the price, floundering about now that her children were grown and out of the house. Denise was adamant that her mother's way of life was not what she envisioned for herself, and concerned lest she "wind up just sort of being a volunteer" at age fifty, she began to peruse the bookstores for official reassurance that women could indeed leave the workplace and return to their careers when their children came of school age.

After gathering the evidence, Denise managed to convince herself that she could leave work temporarily, but unlike her mother, she need not sentence herself to a lifetime of unemployment and domestic isolation. Having quelled her deepest fears, she mustered up the courage and broached the possibility of quitting her job to her husband. But it was not only her husband's response that she had to reckon with.

First there was Aunt Betty, who, despite her controlling and critical manner, was genuinely attached to Madeline.

Moreover, Aunt Betty made it all too clear that she enjoyed being a dominant figure in Madeline's life, with the privileges and responsibilities this entailed. Coming over to visit Madeline when Denise or Marty were at home would be no substitute for the role she had carved out for herself in the family over the course of several months, and Betty did not want to give up what had become her labor of love, her raison d'être.

Of course, Aunt Betty's objections were never voiced in this form; after all nobody could expect Denise to continue to work in order to do Aunt Betty a favor, even though Aunt Betty was a loved and valued member of the family. But what was not put into words could not be subjected to rational argument or even addressed directly at all. So instead of confronting the conflicts of interest within the family head-on, alternative objections to Denise's plan to return home were devised and alliances formed.

Marty's mother was also opposed to Denise's desire to stop working, but for her own reasons. In contrast to Denise's mother, Marty's mother *had* worked when her children were growing up and continued to work to this day. She took pride in having saved money for her children's education and urged Denise and Marty to think about their children's education as well. These were the overt reasons she gave for her conviction that Denise should remain on her job, and it was difficult to argue with them—they made good sense. But there was another, more emotional level to her argument. She sensed that Marty was anxious at the idea that Denise would no longer be supplementing his income, and as Marty's mother she worried about the additional pressure her daughter-in-law's decision would put on her son. And so Marty's aunt and mother joined forces to resist Denise's move back into the home.

With only her mother to back her up—and her mother was not a forceful or convincing ally—when Denise faced an awesome trio consisting of her husband, her mother-in-law, and Aunt Betty (Marty's favorite aunt), her resolve

collapsed. It was not that their arguments were so persua-
sive, but that they were in alliance while *she* was on the
outside; she could not defend her position when all three
opposed her, and her own daughter seemed to be quite
satisfied with the status quo.

Marty had even suggested, at one point, that were
Denise to revert to staying home full-time as she had
during the first seven months, it might have a negative
effect on Madeline. Wouldn't she "regress," he argued,
and become overly dependent upon Denise, as Denise
had been overly dependent on her mother when she was
growing up? This hit upon a sensitive nerve and gave
Denise pause for thought. The idea that her impulse to
stay home with her daughter might be harmful rather
than helpful to Madeline cast a pall over the entire argument, and Denise felt criticized, misunderstood, and isolated within her own family. She began to question her
motives and swallow her feelings.

The turmoil within the family was no longer confined to
the issue of whether Denise worked. The initial conflict
became a conflict of loyalties, and the particular decision
became the vehicle through which the two families—Marty's
and Denise's—struggled to gain control. As Marty's side
of the family joined in an alliance with him in his disagreement with Denise, and Denise's mother quietly lent
her support to her daughter's position, the rift between
the marital pair only deepened. Of course the baby, Madeline, was torn between the two factions, and unbeknownst
to her, she was used as ammunition in her parents' struggle.

Denise acknowledged that despite her own anxiety and
ambivalence about work, about Aunt Betty, and about
Marty, Madeline had adjusted very well to the family
arrangements and was apparently thriving. She was very
attached to Aunt Betty and expressed little sign of distress
when her mother left for work in the morning. Although
Madeline was too young to "take sides" in the dispute
between the adults, her good adjustment indirectly bol-
stered Marty and his family's argument, and placed her

and Denise on opposite sides of the fence—at least for the moment.

By the time Madeline turned one Denise had not yet left her job, Aunt Betty was still setting rules pertaining to Madeline's table manners, and Marty was still refusing to help with the household. Unhappy with the situation, but feeling helpless to change it, Denise became pregnant again. (Nonverbally, she communicated to the family that some new arrangement would be required; that the status quo was not acceptable, and that it was only a question of time—nine months at the very most.) As it turned out, the pregnancy ended suddenly in a miscarriage, but the ramifications were, nevertheless, far-reaching.

Denise stayed in the hospital overnight, and when she returned home Madeline was clinging to her blanket, and moreover, had reverted to crawling when three weeks earlier she had been proudly walking everywhere. Madeline's neediness and her explicit desire for her mother over everyone else, including Aunt Betty, resonated with Denise's own desire to be with her child continuously, a desire that was only intensified by the miscarriage. In terms of the family system, Denise had gained an ally in Madeline, one who could effectively bolster her position by vividly demonstrating to Marty and his family the emotional costs of Denise's absence from the home. Shortly thereafter, the balance in the family tipped in Denise's favor. Denise pointed out to Marty that her absence, *not* her presence, was what fostered Madeline's dependency and inhibited her development, and with *both* his daughter and his wife visibly miserable each morning as Denise prepared to leave for work. Marty's resistance was worn down and he was finally persuaded to switch sides in the family quarrel. As soon as Marty's loyalty to his wife and daughter took precedence over his loyalty to his mother and favorite aunt, the alliance between the two older women disintegrated as Marty's mother realized that she had nothing to gain from joining with her displaced sister. This freed Denise to make her move.

Denise is pleased that she and Marty made the decision they did, and she is happier to be home full-time with Madeline than she was juggling work and motherhood—at least for the time being. But a large part of her satisfaction is in having regained some control over her home. Denise had always found her in-laws to be extremely intrusive, offering advice about everything from refrigerators to how to remedy Madeline's uneven gait, but it was not until the situation had reached near-crisis proportions and threatened to involve even baby Madeline in the family turmoil that she or her husband felt comfortable setting limits on his family's involvement and asserting their identity as a separate unit. It was not until Denise had rallied Marty and Madeline to her side that she felt confident enough to assert her desires over those of her in-laws and exercise her power as a wife and mother.

Aunt Betty is no longer a palpable presence in the house, and her visits are just that—visits. Although we do not have information pertaining to her or her sister's adjustment to the changes in their family roles, we do know that these changes were inevitable. As long as Marty's aunt and mother occupied central positions within the household, the alliance between husband and wife was in jeopardy. Despite their good intentions—and we cannot in all fairness deny them that—mother and aunt had to be moved to the periphery for Denise and Marty to begin to work together as equal parents.

The dynamics of Roseanne's experience with her in-laws were quite similar to Denise's, though the specific content of the family arguments was different. In Roseanne's case, the conflicts focused upon the baby's diet and sleep patterns, with Roseanne taking one position and her husband and his family taking another. For the purposes of this discussion, their respective positions on these issues are irrelevant; what is relevant was the splitting within the marital couple and the intolerance of differences.

Differences between people do not in themselves constitute the basis for hostility and divisiveness. But as sometimes happens in families, "symbolic meanings are attached to these differences" [and] "one side of the difference is felt to be right, the other wrong."[5] Roseanne's reluctance to urge or cajole their daughter into eating three square meals a day symbolized to her husband, Eli, that she was a careless and incompetent person; Eli's insistence that their daughter eat everything on her plate symbolized to Roseanne that he was rigid and controlling. But even more significantly, their positions had meaning in terms of the entire family system—who is allied with whom, who is an authority, and who needs to be told what to do, who is on the outside and who is on the inside. To Roseanne, Eli's position regarding mealtimes represented his overriding loyalty to his mother (who was quite vocal in her agreement with her son), and a betrayal of his bond with Roseanne. As she says, "I was the wierd one." To Eli, Roseanne's position represented her unwillingness to join with him and adopt his family traditions.

The seeds of family conflict were sown well before Roseanne and her husband, Eli, had their daughter, Emma, although until her birth they remained buried beneath the surface. Roseanne and Eli came from very different ethnic and religious backgrounds; during the early days of their marriage these differences contributed to their mutual attraction, but under stress they became convenient targets of blame and disappointment, serving to intensify existing feelings of frustration and alienation and threatening the couple's identity as a family. "I had a very good relationship with my in-laws before Emma was born, and it was totally destroyed. . . . The day my daughter was born my mother-in-law turned into this bizarre person reverting back to her past. . . . I try not to be rude, but she is always trying to convert me to her way of thinking."

By highlighting the interrelationship between the generations, the birth of a baby not only stimulates grandparents' desires to be part of their children's family, but also magnifies whatever barriers to intimacy may exist; irrational fears of abandonment may develop, bringing some

families closer together but wrenching other families farther apart. Scapegoats, who absorb the blame for whatever bad feelings arise, are manufactured in an effort to
protect the family. (By confining bad feelings to one isolated individual, the other members of the family can
preserve the illusion of family unity and harmony.) Roseanne's differences might have been seen by her mother-in-
law as curious or even endearing prior to the birth of baby
Emma, but when it became clear that Roseanne was really
part of the family, they were irritants, shattering her mother-
in-law's illusion of control, marring her vision of what *her*
family *should* be like—and they had to be eliminated.

Emma had suffered nerve damage at the time of delivery, and while this proved to be reversible, it added to the
stress in the family. Most significantly in terms of the
family dynamics, what happened to Emma at birth de-
flated Roseanne's confidence in herself and her decision-
making ability, and because Eli's belief in his wife's good
judgment began to waver, he offered her little in the way
of support, leaving the door wide open for his mother to
edge her way in. It had been Roseanne's decision to go to
a midwife rather than to a physician, and though it remained unclear whether the damage might have been
avoided if she had followed her husband's and her mother-
in-law's advice and gone to a doctor, Roseanne absorbed
the guilt for what had happened—and there was a lot of it
to absorb. The family never spoke openly about their
speculations or their feelings, but in their silence they
condemned her. Feeling guilty, Roseanne found it difficult to set limits on her mother-in-law's intrusiveness,
and she, along with Eli, allowed her authority as the
baby's mother to be subtly undermined. "I wanted to put
together my own little thing, but I felt I was doing it his
mother's way."

Rather than bolstering his wife's self-esteem and supporting her in her disagreements with his mother, Eli
frequently took his mother's part, leaving Roseanne feeling like an outsider in her own family. "I don't know if it

was a rejection of me or just an expression of his over-protectiveness, but everything had to be done like it was done in the old country during the 1950s."

Other members of Roseanne's and Eli's extended family offered Roseanne little in the way of support, which only intensified her feelings of alienation and insecurity. Eli's brother and his wife were planted firmly in the center of the family, and while they were not critical of Roseanne, they were not potential allies in her battles with her husband and mother-in-law; at best they were neutral, at worst they were on the other side of the fence. On the other hand, the idea of allying herself with members of her own family was not at all appealing to Roseanne. Now that she was a mother, she found herself feeling more distant than ever from her single brothers, who liked to "party" on weekends, and who could not possibly understand her concerns. Moreover, her brothers continued to tell the same ethnic jokes they always had, oblivious to the fact that these jokes grated upon Roseanne since her husband and his family were members of the ethnic group that was the target of their humor. Roseanne was unprepared to betray her loyalty to her husband in order to rejoin the sibling fold; there was too little to gain and too much to lose, and so she was betwixt and between.

As far as her parents were concerned, Roseanne had distanced herself emotionally from them years before, and much as she might have benefited from a positive motherly relationship to counterbalance the tense relationship she had with her mother-in-law, Roseanne found it difficult to respond to her mother's gestures of reconciliation. Ironically, however, the conflicts she experienced in relation to her husband and his family cast her mother in a new and more favorable light. Indeed, she sometimes wonders whether her mother's careless insensitivity to her children's needs wasn't preferable to her mother-in-law's self-righteous intrusiveness.

It was not accidental that Roseanne had chosen a husband whose personality and family background were distinctly different from her own—disaffected with her family of childhood and searching for an alternative, the difference was a major part of the attraction. But Roseanne found that, despite her earnest wishes, she could not be integrated into her husband's inflexible family system and still preserve her separate identity. Contrary to what she had supposed when she first got married, this identity of hers was not so easily relinquished. Her husband's loyalty to his family and their traditions, coupled with her mother-in-law's need to control her and her baby, threatened to undermine not only the marriage (two years later Roseanne still speaks bitterly of Eli's betrayals around Emma's eating and sleeping patterns), but also Roseanne's self-esteem. Both were sacrificed to maintain the family system, which had difficulty accommodating someone a little different.

Family therapy would probably have been the best alternative to the martyrdom of Roseanne, but Roseanne reports that Eli was unwilling to participate (therapy was antithetical to his and his family's way of thinking). Eventually, however, Roseanne felt desperate enough, but also deserving enough, to begin to see a therapist herself, and she is beginning to pull herself out of the traps she had fallen into as a new member of her husband's family. She is shedding some of her guilt, and as she feels better about herself, she finds herself less dependent upon her husband (or his mother) for validation. How Roseanne's therapy will affect her marriage will depend on how Eli adjusts to the changes in Roseanne's internal world. Because the family is a system, and all parts are dependent upon all other parts for smooth functioning, an adjustment in one form or another will be necessary. This family is losing the patsy who has doubled as its scapegoat, and it will have to find another way to manage its conflict.

The Older versus the Younger Generation

*My mother thinks it is very important for Tom to be
well behaved. But I'm not so sure it is so important for
a toddler to be so well behaved. I can chafe at the bit in
an instant when I hear her express her concern about
when he'll be able to shake hands with people. That
there is nothing about who Tom is as a person is still
an issue for me.—Laura, thirty-five, mother of a nearly-
three-year-old boy*

*I asked my mother if she would like to spend a week with
us after Billy was born. She made some excuses about
her back, and when she asked, "What help can I be?"
It was like a match in an oil pit. The anger has been
there all the time and something finally ignited it.—Ann,
thirty-seven, mother of a two-and-a-half-year-old boy*

*My father and I have a very distant relationship, so I
was amazed to see how he reacts. . . . I never saw him
smile so much in my life. His feelings are more out there.
—Nancy, twenty-nine, mother of a four-month-old girl*

The relationships that evolve between grandparents and
grandchildren cannot but affect the relationships that exist
between grandparents and parents. The baby may function as a bridge, connecting the generations anew, enabling them to reach out to each other without sinking too
deeply into the muck of past intergenerational conflict, or
it may widen the gulf that already divides one generation
from the other. Through the baby there is the potential for
renewal and progress, but also the potential for repetition
and "remembrance of things past."

The bond between adult children and their parents is
strengthened when, as grandparents, parents are able to
respond freshly and lovingly to their children's children.
What new mother does not feel gratified and given-to
when her parents or in-laws show that they truly love
the baby she loves so much herself? And how can she feel
quite so critical of her parents or her in-laws when they

proudly proclaim that her baby and their grandchild is delightful, intelligent, and altogether quite marvelous? The warm feelings are contagious, and it is difficult to dislike or be angry with people who genuinely and consistently love the child who is closest to your heart.[6]

Many women who remember their fathers as having been remote and emotionally inaccessible while they were growing up are particularly moved when they see them responding in an uncharacteristically tender and loving manner with their grandchildren. Shadowy and elusive figures, these men rarely had time for their daughters and felt awkward expressing their affection directly to them in words or in deeds. Therefore, when, as grandfathers, fathers suddenly light up at the sight of their grandchild, or praise a toddler for his help raking the leaves, or boast of his precociousness, it comes as a surprise and revelation. "Ah!" says the woman. "He does feel deeply and tenderly after all." Before the baby, her father's love could only be inferred; now the baby is a vehicle through which it can comfortably be expressed.

Hurt feelings can be soothed by proxy, as grandparents build relationships with their children's children; they can also be rekindled, however, and inasmuch as desires for love and acceptance from a parent can finally be gratified via the baby, they can also be frustrated once again. With the birth of a baby, intergenerational tensions may resurface with a vengeance when a grandparent's mode of relating to a grandchild recapitulates negative aspects of the original parent-child relationship.

A grandparent may idolize a grandchild, or relate to him or her in a perfectionistic, critical, overprotective, or underinvolved manner. But if this reminds a new parent of his or her own childhood frustrations and disappointments, the grandparent's shortcomings as a grandparent are magnified, and old battles are fought on a new stage with the addition of a couple of supporting characters. Once again, the generations cross swords.

Ann describes her outrage when her mother politely

declined her invitation to come for a visit shortly after the baby was born. Just as in Ann's childhood experience, it was not what her mother did but what she did not do that was so disturbing, that left Ann feeling so needy and so angry. Now an elderly woman with a back problem, Ann's mother was unable to imagine that Ann and her baby might need something other than concrete services from her. Nor did it occur to her that *she* might derive pleasure from a visit with her daughter and new grandchild. But this was no different from when her mother was young and vigorous; then too she was unable to respond to Ann's desires for emotional sustenance. Ann's present anger at her mother for her mother's disinterest in Billy is a delayed response. It has been building up inside her for years.

Thanksgiving dinner with Ann's in-laws was also colored by her general experience of aridity and alienation within her own family. The food was unpalatable, there was no conversation, and her in-laws' mode of relating to Billy was only too familiar to her. "As long as Billy meets their needs and goes over to them, that's fine, but they haven't done a thing to put their arms out to him." A painful replay from the past, her in-laws' rigidity and unforthcoming response to Billy touches a sensitive nerve in Ann and reinforces her desire to distance herself from parental figures, past and present.

In Cheryl's family, conflicts between the generations that were revived with the birth of the baby took a different form. As may be recalled, when she was growing up, Cheryl experienced her mother as overly involved with her, but also overly distant. Protective of her daughter and anxious around points of separation, her mother could not be truly intimate with Cheryl because she never seemed to enjoy her or take pleasure in being her mother. This paradoxical mode of relating was highlighted when Cheryl became a mother, resurfacing as it did in relation to her grandson and again in relation to Cheryl as a new mother. Although her mother was delighted when Cheryl became pregnant, as if in becoming a mother Cheryl were finally fulfilling her "manifest destiny" by following in *her* footsteps, she constantly worried about grandchild Jesse's emotional and physical well-being, and subtly but consistently implied that Cheryl was too lax (or perhaps too relaxed) and should join with her in her worry. Ironically, but in some ways true to her character, Cheryl's mother rarely offered to help with Jesse, but instead made demands upon Cheryl's time and attention. Until Jesse stopped crying at night she was reluctant to baby-sit, and Cheryl understands this withholding type of behavior as an outgrowth of her mother's relationship to her when she was a child: "I think she's resentful because she didn't have opportunities and she was home all the time."

The death of Cheryl's father only fed her mother's chronic neediness and resentment, and she turned, as she always had, to Cheryl to fill up the gaps in her life. "Instead of being the helpful grandma type, she is another person whose demands I have to deal with." Cheryl never questions that on some fundamental level her mother cares for Jesse, just as she never questioned that her mother would always be there for her whenever she needed her as a child or as an adult. But the frustration and guilty disappointment Cheryl now feels in relation to her needy mother is resonant of what she felt growing up. Her mother is involved with Jesse, but as was the case with Cheryl, her focus is on problems (real and anticipated); she gives Cheryl well-intentioned advice but implicitly undermines Cheryl's confidence in herself; she seems to want more from everyone but takes little pleasure in what they have to offer her. Motherhood has drawn Cheryl and her mother closer now that they share something in common, but in their relationship, being too close has always been a source of tension. The question arising now in relation to Jesse is the same one that was never fully resolved thirty-odd years ago between Cheryl and her mother, and that is whether each can give to the other what the other desires without exacting a pound of flesh in return.

The Resuscitation of Sibling Rivalry and Other Horizontal Forms of Competition

> *Now Israel loved Joseph more than all his children, because he was the son of his old age: and he made him a coat of many colours.*
> *And when his brethren saw that their father loved him more than all his brethren, they hated him, and could not speak peaceably unto him.*—Genesis 37:3

> *My sister is very worried about never having a child, and I think she feels a great deal of envy. I'm careful not to rub her nose in it. . . . I wouldn't tell her that it is the most wonderful thing that ever happened to me.*—Susan, forty-four, mother of a three-and-a-half-year-old boy

> *My mother has a boyfriend whom she sees every weekend and so she has a lot less time for me and Sarah than she had for my sister and her children. That she is not as available to me as she was to them has been a big issue for us.*—Deborah, thirty-five, mother of an eighteen-month-old girl

Rivalry between siblings seems to be an inevitable part of growing up in a family.[7] It is not simply a product of modern times or an idea made fashionable by psychologists and their sympathizers. The phenomenon is emblazoned in our consciousness from the biblical stories of Cain and Abel, Jacob and Esau, Joseph and his brothers, and in the fairy tales of the Firebird and Cinderella and her wicked stepsisters. These archetypal stories expose the darker side of brotherly and sisterly love.

Parents are the arbiters of reality for their children, possessing the power to confer on each one an identity, a sense of place, and a feeling of self-worth. But since every child is perceived by his parents differently from every other child, and since even in the most benevolent of families differences in personality, intelligence, hair color, birth order, or sex are often assigned different values, family life is particularly conducive to feelings of competition. To some extent, this is unavoidable. Parents are people and people have preferences. Moreover, what complicates matters further is that their perceptions of their children frequently represent a blend of realistic appraisal, personal fantasy, and irrational biases.

Preferences for one sibling over another are frequently unconscious, and when they become conscious, they are generally rationalized away. (She's the eldest, so of course she's more mature and I can confide in her; he's always been the introvert, so how can I really get close to him? It's because she's so wild that she gets so much of the attention.) While it is anathema to some to concede that there are inequalities within the family and that there are alliances that exclude one member and include another, these are realities of family life that most of us are all too familiar with, and they breed feelings of competition among siblings. Here are some relatively benign examples.

A mother feels a particular affinity to her eldest daughter, whose personality resembles her own, and though she loves both her daughters and makes every effort to divide her attention evenly between them, the younger one senses that her sister shares an intimacy with her mother that she does not. As adults, both sisters live with the legacy that the younger one grew up in the older one's shadow. As mothers, the relationship each sibling has with the other's children is colored by the competitive and guilty feelings that linger on from childhood.

A father finds it easier to relate to his son the athlete than to his son the bookworm. The designated bookworm reminds him of himself and his father, whereas the athlete resembles a favorite uncle. Though he applauds each of his sons' successes, he cannot mask the fact that the athlete embodies his unfulfilled dreams for himself, whereas the student embodies his father's dreams for him and his own uneasy compromise with the contingencies of reality. This father's bookkeeping may be impeccable as he divides attention and money equally between his two sons, but his emotional support is uneven. As an adult with children of his own, the less favored son scrutinizes his father's relationship to *his* son, is hypersensitive to any signs that his brother's son is preferred over his, and is ready to pounce or withdraw, depending upon his personal style of expressing his grievances. He does not need to be convinced that once again he is the victim of injustice, however unintentional, and he may very well be right.

When a family operates on the assumption that there is a finite amount of love, attention, and respect to be divided among the lot, then one child's gain is another's loss, and competition between sister and brothers can only lead to envy, guilt, and divisiveness. With this as a backdrop, the birth of a new baby, which after all is a gift of sorts, may resuscitate old rivalries between siblings for two very different but related reasons. On the one hand, the new mother has taken it upon herself to initiate a change that affects everyone in the family—by her action her sister has become an aunt, her brother an uncle, and her parents grandparents—and the mere fact that she has taken the initiative may disturb the balance of power within the family and precipitate a power struggle to rebalance the scales. Moreover, in the process, she has acquired something of great value that she didn't have before, a loyal ally, and perhaps something her sister or brother would also like to have but cannot for any number of reasons.

On the other hand, when a sister has a baby it may become crystal-clear that the more things change in the family, the more the family dynamics remain the same. Parents, who are now grandparents, often reassert the very same feelings they always had about their various offspring, only now even more indirectly, through their relationships with the new generation of babies. The realization that nothing has changed between parents and children may be disappointing to the new mother, to her siblings, or to both, frustrating their hopes that someday their parents will wake up, see the light, and rectify whatever injustices had previously existed within the family. The baby, who is cast in the role of family Angel, Terror, Genius, or Schlemiel, can be seen as just one more piece of evidence that life is unjust and that one sibling has been dealt a better hand than another.

Rachel recalls that she and her older sister were constantly fighting with each other when they were growing up. Vague about the content and confused as to the origin of their childhood and adolescent feuds, Rachel is, nevertheless, convinced that Caroline resented her from the time she was born and that her parents must have done something (what, she does not know) to have instilled such competitive feelings in their daughters. While *she* remembers her parents as having been very loving, she cannot be certain that her sister Caroline experienced them the same way.

Since Rachel had her baby eight months ago, she has sensed a resurgence of resentment from her sister and has noted that Caroline has become increasingly critical of her for no apparent reason. Caroline is thirty years old and single, and since her career as a lawyer has taken off she often finds herself working eighty hours a week. It is Rachel's impression, however, that, despite her professional success, Caroline is not happy. Caroline loves children and has openly expressed a desire for a husband and a family of her own, and yet she is well aware that the realities of her professional life make it difficult for her to fulfill this desire. Her current work schedule limits the time she has available to devote to her personal life, and at present, the idea of having a baby remains very much an abstraction.

Whatever internal conflicts exist for Caroline have intensified since Rachel, her baby sister, preempted her birthright and went ahead and had a baby herself. Previously, the conflict Caroline was experiencing was her own, between one aspect of her personality and another, but now it has entered the interpersonal realm, and old feelings of resentment (on the part of Caroline) and guilt (on the part of Rachel) have resurfaced. They are acted out through the characters of the New Mother, the Wise Critical Aunt, and the Baby Zachary, with Rachel's husband and parents playing supporting roles.

Although Caroline does not criticize Rachel's relationship with Zachary, she tends to be critical of everything else Rachel does— "In general, she likes to put me down," says Rachel—and when Caroline visits Zachary she makes it clear that she prefers Rachel to leave them to themselves. Evidently it is the sibling relationship that continues to pose a threat to Caroline's good estimation of herself, and the birth of Zachary is but one more dimension in which she compares herself to her younger sister and finds that she falls short (at least according to her own yardstick). Although Caroline genuinely enjoys being an aunt, she does not like sharing her sister's experience of motherhood with her. And although she is grateful for the opportunity to help with her nephew if it means spending some time with him alone and on her terms, as soon as aunt and nephew are placed in the context of the larger family system—Rachel, her husband, and their parents—Caroline feels upstaged. Rather than play a supporting role to her sister's lead, Caroline asserts her primacy by becoming pompously quarrelsome.

Cheryl and her older half-sister, Elise, were also extremely competitive as children. Elise's father died shortly after she was born, her mother remarried, and then Cheryl came along. Cheryl's father naturally became father to Elise, but there was a difference, if not in his mind then in the minds of the two sisters. The man in the house was Cheryl's blood relation, her "real" father and not Elise's, and this colored the girls' relationships to both of their parents as well as to each other. We do not know, but it would not be surprising were Elise to have experienced herself as at a disadvantage in comparison to Cheryl, who was the child of *both* their parents. Moreover, it would not be unusual for Cheryl to feel both pleased and guilty about her "advantaged" position in the family.

But whether or not the two sisters actually experienced the imbalance in the family in precisely these terms, there was an unspoken rivalry between the two, and Cheryl reports feeling that, despite her own extremely close relationship with their mother, Elise was more her mother's "kind of kid" than she was. Cheryl described herself as having always been more rebellious than Elise (perhaps Elise did not feel secure enough in her position to risk her parents' disapproval by rebelling) and is convinced that her mother responded better to her sister's "conventionality" than to her ambitious nonconformism.

As women, Cheryl and her sister have, up until now, managed to carve out their own separate spheres of influence—Elise has been the Competent Mother of Two while Cheryl has been the Professional Woman—and childhood tensions between the sisters have subsided. By becoming a mother Cheryl realizes that she is encroaching upon her sister's designated territory and that by so doing she may disturb the delicate balance they have struck between them. She awaits with some trepidation the ramifications of her daring move.

On the one hand, now that Cheryl is a mother, she and her sister have a mutual interest; on the other hand, Cheryl is worried that her sister may feel overshadowed by her. "Before I had the baby I was very comfortable with her because things felt very even, but now she doesn't have anything over on me anymore. Professionally I'm more accomplished. . . . Now I don't know what she feels." As yet, there have been no invidious comparisons made between the two sisters regarding their work, their mothering, or their children, but Cheryl is aware that this may change. "If there's an underlying competition between us, it has to be passed onto the kids," she says somewhat pessimistically. For now, she is enjoying the hiatus in their rivalrous feelings toward one another and hopes it will last.

Sibling-type rivalry is not always strictly limited to siblings. Just as sisters and brothers are sensitive to any hint of inequality or imbalance between them, new mothers may compare themselves (and be compared) to cousins and find themselves competing for the approval and attention of mothers, fathers, aunts, and uncles. When the older generation colludes in the competition and draws comparisons between one new mother and baby and another new mother and baby, the younger generation is divided as much as they are brought closer together in parenthood.

Deborah felt angry when her mother, her aunt, and her older sister intimated that she and her eighteen-month-old daughter, Sarah, were too enmeshed with one another, and she was infuriated and humiliated when they drew an unfavorable comparison between Sarah and her "well-adjusted" cousin, who purportedly was friendly to everyone in the family and experienced no separation anxiety whatsoever. The comparison between the two toddlers engendered such competitive feelings in Deborah that she felt compelled to find fault with her cousin, the mother of the "model child." "She's not very bonded with her child, and he'll go to anybody because everybody has taken care of him. Sarah is very clingy, but it is appropriate." Regardless of whose assessment of the children is the correct one, the extended family, which in this case included Deborah's mother, aunt, sister, cousin, and cousin's baby, were all implicated in Deborah's feelings about herself, her daughter, and their relationship. Criticisms of Deborah (her family questioned the reasonableness of her decision to work only one day a week) were communicated via the baby, and Deborah retaliated along similar lines. *Her* baby was the one who was better taken care of and who was developmentally "normal"—*not* her cousin's.

Like everyone else, grandparents sometimes respond more to one grandchild than to another—perhaps their personalities mesh with one child more than with another, or they always wanted a boy, or one particular baby reminds them of a dearly beloved sister or mother. Although these preferences may have little impact on the emotional well-being of the baby who is more or less favored by a grandparent, they may be highly significant to the baby's parents when they see history repeating itself. A grandparent's preferences among his or her grandchildren may recapitulate patterns of favoritism that existed within the original family system. When the child of the family extrovert is loved and admired for his friendliness and precocious use of language, and the child of the family introvert is accused of timidity and assumed to be less intelligent, old wounds are reopened and the new generation becomes the arena in which brothers and sisters, mothers and fathers settle or fail to settle old accounts.

Judith is aware that in her husband, Steve's, family, Steve and not his younger brother, Peter, was informally designated as their mother's special confidant—her surrogate husband and father rolled into one. This began after her divorce, when Steve and Peter were still children, and has persisted into their adult lives. While from a psychological point of view Steve's position as the "parentified child" was not an enviable one, in the context of the family system it cast an aura of authority and importance around him, and his younger brother could not but feel diminished in comparison.[8] Consequently, as adults the two brothers are quite competitive with each other—in their work, on the tennis courts, and when discussing politics.

Before Judith and Steve became parents, relations between the two brothers were either purposely superficial or tiresomely combative as each alternately resisted and succumbed to feelings of competition. Having the baby precipitated a change in this pattern of relating, a pattern that had evolved over the years and was as stultifying as it was difficult to break out of. Judith and Steve turned to Peter and his wife, who were already well-seasoned parents, for advice, support, and companionship on cold winter weekends, and by so doing, the imbalance of power gradually evened itself out. Steve's relationship with his brother was no longer merely a reflection of their early family relationships, Steve was no longer the ultimate authority, Peter was no longer the naïve kid brother trailing behind, and the two brothers and their wives began to feel more at ease and less competitive with each other.

However, despite the changes in Steve and Peter's relationship to one another, their mother, Miriam, continued to figure as a divisive presence in the family. Miriam's attachment to Steve and Judith's baby was immediate and intense, but even Judith could see that it was unrealistically positive. In contrast, Miriam's relationships with Peter's children were strained, and love and trust came slowly and painstakingly. Peter could not help but feel that once again he and his were unappreciated, cast in the shadow of his brother Steve's "special" aura. And who can deny his experience, though his own role in perpetuating the past remains obscured? Steve, in turn, felt unfairly accused by his brother of preferential treatment and joined with their mother in characterizing Peter as hypersensitive and defensive. And who can say that his perceptions are not accurate, though he does not see how once again he and his mother are allies and Peter is once again on the outside?

Miriam's varying responses to her two sons' children reflect not only her feelings about her two sons, which have not changed significantly over twenty-five years, but also her two sons' feelings about her, which they communicate subliminally to their children. Peter's suspicion of his mother on account of past and present grievances is transmitted to his children, who are then suspicious of their grandmother's overtures as well. "Why don't you offer to baby-sit for us? You are always baby-sitting for Steve and Judith." Peter makes demands of his mother, who has in fact baby-sat far more frequently for Steve's baby than for Peter's children. "You rarely ask me to," replies Miriam ingenuously, secretly hoping that he will not ask, since his children do not seem to enjoy her visits with them and she feels slighted. A quarrel ensues, with Steve being pulled into the middle by his mother, who urges him to drum some sense into his brother's head. Peter is enraged that Steve has gotten involved (ignoring the fact that it was he who drew his brother into the dispute by implication). The result is that relations between the siblings become tense once again, and the past has managed to insinuate itself into the present.

Whether in becoming a mother a woman hopes to carry on the family traditions she learned as a child or strives to create new, more satisfying forms of relatedness, she is making a commitment to family life—a commitment to living intimately with others over time, through thick and thin. Although her primary loyalty is shifting from the family of the past to the family of the future, the families of origin—where it all originated for her and her husband—remain living presences.

While the baby and its father have become the focus of a woman's dreams and conflicts about being close and being a separate individual, the new mother must also reckon with the fact that her becoming a mother has psychological significance for all members of her extended family. The birth of the baby stimulates feelings of hope, regret, love, and jealousy, as some family members worry about being left out or shunted to the side, while others relax their guards and move in closer to the emotional center.

The fact that a woman is now mother to a baby as well as a daughter, a sister, a wife, or a niece means something different to each and every family member. It can be experienced as a gift or a blow to self-esteem. The new mother must contend with the various and sometimes idiosyncratic responses of her relatives, which are not always communicated to her in words. Although the new mother may not want to alienate anyone in her family or in her husband's, she may find that it is unavoidable and that she must choose between conflicting loyalties. Her relatives' responses to the baby and to her mothering cannot but color her feelings about her relatives and may even become a kind of litmus test by which she determines who is on her side and who is not.

Ideally, the new mother comes to motherhood without too many preconceptions about who her baby is and how she is going to respond to him. And ideally, she is able to absorb herself in the process of gradually discovering what her baby actually is like, what motherhood really means to her, and what parenthood means to her marriage. Often, however, reality falls somewhat short of this ideal. The new family emerges and takes shape within the context of a larger family system, a system that often resists change as much as it embraces it, and every member of the family offers the new mother a different version of the truth. Her family and her husband's family have a myriad of contradictory images of her, her baby, her husband, and their relationships, and valuable insights come to her mixed with personal biases. It is the new mother's job to untangle the one from the other.

The new mother may become so involved in the work of sifting fact from family fiction, wisdom from individual prejudice, that she may forget to take a good look at herself, her baby, and her husband. In deferring to the beliefs and wishes of others, she may neglect to use her own perceptual apparatus to construct her own version of reality.

As a woman learns to discriminate between helpful criticism and defensive maneuvers, alliances that heal and alliances that divide, she struggles to reconcile her needs as an individual with the needs of the family, which is made up of other individuals but is also an entity in itself. Her struggle is, of course, an aspect of the more fundamental human struggle to connect with others without sacrificing one's individual identity, to listen without ignoring one's own voice, to empathize without losing one's convictions. This is the essential problem of the family life that the birth of the baby forces mothers to confront head-on.

Afterword

The latest statistics tell us that more babies were born in 1987 than ever before in the history of this country, so in purely quantitative terms, now as always, there is nothing more ordinary in life than for a woman to become a mother. Psychological reality is, however, quite different, and for many contemporary women there is nothing more extraordinary, nothing that demands quite as much soul-searching, as they attempt to integrate their needs for autonomy, achievement, and power with their desires to belong, to create a home, and to be intimate.

When motherhood was believed to be the only natural and expected vocation for a woman to have, the changes it precipitated in a woman's life were taken for granted. Who questions the natural course of events? And who is aware of her own breathing? As soon as a woman can freely choose not to become a mother, however, her choice to become a mother assumes ever greater significance. Precisely because at this point in history the relationship between anatomy and destiny is no longer immutable— women have more options today than they had in previous generations, and if they choose *not* to be mothers they need not be consigned to poverty, celibacy, or marginality—women are more conscious of themselves as mothers, and, ironically, more conscious of the ways in which motherhood may pose a threat to their identities as people.

Psychologically, the experience of becoming a mother is full of paradoxes. Motherhood forces a woman to confront

326

the future—hers and her baby's—but also heightens her awareness of her origins as she responds to voices and images of babies and mothers past. Motherhood thrusts a woman into adulthood with all the privileges and responsibilities that go along with it and yet seduces her into believing that she can recapture the past and by so doing reshape it to suit her present needs. As a mother, a woman is no longer a child, an adolescent, a "single" woman, however much she remains psychologically wedded to these images of herself, yet as a mother she is often isolated from other adults and spends a good portion of her days at home, playing, babbling, feeling intensely, and trying her best to please someone else—things she did when she was a child and adolescent herself. She is both more and less serious (she is certainly less dignified), more and less respected (she is finally a *real* woman, but then how committed could she be to her work?), and more and less able to live up to her intellectual potential (depending on how it is being defined). Work has become more and less important to her now that she has become a mother: it is at once a source of self-esteem and a source of anxiety, a reprieve from the stormy emotions of family life but also a conflict of interest, a financial necessity, and a form of alienated labor she could easily dispense with.

As a mother, a woman has affirmed her commitment to her marriage, but she and her husband quarrel more frequently, have sex less frequently, and often relate to each other more like adversaries than like partners, let alone lovers and intimates. Grounded more than ever in the details of material reality, interactions between mothers and their husbands, mothers and their babies, mothers and their friends, and mothers and their families of origin are steeped in symbolism. Paradoxically, the baby brings to the surface buried conflicts (personal and interpersonal) while simultaneously deflecting attention away from the seat of conflict and absorbing the heat of the emotion.

Contradictions abound, and the challenge for contemporary women is to learn to live with a certain amount of conflict rather than to deny that it exists, to tolerate a measure of ambiguity and ambivalence rather than search for formulaic certainty. Understanding how past relationships color present relationships and can unnecessarily complicate an already complicated balancing act is also important. The old scripts may be familiar and the action may be comfortably predictable, but the dramas they recreate endlessly repeat themselves, and there can be no new resolutions.

As a mother, success is trusting one's judgment, admitting one's failures, and having the modesty and self-respect to forgive oneself one's imperfections. The quest for perfection is a contradiction in terms, a fantasy that oppresses more than it glorifies. Unique as each woman's experience is, there are universal conflicts of motherhood, and recognizing them can be an antidote to self-blame, an opportunity for communion in an otherwise competitive world.

As a mother, a woman watches her baby develop an identity all its own. The "good-enough" mother encourages him to express his individuality, but knows when to limit his willfulness and temper his narcissism so that he can learn to live peaceably with others. In the process of becoming a "good-enough" mother, a woman must learn how to balance these same tendencies in herself. The evolution of the baby's identity is mirrored by its mother's metamorphosis, a metamorphosis that is never complete, a metamorphosis that expresses with ever greater nuance the woman who was the daughter and who still is the daughter, but who is now the mother herself.

Notes

Chapter 1. Motherhood and the Ghosts of Mothers Past

1. Psychoanalyst Margaret Mahler describes a stage of normal symbiosis between a mother and her baby that, according to her scheme, lasts until the baby is around six months, at which point he gradually continues along a path of increasing differentiation and separation. Although Mahler's formulation of infant development is now quite controversial within psychoanalytic circles, and Daniel Stern, a prominent psychoanalyst and developmental researcher, cites evidence that infants never actually experience themselves as merged with their mothers, it is generally recognized that mothers, babies, and small children sometimes have difficulty separating their experience of themselves from the other's experience of them.

2. Psychoanalyst Erik Erikson, in a controversial article entitled "Womanhood and the Inner Space" (see *Identity, Youth and Crisis* [New York: W. W. Norton, 1968]), proposed that differences in girls' and boys' fantasy play conformed to and reflected anatomical differences. He observed that girls tended to create more tranquil domestic scenes within enclosed spaces, while boys tended to invent scenes in which precariously balanced towers set the stage for action-packed adventure. But there have been numerous rebuttals to his biologically linked interpretation. Many argue that the differences he observed between girls' and boys' play is more likely a function of early socialization experiences than reproductive functions.

3. The idea that it is through the process of identification with her mother that a daughter can separate and establish her own life apart is a central thesis of Nancy Chodorow's argument in *The Reproduction*

of Mothering (Berkeley and Los Angeles: University of California Press, 1978).

4. Winnicott goes on to explain: "Whether a woman has babies or not, she is in this infinite series; she is baby, mother and grandmother . . ." By this I take him to mean that all women retain within themselves an identity as a girl/baby (their mother's daughter), an identity as a mother via an early identification with their mother, and an image of their mother which, in this configuration, figures as "mother's mother."

5. I thank Amos Gunsberg for this vivid evocation of a child's dependency upon its parents. I would like to suggest that in some ways this experience of interdependency is recapitulated in motherhood.

6. Joyce McDougall, *Theaters of the Mind* (New York: Basic Books, 1985), p. 6.

7. Harry Stack Sullivan, *The Interpersonal Theory of Psychiatry* (New York: W. W. Norton, 1953), p. 41.

8. Erik Erikson's stage theory of psychosocial development is reproduced diagrammatically in nearly every introductory psychology text I have seen. Surely it is a helpful visual guide and is an important supplement to a discussion of Freud's psychosexual stages of development. However, even as early as 1968, Erikson himself acknowledged that normal psychological development is different for the female than for the male, and that the difference pivots around the issues of intimacy and identity. See *Identity, Youth and Crisis*.

9. See Carol Gilligan, *In a Different Voice* (Cambridge, MA: Harvard University Press, 1982); Daniel Stern, *The Interpersonal World of the Infant* (New York: Basic Books, 1985).

10. See Freud's discussion on "The return of the repressed" in *Moses and Monotheism* (1939), The Standard Edition of the Complete Psycho-

logical Works of Sigmund Freud, Translated from the German under the general editorship of James Strachey, Hogarth Press and Institute of Psychoanalysis, Vol. 23, pp. 125–127.

11. Therese Benedek, "Parenthood As a Developmental Phase: A Contribution to Libido Theory." *Journal of the American Psychoanalytic Association*, Vol. VII, No. 3 (1959), pp. 389–417.

12. Joyce McDougall, *Theaters of the Mind*, p. 7.

Chapter 2. Becoming the Mother You Had (or Never Had)

1. Simone de Beauvoir analyzes this kind of mother-child relationship in a chapter on the mother in *The Second Sex*. De Beauvoir draws connections between attitudes of self-sacrifice and desires for domination, between altruistic behavior and future recriminations. She seems to be describing the mother whom I have referred to as overly enmeshed, and we shall see in our analysis of case study material how these contradictory tendencies coexist.

2. See J. H. Harvey and G. Weary, "Current Issues in Attribution Theory and Research," *Annual Review of Psychology*, Vol. XXXV (1984).

3. In psychoanalytic theory the term "object" is used to refer to a person who is an object of desire.

4. Nancy Chodorow, *The Reproduction of Mothering* (Berkeley and Los Angeles, University of California Press, 1978).

Chapter 3. Life with Baby: A Radical Transformation of Time and Space

1. In *Mary Poppins Comes Back* (Harcourt, Brace and World, 1935) P. L. Travers imaginatively plays with the notion that babies understand aspects of life that are beyond the grasp of adults or even children. In the chapter entitled "The New One," baby Annabel talks to the birds and understands the origin of life. But this knowledge is hers for only a brief period of time, and soon she, like all of us before her, forgets her vision and gradually succumbs to the more "rational," allbeit duller, forms of discourse.

2. This point is made by Erving Goffman in *Interaction Ritual: Essays on Face to Face Behavior* (Chicago, Aldine Publishers, 1967). Psychologists have found that when people (and animals for that matter) are able to predict and control even minor aspects of their environment they experience less stress than when they are unable to do so. Even our experience of physical pain has a psychological component, and it is generally recognized that by understanding and anticipating discomfort we can help alleviate it. (See J. M. Weiss, "Psychological Factors in Stress and Disease," *Scientific American*, 226, 1972, 104–113.) This is one of the rationales for preparing women for childbirth beforehand.

3. See M. J. Lerner, "The Justice Motive in Social Behavior," *Journal of Social Issues*, Vol. XXXI, No. 3 (1975), pp. 1–19. Lerner and his colleagues suggest that people are motivated to believe in a "just world" in which events are never random because then they can feel in control of their lives. This form of reasoning is reassuring but can lead to a tendency to "blame the victim" rather than acknowledge that some things in life just aren't fair.

4. Psychoanalyst Else Frenkel-Brunswik argues that the ability to tolerate ambiguity is a relatively stable personality characteristic. According to her research, people who see the world in black-and-white terms (good guys, bad guys, us, them) and who are unable to acknowledge all the complexities and shadings of reality are more likely to be rigidly authoritarian and conformist. See Else Frenkel-Brunswik, *Selected Papers*, ed. Nanette Heiman and Joan Grant. In *Psychological Issues*, Vol. VIII, No. 3, Monograph 31 (New York: International Universities Press, 1974).

5. D. W. Winnicott, *The Child, The Family, and the Outside World* (Hammondsworth, U.K.: Penguin Books, 1964), p. 120.

6. Ibid., pp. 120–121.

7. As quoted in an article by Carin Rubenstein entitled ''The Baby Bomb,'' which appeared in the *New York Times Magazine* (Health Section) October 8, 1989, psychological research findings suggest that age is not a reliable predictor of adjustment to parenthood and that there seem to be psychological advantages and disadvantages to both early and late motherhood.

8. Erich Fromm, *Escape From Freedom* (New York: Farrar and Rinehart, 1941).

9. Edward T. Hall, *The Hidden Dimension* (Garden City, NY: Doubleday, 1966).

10. I. H. Frieze, J. E. Parsons, P. B. Johnson, D. N. Ruble, and G. L. Zellman, *Women and Sex Roles: A Social Psychological Perspective* (New York: W. W. Norton, 1978), pp. 326–328.

11. Karen Horney, *Neurosis and Human Growth* (New York: W. W. Norton, 1950).

Chapter 4. The Initiation into Motherhood: Communion, Alienation, and Competition

1. Leon Festinger, among other social psychologists interested in the relationship between attitudes and behavior, has suggested that, contrary to common-sense notions of casuality, our behavior influences our attitudes and values as much as our attitudes and values

influence our behavior. By way of explanation, he argues that people strive to reduce the "cognitive dissonance" that results when they see themselves behaving in a way that is inconsistent with their beliefs. One way of reducing dissonance is by modifying beliefs so that they are no longer inconsistent with current behavior. When, under changing life circumstances, we befriend people whose ideas and values are different from our own, we attempt to bridge the gulf and reduce the potential source of dissonance by gradually changing our ideas and values so that they no longer threaten our friendships with contradiction. See also Kurt Lewin's paper "Behavior as a function of the total situation" in *Field Theory in Social Science* (New York: Harper and Brothers, 1951). Lewin's analysis of group dynamics and the convergence of past and present influences on an individual's behavior and ideas has been an important influence on my thinking.

2. Psychologists have found that people generally choose friends who share similar attitudes and values. (See for example, T. M. Newcomb, "The Prediction of Interpersonal Attraction," *The American Psychologist*, Vol. XI [1956] pp. 575–586.) And Muzafer Sherif and his colleagues found, moreover, that they could artificially engender feelings of hostility within a group of children by arbitrarily dividing them into two subgroups, separating them for a limited period of time, and assigning them different names (*Intergroup Conflict and Cooperation: The Robbers Cave Experiment* [Norman, OK: Institute of Group Relations, 1961]).

3. See Festinger, "A Theory of Social Comparison Processes," *Human Relations*, Vol. VII (1954), pp. 117–140.

4. Stanley Schachter *The Psychology of Affiliation* (Stanford, CA: Stanford University Press, 1959).

5. "For better or worse," because a consensus of opinion is no guarantee of the opinion's ultimate value, and the beliefs and feelings of a particular group may simply reflect its own biases. Examples abound in real life of situations in which, from the point of view of an outsider, an individual's peer group has exerted a tragic influence on the course of his life. In his classic psychological study of conformity, "Effects of group pressure upon the modification and distortion of judgments," in *Groups, Leadership, and Men*, ed. Harold

Guetzkow (Pittsburgh: Carnegie Press, 1951); Solomon Asch demonstrated how easily we allow our perceptions to be influenced by others. Subjects in his experiment were asked to estimate the length of a line, a simple task in which there is clearly a right and a wrong answer, and the majority made grossly inaccurate judgments after being led to believe that those were the unanimous judgments of their peers.

6. M. Sherif, and C. W. Sherif, *Reference Groups: Exploration into Conformity and Deviation of Adolescents* (New York: Harper and Row, 1964).

7. The "illusion of unanimity" is a term social psychologists have used to refer to what happens when a group has successfully pressured its members to conform to the prevailing set of ideas. As a result of such conformity, members of the group share in the illusion that what they believe is, without question, the Truth, and that they are invulnerable. Under the sway of this illusion, the group may be spurred to act impulsively on its beliefs.

8. Charles Horton Cooley, *Human Nature and the Social Order* (New York: Schocken Books, 1902), p. 296.

9. It is important to remember that it is a woman's *perceptions* of motherhood and other mothers that are psychologically real to her. So, for example, a woman who lives within a particular subculture in which mothers do *not* work outside the home might find it difficult to return to work because that would mean that she would be deviating from the norms of her reference group. The fact that the majority of women in the United States as a whole *are* working by the time their children are school age may not be a part of her psychic reality.

10. "Separation" is a psychological term that refers not only to the capacity to tolerate physical separation from the mother or mother figure, but also to the capacity to understand that one's thoughts and feelings are one's own and nobody else's, and that one's very existence is not dependent on the presence of another person, or vice versa. "I do not disappear or disintegrate if mommy is not there to see or touch me, and mommy does not disappear or disintegrate if I

do not see or touch her." Developmental theorists generally agree that at around eighteen months children experience "normal" separation anxiety as they become increasingly aware that they are indeed separate individuals.

11. Psychologists studying persuasion and persuasibility have found that people with low self-esteem are more vulnerable to the influence of others than people with high self-esteem. If a person has little confidence in himself, it often follows that he is more ready to defer to the opinions of others who appear to him to be more knowledgeable. Although low self-esteem is often conceived of as a general personality characteristic (something a person carries around with him everywhere he goes), some psychologists have pointed out that a person's estimation of his ability is quite variable, and will depend upon the situation. Since many new mothers are women who are very confident of their abilities at work, yet are nevertheless insecure about their mothering decisions, it may be more useful to talk about how secure a woman feels in regard to her ability to mother rather than about her global estimation of herself and her competency in general. In other words, it is not only the psychologically fragile woman who is susceptible to the influence of the group of other mothers.

12. Research studies indicate that particularly when people feel insecure about themselves they tend to prefer to associate with people who are similar to them, as a kind of self-protective measure. (See J. W. Goldstein and H. W. Rosenfeld, "Insecurity and Preference for Persons Similar to Oneself," *Journal of Personality*, Vol. XXXVII [1969], pp. 253–268.)

13. When another person is perceived as completely different, what he does or thinks or feels is irrelevant to one's life and life decisions. (Comparing apples with oranges provides little basis for choosing the best apple.) It is when we perceive people as similiar to ourselves on some important dimension that we have difficulty dismissing their opinions and beliefs. (See Festinger, "Theory of Social Comparison Processes.")

Chapter 5. Values in Collision: The "Perfect" Mother, the "Perfect" Woman, and the Imperfect Self

1. Alfred Adler, an early follower of Freud who broke ties with the psychoanalytic movement to found what he termed the school of Individual Psychology, believed that the central motive for all human beings is the striving for perfection. Dependent and fragile as infants and children, we create our own unique self-ideal in compensation for deep feelings of inferiority. Unconscious as we may be of our ideals and the reasons for them, we shape our lives so that we can achieve the goals we have set for ourselves. (See H. L. Ansbacher and R. R. Ansbacher, eds., *The Individual Psychology of Alfred Adler* [New York: Harper, 1956].) Karen Horney also discusses at length what she terms "the search for glory" and the pursuit of the "idealized self." However, in contrast to Adler she sees this as "neurotic," though perhaps quite common, and not an inevitable aspect of personality development. Horney distinguishes between the idealized image of the self and the real self which, under optimal conditions, finds expression in the course of natural development. She maintains that in pursuing the ideal an individual invariably becomes alienated from his true potentialities, living under the "tyranny of the shoulds." (See Karen Horney, *Neurosis and Human Growth* [New York: W. W. Norton, 1950]).

2. Horney, Ibid., p. 78.

3. The 1987 movie *Fatal Attraction* comes to mind in its portrayal of a beautiful, sexy, seemingly independent female literary editor who by the end of the movie is literally crazed after having become entangled in a love triangle. Her veneer of successful composure is quickly shattered when her married lover regrets his sudden passion and attempts to retreat to the comfort of his family and home. The wife in the threesome is also sexy and beautiful, but unworldly and a loving mother. At the conclusion of the film she is clearly victorious. The Woody Allen film *Another Woman* portrays a very different kind of woman, but also untraditional in her childlessness. She is a distinguished philosophy professor who had devoted her life to scholarship and, in contrast to the literary editor, suffers from a lack of passion rather than an overabundance of it. Though her fate is not as grim as the editor's, the message is clear: The life of the intellect is a very partial life for both women and men. Intimacy and "feminine" virtues are a necessary part of a happy life.

4. A slogan Merrill Lynch used in one of its television advertising campaigns.

5. In her book *Mothers and Such: Views of American Women and Why They Changed* (Berkeley and Los Angeles: University of California Press, 1984), anthropologist Maxine Margolis documents extensively the transformations in the role of mother from the colonial period up until the present. She maintains that it was only beginning in the nineteenth century that women were called upon to devote themselves to full-time mothering. Before the industrial revolution, when much of a family's productive activity occurred within the home (women made candles, spun cloth, preserved food, and tended gardens), child-rearing was not perceived as a function in and of itself, let alone a woman's mission in life. Moreover, child care was typically shared within the extended family, and the mother was but one among a number of other adults and older children to look after the young ones. The issue here is not whether the present arrangement is better or worse than any other, for the mother or for the child, but rather that there is no one "natural" way to mother. Moreover, the psychological significance of motherhood to a woman's identity varies as a function of the historical and cultural context in which she lives. Ann Dally also provides an historical overview of concepts and ideals relating to motherhood in her book *Inventing Motherhood. The Consequences of an Ideal* (New York: Schocken Books, 1983). Dally maintains that until relatively recently it would not have occurred to women to feel guilty about leaving their young children in the care of someone else. This was standard practice among middle- and upperclass British mothers before World War II. However, economic and ideological changes transformed our understanding of what constitutes a good mother, and John Bowlby's research documenting the effects of maternal deprivation on institutionalized children was used as justification for why women are morally obligated to remain at home full-time if they wish to raise healthy and happy children.

6. When the women's movement gained momentum toward the end of the 1960s, the cultural climate as a whole was ripe for the development of an ideology promoting equality between the sexes. Black Americans had been challenging the doctrine of "separate but equal," a doctrine that had been used to justify racial segregation, for years before the women's movement took hold. In its 1954 decision, *Brown* v. *the Board of Education*, the Supreme Court of the United States declared the doctrine unconstitutional and legitimized the challenge.

7. Most psychologists specializing in research on sex differences would agree that psychological differences within each sex are far greater than the average differences between the sexes and that socialization experiences and social norms are significant factors in the development and maintenance of sex-typed behavior. E. E. Maccoby and C. Jacklin summarize much of this research in their book *The Psychology of Sex Differences* (Stanford, CA: Stanford University Press, 1974).

8. Margolis suggests in *Mothers and Such* that the "cult of motherhood" developed as a result of economic and structural changes associated with industrialization. Her argument is something like this: with the newfound capability for mass production, work life and home life were divided as never before. What had previously been manufactured at home was now manufactured outside the home, in factories, and the home became "a retreat from the competitive world of commerce and industry, a place of warmth and respite." Women became caretakers of the home and of the family, and their relationship to their family changed as a result of the changes in their relationship to the world of work and money. While Margolis argues that the idealization of motherhood in America is a consequence of changes in the material conditions of life, I hope to demonstrate how this idealization is in itself an important influence on women from a psychological point of view.

9. See Helene Deutsch's discussion of motherhood in *Psychology of Women. A Psychoanalytic Interpretation*, Vol. II (New York: Grune and Stratton, 1945). Many psychoanalysts of that era incorporated these ideals into a psychoanalytic theory of "normal" female development. As a result, women whose aspirations were inconsistent with these ideals were diagnosed as having penis-envy and masculinity complexes. See also Betty Friedan's discussion in *The Feminine Mystique* (New York: Dell Publishing, 1963).

10. Margolis, op. cit. p. 48.

11. John B. Watson, *Psychological Care of Infant and Child* (New York: W. W. Norton, 1928), as quoted in Margolis, *Mothers and Such*, p. 52.

12. D. W. Winnicott, *Playing and Reality* (London: Tavistock, 1971).

13. Talcott Parsons, "Age and Sex in the Social Structure of the United States," *American Sociological Review*, Vol. VII (1942), pp. 604–620.

14. Labor Department statistics tell us that women make up nearly 45 percent of the labor force today and project that by the year 2000 this will rise to nearly 50 percent (*New York Times*, November 27, 1988). Moreover, more than 50 percent of mothers with preschool children work outside the home, and as of 1987 53 percent of married mothers with children age one year or under were in the labor force. Lois Hoffman, "The Effects of Maternal Employment in the Two-Parent Family" *The American Psychologist*, Vol. XXIV, No. 2 (February 1989), pp. 283–292.

15. Sociologist Jesse Bernard discusses the inconsistency between women's actual and ideal roles, and the strain it creates when women continue to feel that they should be doing what they cannot possibly do. She argues that during periods of rapid social change the gap between the ideal and the real widens, since changes in ideas are more gradual than economic changes. Consequently, our norms and ideals continue to reflect a reality that no longer is. (Jesse Bernard, "Change and Stability in Sex Role Norms and Behavior," *Journal of Social Issues*, Vol. XXXII, No. 3 (1974), pp. 207–223.)

16. The results of my 1982 doctoral-dissertation research suggested that in the context of professional relationships women respond to male colleagues in much the same manner as they respond to female colleagues. This was contrary to my predictions, but in trying to make sense of the results I concluded that women no longer see themselves as fundamentally different from men, at least not on work-related dimensions, and therefore apply the same norms of behavior in their interactions with them.

17. Clara Thompson, "Cultural Pressures in the Psychology of Women," in *Psychoanalysis and Women*, Jean Baker Miller (ed.) (New York: Penguin Books, 1973), p. 82.

18. Betty Friedan discusses this in *The Second Stage* (New York: Summit Books, 1981), a book in which she addresses the problems women encounter as they leave the "feminine mystique" behind. Friedan

decries the "feminist mystique," which simultaneously denies women their needs for intimacy, family, nurturance, and nurturing and creates the myth of the superwoman who can have it all and do it all. She argues that the myth of the superwoman, who is everything for everybody and a successful career woman to boot, only skirts the issue of men's participation in parenting and in the home, and ignores the need for broad changes in the organization of the workplace.

19. Women have always worked outside their homes when it was financially necessary, but their work was generally low-status and poorly paid, which only testifies to the fact that the world of work has been a traditionally male domain. Of course there were always exceptions—the singular woman doctor, politician, executive, or artist—but their singularity posed no threat to the prevailing norms, which were devised by men, with men in mind.

20. Bernard, "Change and Stability."

21. Daniel Stern's research on early child development and mother-infant interactions has also challenged the notion that psychological autonomy and separation are later, and hence more sophisticated, developments than relatedness and connection. These findings call into question many of the traditional assumptions about psychological maturity and moral development that have identified women as less mature than men.

22. The question of whether stereotypes reflect real or superficial differences between the sexes is further complicated by the fact that early socialization experiences of girls and boys are fundamentally different, even when parents make conscious efforts not to sex-type their children and educators encourage a child's individual growth and development regardless of sex. The difference is that in all but a small minority of cases girls are raised primarily by someone of the same sex, and boys are raised primarily by someone of the other sex. In other words, women are primarily responsible for raising the children, even if the women are relatives or hired help. Thus, if psychological differences persist, and girls tend to behave one way and boys tend to behave another, it is difficult if not impossible to say definitely whether this reflects some innate, biological difference

or whether it is a result of their experiences growing up in relation to a mother or mother figure. Nancy Chodorow discusses this extensively in her book *The Reproduction of Mothering: Psychoanalysis and the Sociology of Gender* (Berkeley and Los Angeles: University of California Press, 1978).

23. As the ideology of the women's movement permeated all aspects of the culture, psychologists become interested in sex-role stereotypes and the "social construction" of "femininity" and "masculinity." Numerous research studies conducted during the 1960s and 1970s provided evidence that there are particular personality traits consistently associated with one sex more than the other. Psychologists have suggested that people's beliefs concerning the varying capabilities and characteristics of men and women shape their concepts of themselves, their expectations of other people, and their behavior in relation to members of each sex. See P. Rosenkrantz, S. Bee Vogel, I. H. Broverman, and D. Broverman, "Sex-role Stereotypes and Self-concepts in College Students," *Journal of Consulting and Clinical Psychology*, Vol. XXXII (1968) pp. 287–295.

24. Thompson, "Cultural Pressures," p. 81.

25. For reasons discussed further below, women are more likely to aspire to traditionally "masculine" goals than men are likely to aspire to traditionally "feminine" goals. This is probably due to the fact that in our culture "masculine" characteristics have been accorded more value than "feminine" characteristics, and "women's work" has typically commanded lower wages and lower status than men's. Compare the salaries of elementary school teachers and secretaries, let alone child-care workers, with the salaries of construction workers and firemen. It is as if the former were unskilled and required less education or training than the latter. Moreover, although an increasing number of women are working outside the home, by all accounts men are not eagerly taking this opportunity to hone their domestic skills. Women continue to take primary responsibility for cleaning, cooking, and child care, with husbands "helping out" or sharing, but not equally. The reasons for this are psychologically complex, and I would venture to say that while many men resist doing "women's work," many women feel uneasy abdicating what they feel is their responsibility to care for the home and the family. What's more, at least when it comes to child care, they are reluctant to give up the pleasure they drive from being primary. Research reported in Carin

Rubenstein, "The Baby Bomb, *New York Times Magazine*, October 8, 1989, documents this kind of ambivalence.

26. The ideal man and the ideal father and the ideal person (one who is respected, valued, and admired in the world at large) propel a man in one general direction, along a difficult but relatively straightforward path. At least up until recently, the man who "provided" well for his family was by definition a good husband and father; a good wife would be sympathetic, not critical, when his long hours on the job made him unavailable for companionship and emotional support. Nobody would criticize him moreover, if, on account of his work, he rarely spent time with his children. The ideal woman and the ideal mother bear little resemblance to the ideal person, however, and a woman who aspires to worldly success may feel that she is forced to choose between two divergent paths, each representing a different set of ideals.

27. Abraham Maslow, *Motivation and Personality* (New York: Harper and Row, 1970).

28. Christopher Lasch, *The Culture of Narcissism* (New York: W. W. Norton, 1978), p. 13.

29. In *The Second Sex* (New York: Knopf, 1953), Simone de Beauvoir argued that whereas men strive for transcendence, women have historically been grounded in immanent reality—conscious of what is, in contrast to what could be. From de Beauvoir's perspective this difference between the sexes is a result of women being objects rather than subjects of history.

Chapter 6. The Subjective Self

1. Erik Erikson uses the term "crisis" to refer to normal turning points in the course of human development. According to his scheme, it is at these points in the life cycle that each of us attempts to master

new psychic challenges, building on the foundation we have laid at previous stages. In his book *Childhood and Society* (New York: W. W. Norton, 1950), Erikson identifies adolescence as a time during which each individual struggles to consolidate his or her identity against the threat of potential identity diffusion. While Erikson believes that this and other "crises" are normal aspects of development, he argues that their ultimate resolution depends to a large extent on the strengths and weaknesses of our individual personality organization.

2. Harry Stack Sullivan refers to "selective inattention" as a psychological defensive strategy in his book *The Interpersonal Theory of Psychiatry* (New York: W. W. Norton, 1953).

3. In his book *The Shadow of the Object: Psychoanalysis of the Unthought Known* (New York: Columbia University Press, 1987), psychoanalyst Christopher Bollas refers to the mother as a "transformational object" in relation to her preverbal baby. The mother at this early stage has the power to transform her baby's experience of himself and the world without his understanding how and why, or even his understanding that *she* is doing it.

4. In her book *The Second Sex* (New York: Knopf, 1953), Simone de Beauvoir cast a critical eye on motherly devotion, self-sacrifice, and overprotection, arguing that these qualities often represent women's compensation for feelings of emptiness, sexual frustration, and discontent with their lives generally.

5. One study has demonstrated that babies responded differently to music or to a story they had "heard" repeatedly *in utero*.

6. When I suggest that the attachment between a mother and infant is not subject to reason I mean that it is not logical or grounded in objective reality. A mother does not love her baby more than her neighbor's baby because her baby is objectively more lovable, and even children who have been abused by their mothers are extremely attached to them. Only the most inexperienced therapist falls into the trap of disparaging his patient's parents, as if a "negative" parent-child attachment could be argued away.

7. Christopher Bollas, *The Shadow of the Object: Psychoanalysis and the Unthought Known* (New York: Columbia University Press, 1987).

8. See Daniel Stern, *The Interpersonal World of the Infant* (New York: Basic Books, 1985) for a detailed explication of the findings of recent infant research studies.

9. Of course, since all mothers were once infants and small children themselves, developmental research findings can contribute to an understanding of the origin of a mother's experience in relation to her baby. If boundaries between herself and her infant are blurred, we might well ask whether this is because she is reliving what was actually her experience of merging when she was an infant, or whether she is fantasizing about union with her mother as she did when she was a young child.

10. Jean Piaget, the Swiss psychologist who is renowned for his theories of cognitive development, maintained that throughout the life cycle all learning involves two complementary and alternating processes: assimilation and accommodation. Assimilation is the process by which we try to understand new experiences by relating them to what we already know. Accommodation is the process by which we modify our concepts so that they can encompass new and different realities. Too much assimilation would result in a false sense of continuity and stasis, whereas too much accommodation would result in a sense of discontinuity between past and present, and fragmentation. See for example Jean Piaget, *Play, Dreams and Imitation in Childhood*, translated by C. Gattegno and F. M. Hodgson (New York: W. W. Norton and Co. Inc., 1962).

11. Many people have observed differences in how little girls and little boys play, beginning at around the age of three. These differences mirror traditional sex-role stereotypes. Often they emerge even when parents and teachers conscientiously avoid rewarding or modeling different behaviors for boys and girls. For example, even in the most "modern" of households, little girls often go through a phase in which they refuse to wear pants, insist upon wearing dresses and skirts, and plead with their mothers to let them don nail polish and lipstick, even when their own mothers do not. While there are many possible explanations for the emergence of "feminine" characteristics in girls and "masculine" characteristics in boys, some psychologists have suggested that what we are seeing is part of a larger struggle

over identity. When a little girl first becomes aware that there are two sexes and that she belongs to the group that includes all other girls and women, she strives to fulfill her newfound identity and become the most and the best of what she is—that is, female. This means looking around her and observing what characteristics distinguish men and women, girls and boys, in the culture at large, and emulating those that are consistent with her identity as a girl. (Boys would be similarly motivated to fulfill their male identities by doing what is "masculine.") Of course, by the time we reach adulthood, assuming we feel relatively secure in our identities, we need not exaggerate feminine or masculine qualities in order to affirm that we are women or men. We may even be able to broaden our definitions of femininity and masculinity so that they overlap, and so that we can borrow from each without threatening our essential sense of femaleness or maleness. Nevertheless, we cannot rid ourselves of these categories, and however femininity is defined, it is bound to be an important dimension in a woman's self-concept.

12. Because the birth of a baby places a strain on the marital relationship, and partners vie with one another for equal time, space, love, and attention (see Chapter 7), differences between a husband's and a wife's sexual needs may be magnified in importance and heavily infused with symbolism. ("You never have time for me anymore." "You are only interested in having sex.")

13. Helen Deutsch, a psychoanalyst whose elaborations of Freud's theories of female sexuality have generated considerable controversy within and outside psychoanalytic circles, argued that for the "normal" woman, coitus, impregnation, and childbirth are unconsciously identified, and that for women sexual pleasure and orgasm are not ends in themselves. A woman's gratification comes indirectly, through satisfying a man, and self-renunciation is the solution to a woman's sexual conflicts, not the problem. See Helene Deutsch, *The Psychology of Women. A Psychoanalytic Interpretation* (New York: Grune and Stratton, Vol. I, 1944).

14. Erik H. Erikson, *Identity, Youth and Crisis* (New York: W. W. Norton, 1968), p. 136. This apparently was Freud's conception of the normal life (Lieben and Arbeiten).

15. According to a report published in a special issue of the *American Psychologist* devoted to children, mothers of half the infants in the

United States work outside the home, and "mothers of young infants are the fastest growing segment of the labor market." See K. Alison Clarke-Stewart, "Infant Day Care: Maligned or Malignant?" *American Psychologist Special Issue: Children and Their Development: Knowledge Base, Research Agenda, and Social Policy Application*, Vol. XLIV, 2 (February 1989), p. 266–273. See also K. A. Matthews, and J. Rodin, "Women's Changing Work Roles. Impact on Health, Family and Public Policy," *American Psychologist*, November, Vol. XLIV, 11 (1989), pp. 1389–1393. According to this article, in 1986 51 percent of women with children under three years of age were working. Contrast this with 25.8 percent in 1970 to appreciate how rapid and dramatic the changes have been.

16. See C. F. Epstein, "Encountering the Male Establishment: Sex Status Limits on Women's Careers in the Professions," *American Journal of Sociology*, Vol. LXXV, No. 6 (1970), pp. 965–982.

17. See R. L. Coser and G. Rokoff, "Women in the Occupational World: Social Disruption and Conflict," *Social Problems*, Vol. XVIII (1971), pp. 535–554.

18. Karen Horney, *New Ways in Psychoanalysis* (New York: W. W. Norton, 1939), p. 117.

19. Sigmund Freud, *The Problem of Anxiety*, translated from the German by Henry Alden Brunker (New York: Psychoanalytic Quarterly Press and W. W. Norton, 1936), p. 23.

20. Salvador Minuchin, *Families and Family Therapy*, (Cambridge, MA: Harvard University Press, 1974), p. 58.

21. S. D. Sieber, "Toward a Theory of Role Accumulation," *American Sociological Review*, Vol. XXXIX, No. 4 (1974), p. 573.

22. E. Mostow and P. Newberry, "Work Role and Depression in Women: A Comparison of Workers and Housewives in Treatment,

American Journal of Orthopsychiatry, Vol. XLV (1975), pp. 538–548. See also R. L. Repetti, K. A. Matthews, and I. Waldron, "Employment and Women's Health. Effects of Paid Employment on Women's Mental and Physical Health," *American Psychologist*, Vol. XLIV, 11 (1989), pp. 1394–1401, for a review of more recent studies of the relationship between women's employment and psychological and physical health. According to these writers, there is no substantiating evidence that multiple roles have a deleterious effect on women, and there is even some support for the idea that work can function as a buffer against stress. "Among married women and mothers, stress is more strongly linked to psychological symptoms, particularly depression, for women who are not employed" (p. 1399).

Chapter 7. The Marital Relationship

1. Social psychologists have observed that there is not a linear relationship between feelings of anger or injustice over differential treatment and objective measures of inequality. So, for example, differences in men's and women's roles may be perceived as justifiable on account of psychological, biological, moral, or economic differences. As long as women consider men to be in a fundamentally different category of human being, they would not necessarily expect to have similar rights and privileges, and would not balk when they do not. Similarly, when generational boundaries are clearly delineated within a family, children do not expect to be able to do the things their parents do, and whatever differences in rights and rules exist are not experienced as unjust. When boundaries between men and women, or for that matter children and adults, become fuzzy, however, there is the potential for outrage when inequality occurs.

2. Similarly, women are not subject to the sanctions men are, if upon becoming mothers they choose to withdraw from their careers and assume a more stereotypically feminine role.

3. This is once again an allusion to psychoanalyst and pediatrician D. W. Winnicott, who speaks of the "good-enough" mother in contrast to the mythical mother who is always attuned, always empathic with her children.

4. Jules Henry, *Pathways to Madness* (New York: Vintage Books, 1965), p. 196.

5. Philip Reif, *Freud: The Mind of the Moralist* (Chicago: University of Chicago Press, 1959), is an excellent analysis of Freud's theory and its implications for human life in general, beyond the psychoanalytic relationship.

6. Family therapist Ivan Boszormenyi-Nagy refers to the intergenerational bonds that develop within all families as "invisible loyalties"—invisible because we are unaware of how tenaciously we hold onto the roles we were cast in as children despite our conscious repudiation of them and our apparent distancing. See Ivan Boszormenyi-Nagy and Geraldine Spark, *Invisible Loyalties: Reciprocity in Intergenerational Family Therapy* (New York: Harper and Row, 1973). This text is where I was introduced to the language of bookkeeping as it applies to interpersonal loyalty and betrayal. One of Nagy's theses is that until a person can feel as if he has repaid or been repaid the debts he has accrued in his family—balanced the accounts between giving and having been given to—he will be unable to disengage from the family system, however destructive it is to him.

7. Salvador Minuchin, *Families and Family Therapy* (Cambridge, MA: Harvard University Press, 1974)) p. 57.

8. This is the theme of a very interesting study of the novel by the French critic René Girard, *Deceit, Desire and the Novel*.

9. We shall see, in the following chapter on the extended family system, how actual flesh-and-blood parents and siblings figure as presences within a marriage, particularly in relation to a new baby. Here, however, we are referring to the ghosts of childhood who inhabit our psyches, and who have become aspects of our personalities that we bring with us unaware to every relationship. Freud talks of the "family romance," and argues that there are always four in the marriage bed, not just two. And Eric Berne, the founder of Transactional Analysis and author of *Games People Play* (New York: Grove Press, 1964), speaks of the Child, the Parent, and the Adult within us all.

10. In social psychology the theory of relative deprivation suggests that people's experience of deprivation or jealousy is not solely a function of their objective conditions. Rather, their subjective experience depends on who they compare themselves to, and whether these comparison-others are receiving more, the same, or less of whatever is deemed desirable. Faye Crosby's article "A Model of Egoistical Relative Deprivation, *Psychological Review*, Vol. LXXXIII (1976), pp. 85–113, is an excellent synthesis of the theoretical argument.

11. Nathan W. Ackerman, *Treating the Troubled Family* (New York: Basic Books, 1966), p. 114.

12. There is a consensus among family systems theorists that symptomatic children—that is children who are identified as having a psychiatric problem—are actually bearers of the family pathology, which is rooted in marital conflicts. These symptom-bearers are often children who have served as buffers between their parents, and their symptomatic behavior may actually function as a safety valve through which the family pain can be expressed without jeopardizing the marriage. The child is thus simultaneously buffer, scapegoat, and sacrificial lamb, sacrificing his own psychological well-being so that other members of the family, his parents in particular, need not confront their own inadmissible feelings. See also Virginia Satir, *Conjoint Family Therapy* (Palo Alto, CA: Science and Behavior Books, Inc., 1967).

13. Here, as elsewhere, I use the generic "he" only for convenience, without intending to imply that boys are more likely than girls to be cast in this role.

14. In a poem entitled "The Book of Sir Tristram," by Henry Weinfield, the line goes "the Golden Age is always of the past." And there is the inverted allusion to Bruno Bettelheim's famous book *Love Is Not Enough; The Treatment of Emotionally Disturbed Children* (New York: Free Press, 1950).

15. The reason psychologists give projective tests such as an inkblot test is precisely because when there are no clear guidelines as to how to respond or what is the right answer a person is forced to fall back

on his preconceptions; his response will reflect his personality and his individualized approach to problem-solving. When there are clear structures, most of us conform more or less to the guidelines given us. I would argue that at this point in history, when ideas about sex roles, parenting, marriage are in flux and there is no clear consensus or certainty about one right approach, husbands and wives are more likely to rely on their own individual feelings, memories, and ideas and to understand present-day relationships in these terms. While the potential for creativity is greater, there is also a greater potential for individual distortion.

Chapter 8. Beyond the Nuclear Family: How Your Baby Fits into the "Family System"

1. Ivan Boszormenyi-Nagy and Geraldine M. Spark, *Invisible Loyalties* (Hagerstown, MD, Harper and Row, 1973), p. 2.

2. Again I use the term "crisis" in the sense intended by Erik Erikson. The birth of a baby requires a shift in family relationships, and as such the family system, as it exists, is destabilized. Each member of the family must adapt in one way or another to his or her new role if a new equilibrium is to be found.

3. Nathan W. Ackerman, *Treating the Troubled Family* (New York: Basic Books, 1966), p. 72.

4. Ivan Boszormenyi-Nagy uses this metaphor in his discussion of loyalty and equity within the family. According to Nagy, we all struggle to repay our debts to our parents and collect that which is owed to us. Until the accounts are balanced, we are unable to extricate ourselves from the invisible bonds that link us to our early family relationships at the expense of forging a separate identity. See in particular Boszormenyi-Nagy and Spark, *Invisible Loyalties*, p. 107.

5. Ackerman, *Treating the Troubled Family*, p. 81.

6. One theory in social psychology, called balance theory, formulated originally by Fritz Heider, essentially states that people strive to maintain a sense of psychological balance. This means that if A likes B and A likes C then B and C should like each other. If in fact they do not, A might find some reason to change his feelings about either B or C in order to reestablish a sense of balance or consistency. See Fritz Heider, *The Psychology of Interpersonal Relations* (New York: Wiley, 1958).

7. I am not familiar with any research investigating competitive feelings within groups of children who are raised communally, but it would be interesting to see whether these children develop sibling-type rivalries in the context of other peer relationships. One question that might be explored is whether the family system creates the conditions wherein such competition thrives and proliferates, or whether the family is just one of many arenas in which we express our desire to excel and surpass others.

8. In the language of family systems theory, when a child is treated by a parent as if he were another adult, generational boundaries have been violated, and the child is considered parentified. Although the parentified child may himself enjoy some of the privileges of being treated as an adult, he has been forced to grow up too quickly in order to satisfy his parent's needs rather than his own, and if he appears to be particularly mature for his age, it is actually a pseudo-maturity he has adopted.

Bibliography

Ackerman, Nathan W. *Treating the Troubled Family.* New York: Basic Books, 1966.

Adler, Alfred. *The Individual Psychology of Alfred Adler*, ed. H. L. Ansbacher and R. R. Ansbacher. New York: Basic Books, 1956.

Asch, Solomon E. "Effects of Group Pressure upon the Modification and Distortion of Judgments," in Harold Guetzkow, ed., *Groups, Leadership, and Men.* Pittsburgh: Carnegie Press, 1951.

Benedek, Therese. "Parenthood as a Developmental Phase: A Contribution to Libido Theory." *Journal of the American Psychoanalytic Association*, Vol. VII, No. 3 (1959), pp. 389–417.

Bernard, Jesse. "Change and Stability in Sex Role Norms and Behavior." *Journal of Social Issues*, Vol. XXXII, No. 3 (1974), pp. 207–223.

Berne, Eric. *Games People Play.* New York: Grove Press, 1964.

Blake, William. "Auguries of Innocence," in *The Poetry and Prose of William Blake*, ed. David V. Erdman. New York: Doubleday, 1965.

Bollas, Christopher. *The Shadow of the Object. Psychoanalysis of the Unthought Known.* New York: Columbia University Press, 1987.

Boszormenyi-Nagy, Ivan, and Spark, Geraldine M. *Invisible Loyalties: Reciprocity in Intergenerational Family Therapy.* Hagerstown, MD: Harper and Row, 1973.

Chodorow, Nancy. *The Reproduction of Mothering: Psychoanalysis and the Sociology of Gender.* Berkeley and Los Angeles: University of California Press, 1978.

Clarke-Stewart, K. A. "Infant Day Care: Maligned or Malignant?" *American Psychologist Special Issue: Children and Their Development: Knowledge Base, Research Agenda, and Social Policy Application,* Vol. XLIV, No. 2 (February 1989), pp. 266–273.

Cooley, Charles Horton. *Human Nature and the Social Order.* New York: Schocken Books, 1902.

Coser, R. L., and Rokoff, G. "Women in the Occupational World: Social Disruption and Conflict." *Social Problems,* Vol. XVIII (1971), pp. 535–554.

Crosby, F. "A Model of Egoistical Relative Deprivation." *Psychological Review,* Vol. LXXXIII (1976), pp. 85–113.

De Beauvoir, Simone. *The Second Sex.* New York: Knopf, 1953.

Dally, Ann. *Inventing Motherhood: The Consequences of an Ideal.* New York: Schocken Books, 1983.

Deutsch, Helene. *The Psychology of Women: A Psychoanalytic Interpretation,* Vol. I. New York: Grune and Stratton, 1944. (See also Vol. II, *Motherhood,* 1945.)

Epstein, C. F. "Encountering the Male Establishment: Sex Status Limits on Women's Careers in the Professions." *American Journal of Sociology,* Vol. LXXV, No. 6 (1970), pp. 965–982.

Erikson, Erik H. *Childhood and Society.* New York: W. W. Norton, 1950.

———. *Identity, Youth and Crisis.* New York: W. W. Norton, 1968.

Festinger, Leon. "A Theory of Social Comparison Processes." *Human Relations,* Vol. VII (1954) pp. 117–140.

Frenkel-Brunswik, Else. "Intolerance of Ambiguity as an Emotional and Perceptual Personality Variable," in Nanette Heiman and Joan Grant, eds., *Else Frenkel-Brunswik: Selected Papers, Psychological Issues,* Vol. VIII, No. 3, Monograph 31, New York: International Universities Press, 1974.

Freud, Sigmund. *The Problem of Anxiety*, trans. Henry Alden Brunker, M.D., New York: Psychoanalytic Press and W. W. Norton, 1936.

————. *The Standard Edition of the Complete Psychological Works of Sigmund Freud*, trans, under the general editorship of James Strachey. Vol. II, *Studies on Hysteria;* Vols. IV and V, *The Interpretation of Dreams;* Vol. VI, *The Psychopathology of Everyday Life;* Vol. XIX, Some Psychological Consequences of the Anatomical Distinctions Between the Sexes; Vol. XXI, *Civilization and Its Discontents;* Vol. XXI, Female Sexuality; Vol. XXII, Femininity. In *New Introductory Lectures on Psychoanalysis;* Vol. XXIII, *Moses and Monotheism.* London: The Hogarth Press and Institute of Psychoanalysis, 1966.

Friedan, Betty. *The Feminine Mystique.* New York: Dell, 1963.

————. *The Second Stage.* New York, Summit Books, 1981.

Frieze, I. H., Parsons, J. E., Johnson, P. B., Ruble, D. N., and Zellman, G. L. *Women and Sex Roles: A Social Psychological Perspective.* New York: W. W. Norton, 1978.

Fromm, Erich. *Escape from Freedom.* New York: Holt, Rinehart and Winston, 1941.

Gilligan, Carol. *In a Different Voice: Psychological Theory and Women's Development.* Cambridge, MA: Harvard University Press, 1982.

Girard, René. *Deceit, Desire and the Novel: Self and Other in Literary Structure*, trans. Yvonne Freccero. Baltimore and London: The Johns Hopkins Press, 1965.

Goffman, Erving. *Interaction Ritual. Essays on Face-to-face Behavior.* Chicago: Aldine, 1967.

Goldstein, J. W., and Rosenfeld, H. W. "Insecurity and Preference for Persons Similar to Oneself. *Journal of Personality*, Vol. XXXVII (1969), pp. 253–268.

Graves, Robert. *The Greek Myths*, Vol. I. New York: George Braziller, 1959.

Hall, Edward T. *The Hidden Dimension.* Garden City, NY: Doubleday, 1966.

Harvey, J. H., and Weary, G. "Current Issues in Attribution Theory and Research," in *Annual Review of Psychology*, Vol. XXXV. Palo Alto, CA: Annual Reviews, 1984.

Heider, Fritz. *The Psychology of Interpersonal Relations*. New York: Wiley, 1958.

Henry, Jules. *Pathways to Madness*. New York: Vintage Books, 1965.

Hoffman, Lois. "The Effects of Maternal Employment in the Two-Parent Family." *The American Psychologist*, Vol. XLIV, No. 2 (February 1989), pp. 283–292.

Horney, Karen. *Neurosis and Human Growth*. New York: W. W. Norton, 1950.

———. *New Ways in Psychoanalysis*. New York: W. W. Norton, 1939.

Kipling, Rudyard. "Our Lady of the Snows" (1897), *Collected Verse*. New York: Doubleday, Page, 1907. p. 96.

Lewin, Kurt. *Field Theory in Social Science: Selected Theoretical Papers*, ed. Dorwin Cartwright. New York: Harper, 1951.

LeMasters, E. E. "Parenthood as Crisis." *Marriage and Family Living*, November 1957, pp. 352–355.

Lasch, Christopher. *The Culture of Narcissism*. New York: W. W. Norton, 1978.

Lerner, M. J. "The Justice Motive in Social Behavior." *Journal of Social Issues*, Vol. XXXI, No. 3 (1975), pp. 1–19.

Maccoby, E. E., and Jacklin, C. *The Psychology of Sex Differences*. Stanford, CA: Stanford University Press, 1974.

Mahler, Margaret S., Pine, F., and Bergman, A. *The Psychological Birth of the Human Infant*. New York: Basic Books, 1975.

Margolis, Maxine. *Mothers and Such: Views of American Women and Why They Changed*. Berkeley and Los Angeles: University of California Press, 1984.

Maslow, Abraham. *Motivation and Personality*. New York: Harper and Row, 1970.

Matthews, K. A., and Rodin J. "Women's Changing Work Roles: Impact on Health, Family, and Public Policy."

American Psychologist, Vol. XLIV, No. 11 (November 1989), pp. 1389–1393.

McDougall, Joyce. *Theaters of the Mind: Illusion and Truth on the Psychoanalytic Stage*. New York: Basic Books, 1985.

Merkin, Daphne. *Enchantment*. San Diego: Harcourt, Brace Jovanovich, 1986.

Minuchin, Salvador. *Families and Family Therapy*. Cambridge, MA: Harvard University Press, 1974.

Mostow, E., and Newberry, P. "Work Role and Depression in Women: A Comparison of Workers and Housewives in Treatment." *American Journal of Orthopsychiatry*, Vol. XLV (1975), pp. 538–548.

Newcomb, T. M. "The Prediction of Interpersonal Attraction." *The American Psychologist*, Vol. XI (1956) pp. 575–586.

Parsons, Talcott. "Age and Sex in the Social Structure of the United States." *American Sociological Review*, Vol. VII (1942), pp. 604–620.

Piaget, Jean. *Play, Dreams and Imitation in Childhood*, trans. C. Gattegno and F. M. Hodgson. New York: W. W. Norton, 1962.

Proust, Marcel. *Swann's Way*, trans. C. K. Scott Moncrieff and Terence Kilmartin. New York: Random House, 1981.

Repetti, R. L. Matthews, K. A., and Waldron, I. "Employment and Women's Health: Effects of Paid Employment on Women's Mental and Physical Health." *American Psychologist*, Vol. XLIV, No. 11 (1989), pp. 1394–1401.

Rieff, Philip. *Freud: The Mind of the Moralist*. Chicago: University of Chicago Press, 1959.

Rosenkrantz, P., Vogel, S., Bee, H., Broverman, I., and Broverman, D. "Sex-role Stereotypes and Self-concepts in College Students." *Journal of Consulting and Clinical Psychology*, Vol. XXXII (1968), pp. 287–295.

Rubenstein, Carin. "The Baby Bomb." *The New York Times Magazine* (Health Section), October 8, 1989.

Satir, Virginia. *Conjoint Family Therapy*. Rev. ed. Palo Alto, CA: Science and Behavior Books, 1967.

Schachter, Stanley. *The Psychology of Affiliation*. Stanford, CA: Stanford University Press, 1959.

Sherif, M., Harvey, O. J., White, B. J., Hood, W. R., and Sherif, C. W. *Intergroup Conflict and Cooperation: The Robbers Cave Experiment*. Norman OK: Institute of Group Relations, University of Oklahoma Press, 1961.

Sherif, M., and Sherif, C. W. *Reference Groups: Exploration into Conformity and Deviation of Adolescents*. New York: Harper and Row, 1964.

Sieber, S. D. "Toward a Theory of Role Accumulation." *American Sociological Review*, Vol. XXXIX, No. 4 (1974), pp. 567–579.

Stern, Daniel. *The Interpersonal World of the Human Infant*. New York: Basic Books, 1985.

Sullivan, H. S. *The Interpersonal Theory of Psychiatry*. New York: W. W. Norton, 1953.

Thompson, Clara. "Cultural Pressures in the Psychology of Women." Reprinted in *Psychoanalysis and Women*, Jean Baker Miller, M.D., ed. New York: Penguin Books, 1973.

Tolstoy, Leo. *Anna Karenina*, trans. Constance Garnett. Garden City, NY: Nelson Doubleday, 1944.

Weinfield, Henry. "The Book of Sir Tristram," *In the Sweetness of the New Time*. Atlanta: House of Keys, 1980.

Weiss, J. M. "Psychological Factors in Stress and Disease." *Scientific American*, Vol. CCXXVI (1972), pp. 104–113.

Winnicott, D. W. *The Child, the Family, and the Outside World*. Hammondsworth U.K.: Penguin Books, 1964

———. *Home Is Where We Start From*. New York: W. W. Norton, 1986.

———. *Playing and Reality*. London: Tavistock, 1971.

Woolf, Virginia. *A Room of One's Own*. New York: Harcourt Brace and World, 1929.

———. *To the Lighthouse*. New York: Harcourt Brace, 1927.

———. *The Voyage Out*. New York: Harcourt Brace and World, 1920.

Yeats, William Butler. "The Second Coming," in *The Poems of W. B. Yeats*. New York: Macmillan, 1983. p. 187.

Index